third edi

# Teaching Science for All Children

## Inquiry Lessons for Constructing Understanding

**Ralph Martin**
*Ohio University*

**Colleen Sexton**
*Ohio University*

**Teresa Franklin**
*Ohio University*

PEARSON

A and B

Boston ✦ New York ✦ San Francisco

Mexico City ✦ Montreal ✦ Toronto ✦ London ✦ Madrid ✦ Munich ✦ Paris

Hong Kong ✦ Singapore ✦ Tokyo ✦ Cape Town ✦ Sydney

| | |
|---|---|
| *Series Editor:*  Traci Mueller | *Photo Editor:*  Katharine S. Cook |
| *Editorial Assistant:*  Janice Hackenberg | *Electronic Composition:*  Omegatype Typography, Inc. |
| *Executive Marketing Manager:*  Amy Cronin Jordan | *Composition Buyer:*  Linda Cox |
| *Editorial-Production Administrator:*  Annette Joseph | *Manufacturing Buyer:*  Andrew Turso |
| *Editorial-Production Coordinator:*  Barbara Gracia | *Cover Designer:*  Kristina Mose-Libon |
| *Text Designer:*  Denise Hoffman | |

The material in this textbook is based upon work supported by the National Science Foundation under grant No. 91-47392. Any opinions, findings, conclusions, or recommendations expressed in this publication are those of the authors and do not necessarily reflect the views of the Foundation.

For related titles and support materials, visit our online catalog at www.ablongman.com.

Portions of this book first appeared in *Teaching Science for All Children: An Inquiry Approach,* Fourth Edition, by Ralph Martin, Colleen Sexton, Teresa Franklin, and with Jack Gerlovich, copyright © 2005, 2001, 1997, 1994 by Pearson Education, Inc.

To obtain permission(s) to use material from this work, please submit a written request to Allyn and Bacon, Permissions Department, 75 Arlington Street, Suite 300, Boston, MA 02116 or fax your request to 617-848-7320.

Between the time website information is gathered and then published, it is not unusual for some sites to have closed. Also, the transcription of URLs can result in typographical errors. The publisher would appreciate notification where these errors occur so that they may be corrected in subsequent editions.

**Library of Congress Cataloging-in-Publication Data**

Ralph Martin
  Teaching science for all children: Inquiry lessons for constructing understanding—3rd ed. /
Ralph Martin, Colleen M. Sexton, Teresa Franklin.
      p. cm.
    Includes index.
    ISBN 0-205-43152-6 (pbk.)
      1. Science—Study and teaching—Methodology. 2. Science—Study and teaching (Elementary)—
Methodology. 3. Teachers—Training of. 4. Constructivism (Education).  I. Sexton, Colleen M.
II. Teresa Franklin   III. Title

Q181.M1778 2005
372.3'5044—dc21                                                                                       200426027

**Photo Credits:** Special thanks to the following companies for use of their photos on p. 9: (from top), Courtesy of H. L. Bouton Co., Inc.; Courtesy of Sargent-Welch Company; Courtesy of Boekel Industries, Inc.; Courtesy of Lab Safety Supply. p. 10: Courtesy of Sargent-Welch Company.

Printed in the United States of America

10   9   8   7   6   5   4   3           RRD-IN     09   08   07

*For Jessica, whose curiosity and quick wit continues to inspire and amaze Dad.*
*Our nation's children's successes depend upon teachers like you. Spread the inspiration!*
*Become all that you can!*—R. M.

*For Jimmy, whose energy, enthusiasm, and passion for life help me*
*see science in things I would have missed, and for Sarah and Celeste,*
*who continuously motivate and inspire me!*—C. S.

*To my best friend and husband, Doug. Keep sailing!*—T. F.

*Preface* *vii*

### chapter 1

## *Who, What, Why, and How?*
### *Things You Want To Know About Inquiry Science Lessons* 1

### chapter 2

## *Does Educational Technology Make A Difference?*
### *Using Educational Technology to Enrich Your Science Lessons* 13

### chapter 3

## *Lessons for Constructing Understanding* 25

### s e c t i o n 1

## *Life Science Lessons* 26

## section II

## *Physical Science Lessons   97*

## section III

## *Earth and Space
Science Lessons   170*

## *Appendix A: National Science Education Standards: Content Standards for K–4 and 5–8   245*

## *Appendix B: NSTA Position Statement: Guidelines for Responsible Use of Animals in the Classroom   251*

## *Appendix C: NSTA Position Statement: Liability of Teachers for Laboratory Safety and Field Trips   252*

## *Appendix D: NSTA Position Statement: Laboratory Science   253*

## *References   255*

## *Index   257*

*Teaching Science for All Children: Inquiry Lessons for Constructing Understanding,* Third Edition, is designed to help you help children *do* and *learn* essential science concepts and skills. The amount of science information is increasing at a rapid rate. At the same time newer tools are being developed for us to manage all of this information. Oftentimes the dilemma is: Do I give up learning the new tools or learning the new content? This book provides you with strategies to have the best of both worlds. It does not have to be an either/or decision when it comes to effective science teaching.

This book is written for the classroom teacher, the home schooling teacher, and parents interested in sound, holistic science lessons that address the National Science Education Standards (NSES) and the National Educational Technology Standards (NETS).

In Chapter 1, our emphasis is on proper science concept formation. This strategy requires students to engage in the processes of science, reflect upon their experiences, and through carefully guided questioning, make the concept concrete. The use of the 4–E learning cycle of *exploration, explanation, expansion,* and *evaluation* is examined. This teaching strategy is consistent with our views of how children construct their understanding of a concept through constructivist teaching practices. While student action is important for proper concept formation, their participation cannot happen without attention to safety. Included in Chapter 1 is a quick reference guide to help you consider some safety essentials for the types of lessons you will find in this book.

Chapter 2 provides a vision for educational technology: what it is and how the tools can be applied appropriately. This chapter relates the National Educational Technology Standards for educational technology, an expectation that the International Society for Technology Education (ISTE) has set for all children K–12. We show how these standards for educational technology can be applied to teaching science lessons included in Chapter 3. Our intent is to give you a vision of what a science classroom looks like when educational technology tools are appropriately applied.

Chapter 3 contains 65 complete science lessons, organized according to the disciplines identified by the National Science Education Standards (NSES): life, physical, and earth and space sciences. Each lesson is correlated with the grade levels and concepts recommended by the NSES framework. These lessons contain more than 150 different activities that are experienced in a very powerful way–a way that encourages the highest level of hands-on, minds-on student activity and stimulates high levels of concept formation. Our lesson plans are consistent with the 4–E learning cycle detailed in Chapter 1. The exploration phase stimulates the learner to construct conceptual understanding. This fundamental understanding is expanded by addressing the new dimensions of the NSES content standards, such as the history and nature of science, the interrelationship of science and technology, and science in personal and social perspectives. Evaluation and assessment are embedded in the instruction throughout the cycle and use performance-based techniques such as pictorial assessment, reflective questioning, and hands-on assessment. The evaluation expectations are written as performance outcomes. As you use the lessons, the outcomes listed will guide the type of assessment you create to provide your students with a variety of opportunities to demonstrate that students truly have grasped the science concept. The lessons provided have been classroom-tested by our own undergraduate and graduate students as well as by practicing teachers.

The National Science Education Standards content standards are provided in Appendix A. The spirit of the NSES content standards is reflected in the lessons found in this book. As you gain experience in using these lessons, we encourage you to choose from the NSES concepts and try your hand at creating your own 4–E learning cycle science lessons.

## Supplements

### Instructor's Manual and Test Bank

Prepared by the authors, this manual contains five parts:

- *Teaching Suggestions*—A model syllabus with assignment guides and grading rubrics for field experience, draw-a-scientist, concept mapping, learning cycle lesson planning, peer-taught demonstration lessons, self-analysis of teaching papers
- *Chapter Outlines*—Capsule descriptions of the material and concepts for each chapter; useful for lecture preparation
- *Test Item Bank*—Hundreds of test items; when used with the test generator, provide custom quizzes and examinations
- *Concept Maps*—Multiple uses as exemplars for each chapter, study guides, and presentation graphics
- *Transparency Masters*—PowerPoint files are provided on the companion website and in the Instructor's Manual in hard copy as student handouts.

### Companion Website (www.ablongman.com/martin4e)

Our new companion website contains several helpful learning and teaching aids, such as:

- *Chapter objectives* for quick summary of each chapter's mission
- *Concept maps* that provide a visual graphic story of each chapter's concepts
- *Practice tests* that support study and preparation for examinations by giving instant feedback
- *Additional readings* that contain annotations for further reading and study on the important topics of each chapter
- *PowerPoint* slides for teaching and learning about the main features in each chapter

- *Resources,* as exemplars of best practices, that include modern or historically significant examples of innovation in science teaching and learning
- *Sample 4–E lesson,* created using an activity from the "Project Learning Tree" environmental science curriculum

## New! Allyn & Bacon "mylabschool" Web Resource

Free when packaged with a student access code. Contact your local representative for more details!

Discover where the classroom comes to life! From video clips of teachers and students interacting to sample lessons, portfolio templates, and standards integration, Allyn & Bacon brings your students the tools they'll need to succeed in the classroom—with content easily integrated into your existing course.

Delivered within Course Compass, Allyn & Bacon's course management system, this program gives your students powerful insights into how real classrooms work and a rich array of tools that will support them on their journey from their first class to their first classroom.

## Related Text

*Teaching Science for All Children: Inquiry Methods for Constructing Understanding, with "Video Explorations" VideoWorkshop Student CD-ROM,* **Third Edition,** provides methods for future teachers to foster awareness among their students of the nature of science; to implement skills in the classroom using science inquiry processes; and to develop in their students an understanding of the interactions among science, technology, and society. ISBN: 0205431534

## Acknowledgments

It is a wonderful feeling to work with colleagues who are intelligent, enthusiastic, and passionate about science education and the preparation of teachers. Being able to call these same colleagues your friends is even better. The creation of this book came out of the mutual respect and value each of us has for what we bring to the table. Our shared beliefs in the integration of good science teaching with appropriately applied educational technology tools are reflected in this work. We offer special thanks for the guidance and encouragement provided by our editors, Traci Mueller and Erin Liedel.

We also are thankful to our families for their support and understanding as we monopolized the family computers late into the evening to complete our parts. Special thanks to Marilyn, Jennifer, Jessica, Jonathan, Sarah, Celeste, Doug, and Matthew.

### chapter 1

# Who, What, Why, and How?

## Things You Want To Know About Inquiry Science Lessons

## Users of This Text

*Teaching Science for All Children: Inquiry Lessons for Constructing Understanding,* 3rd edition, features many of the same lessons as our *Teaching Science for All Children: An Inquiry Approach,* 4th edition. This streamlined book focuses on formulating essential science concepts and skills with children. Our target audience is children in the early grades—elementary through the middle school years.

Potential users for this book are:

+ teacher preparation programs that are acutely focused and benefit from quick immersion into science lessons for and with children
+ teacher development and continuous improvement programs for use as a professional trade book
+ leaders who need an effective resource for school science curriculum development
+ individual teachers who wish to have a high quality science curriculum supplement that presents for easy use up-to-date science and technology standards for children
+ professionals who eschew the gimmicky fragmentation of science activities in favor of the effectiveness of holistic lessons
+ parents of home-schooled children and charter school educators who want to build a selective science curriculum that helps their learners benefit from national science and technology standards
+ paraprofessionals who want materials that guide them with assurance that their learners will be successful learners

## Objectives of This Text

This book uses the *National Science Education Standards* (NSES) and the *National Educational Technology Standards* (NETS) to help those who teach help children become successful learners in science. A successful learner overcomes the performance limitations that are common to many elementary and middle-school children in today's era of achievement and performance testing. Major assessment initiatives, such as the *National Assessment of Educational Progress* (NAEP) and the *Third International Mathematics and Science Study* (TIMSS), reveal that youth typically perform well on science tests of factual knowledge, but become frustrated and perform poorly when they are expected to use scientific information to solve lifelike problems. Children perform much better when they have deep conceptual (rather than more limited factual) understandings, a healthy array of inquiry and problem-solving skills, and positive attitudes supported by productive curiosity. Indeed, these are the traits of a literate learner who can build fundamental understandings and construct meaningful connections within the fields of science and among other major school subject and skill areas. The lessons in our book are designed to help learners overcome the limitations of typical school science experiences and to help them excel while becoming more widely literate.

## Beliefs About Learning and Teaching

Our beliefs and their rationale are detailed in a companion book, *Teaching Science for All Children: Inquiry Methods for Constructing Understanding*, 3rd edition. For purposes of this book and helping you to understand why our lessons are constructed with considerable detail and care, let us simply share:

> *Learners may believe what they see, but they actually* understand *what they do.*

Understanding is rather simple to describe in theoretical terms, but it is difficult to achieve with the limits, pressures, and busyness of schooling. "Hands-on" learning is a teaching concept often expressed and supported by educators. However, it may be misinterpreted or misused. It is important that children's hands stimulate their senses, but it is perhaps more important that children's minds be strongly connected to what their hands *do*. Hands-on, minds-on learning can be effective, but only if *both* occur together. The lessons in our book connect hands and minds through opportunities for natural and guided inquiry.

Inquiry teaching and learning processes connect the minds' thinking with what the hands do. The lessons in this book will help to assure that children's thoughts and senses help them create understanding from what they *do*. Our book expands its long-standing constructivist approach to help you help learners make important learning connections by stimulating and guiding their thinking through processes of science inquiry. Simply stated, the lessons in this book will help you to help learners construct their own understanding by connecting their ideas into a fabric of science concepts, attitudes, and skills that carries meaning for them personally and academically. This success is possible because the *National Science Education Standards* (NSES) are used to select the core concepts and skills for each lesson and are fully integrated throughout this book. Each lesson is also technology rich or enriched by using the *National Educational Technology Standards* (NETS), which are discussed in Chapter 2.

## Beliefs into Action

Most notably, these science lessons consist of carefully constructed activities woven into holistic lessons that provide experiences with a specific focus on the concepts that are recommended by the NSES. As well, each lesson addresses the new science content dimensions contained in the NSES, such as helping learners to develop:

+ an awareness of the history and nature of science,
+ an understanding of the influence of science in personal and social perspectives,
+ skills in using science inquiry processes, and
+ an understanding of the complex interrelationships between science and technology.

These new content dimensions offer special curriculum challenges for educators and often are "pulled out" into stand-alone lessons in a typical science program or school curriculum. Pulling out does help to assure that the standard is addressed, but it may not assure that learners sufficiently understand and can connect these special individual lessons with the more essential concepts of science. The same can happen to treatments of technology and its many tools; separate technology lessons may not assure that learners can use the tools and skills to solve meaningful problems in other settings. We do not pull out. We pull together. We use an effective inquiry teaching and learning model, called a *learning cycle*, to connect these new challenges in a meaningful way.

## The 4–E Science Learning Cycle

A learning cycle is a method for planning lessons, teaching, learning, and developing curricula. This teaching method was orginally designed for the Science Curriculum Improvement Study and has produced the largest achievement gains of the experimental elementary science programs of the 1960s. These increases are largely a result of the learning cycle as an inquiry teaching and learning method, because the cycle is a way of thinking and acting that is consistent with how pupils naturally inquire and make discoveries

The science learning cycle originally consisted of three phases: exploration, concept invention, and application. Several modifications have been made to the original learning cycle over the past four decades, and the literature reports several popular iterations. We recommend a 4–E learning cycle, which is specifically designed to accommodate all the new science goals emphasizing mastery of specific concepts, developing reasoning and problem-solving skills, and addressing new dimensions of science and accountability.

The 4–E learning cycle consists of four phases: Exploration, Explanation, Expansion, and Evaluation (see Figure 1.1). Each phase, when followed in sequence, has sound

**FIGURE 1.1** The 4–E Science Learning Cycle

*Source:* Adapted from a figure by Charles Barman, "The Learning Cycle: Making It Work," *Science Scope* (February 1989): 28–31.

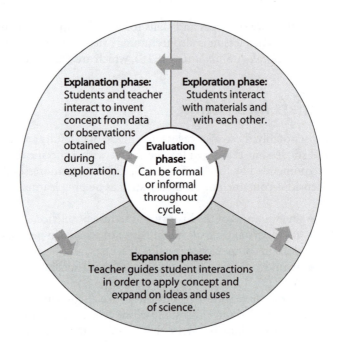

**Explanation phase:** Students and teacher interact to invent concept from data or observations obtained during exploration.

**Exploration phase:** Students interact with materials and with each other.

**Evaluation phase:** Can be formal or informal throughout cycle.

**Expansion phase:** Teacher guides student interactions in order to apply concept and expand on ideas and uses of science.

theoretical support from the cognitive development theory of Jean Piaget (Renner & Marek, 1988; Marek & Cavallo, 1997) and applies constructivist learning procedures (see Chapter 2). The 4–E learning cycle produced significant gains in pupil achievement, skills, and scientific attitudes during the authors' successful Lead Teacher Project for K–6 science funded by the National Science Foundation. Table 1.1 presents an overview of the cycle's phases. A quick primer about how to go through a successful learning cycle follows.

*Let's explore!* First, engage the learner with an interesting problem or challenge and encourage the learner to EXPLORE it. Exploring could require a single class period, or longer, if you have a traditional school structure. Exploring is important because it affords a learner time to manipulate objects, make important observations, puzzle over the unknown, and develop preliminary understandings and intuitive rudimentary science explanations. Begin an exploration without telling learners what they will learn— that comes later and occurs naturally. As a teacher your role is to guide a learner's curiosity, ask questions, and to give hints and cues that keep the exploration going until it has reached its climax.

Questions will help to guide the exploration and we offer examples in our lessons. Figure 1.2 shows how questions play an important part in the processes of inquiry and help to keep the learning cycle moving productively. As an example, divergent (or open-ended) questions particularly help learners to explore. Ask questions that will help learners to sharpen their observations of phenomena and their exploration of potential cause and effect relationships, such as: "What do you think the putty's temperature will feel like after you have rolled it in your hands?", "What familiar odor does the gas smell

**TABLE 1.1** 4–E Learning Cycle Summary

| Phase | Focus | What Students Do | What Teachers Do | Outcome |
|---|---|---|---|---|
| Exploration | Inquiry<br><br>Engaged learning | Hands-on investigations<br><br>Use process skills and tools<br><br>Cooperative investigation | Establish the inquiry<br><br>Interact with student groups<br><br>Guide exploration<br><br>Informal assessment | Process skill development<br><br>Preconceptions formed |
| Explanation | Convergent thinking for conceptualization<br><br>Processing the exploration | Respond to teacher's guidance<br><br>Examine collected information<br><br>Respond to questioning<br><br>Understand the concept | Direct investigation of the information<br><br>Use questioning<br><br>Coach toward explicitness<br><br>Identify the concept<br><br>Form operational definition for concept | Concept identified and described |
| Expansion | Expanding understanding of concept<br><br>Address new dimensions of the National Science Education Standards | Teacher-directed activity<br><br>Student-directed projects<br><br>Use concept and skills in new situation<br><br>Think, reason, apply | Direct additional activity<br><br>Guide student projects<br><br>Continue the inquiry<br><br>Questioning<br><br>Practical applications<br><br>Informal assessment | Deeper conceptual understanding<br><br>Substantive accomplishment of standards |
| Evaluation | Discern what students know and can do | Respond to teacher<br><br>Demonstrate understanding<br><br>Demonstrate skills<br><br>Express attitudes | Interact with students and groups<br><br>Focus on what students know and can do<br><br>Plan next steps | Demonstration of conceptual understanding, proficiency in using skills, degree of attitudes |

like?", "What do you think you can do to find out what is inside the box without opening it?" After you have exhausted all of your questions and the learners have explored all possibilities, it is time to move on to the next step.

*Let's construct an explanation!* To EXPLAIN means to guide learners toward the point of the lesson so that they construct and provide a scientific conceptual explanation in their own words, with our assistance. This is the succinct point of the whole lesson and must be done with forethought and care and not be rushed. Your role is to help learners use what they have learned previously during their explorations to make meanings that are new to them. Guide their thinking rather than tell learners what they should think. Encourage learners to make definitions that explain the meaning of new science words and concepts. Guide them so that the science point of the lesson is brought into a sharp focus. Strive to help learners have "Aha!" moments by helping them

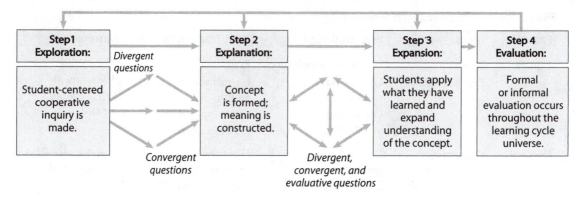

**FIGURE 1.2** Using Questions During a Learning Cycle

to organize the products of their prior exploration into meaningful patterns and relationships, such as measurements, observations, brainstorms, and the like. Convergent questions (see Figure 1.2) will help you to do this.

Convergent questions are focused and cause learners to reason from information toward a common point, and it is this point of your lesson that is so important. Examples: "What happened to the bar magnets when N and S were close together?", "What happened to the bar magnets when both N's were put close together?", "Did your magnets always behave this way?", "Did the same thing happen when both S's were pushed together?", "Why do you suppose this always happened?", and "What is it about magnets that seems to cause this to happen?" Questions like these, following on the heels of sufficient exploration with magnets, will help a learner construct a preliminary conception of magnetic poles—opposite poles attracting, like poles repelling, and lines of magnetic force. But, it would be a mistake to stop and move on to a different concept after achieving only this level of understanding, for it is preliminary and shallow. The result would be similar to memorizing without understanding how to apply a concept. The smart move, then, is to spend some additional time in related activity to deepen the understanding and to help learners connect the new learning with prior experiences and to do so in a multitude of settings. This also helps the teacher connect with different learner style preferences and the learning cycle expansion phase, which is where the NSES and NETS become very helpful.

*Let's now take what we have discovered and expand upon it!* EXPANSION helps a learner to deepen understanding, to overcome superficial familiarity that may be mistaken for learning. Our lessons contain many activities, projects, and research ideas that will help you help learners expand their understanding and sharpen their skills, and all of this revolves around the lesson's central concept. We offer key questions that you may use to challenge and guide this expansion. Many of these questions are clustered under four important new science content dimensions provided by the NSES:

✦ *Science as Inquiry,* which includes uses of the science processes, scientific knowledge, and attitudes to help learners to reason and to think critically as a way to construct understanding of science ideas.

- *Science and Technology,* which helps learners to develop scientific abilities and science understanding in order to establish connections between the natural and the human-designed world.
- *Science in Personal and Social Perspectives,* which develops decision-making skills for solving personal and community problems, making personal health choices, understanding changes in populations and the complications of resource usage, and becoming aware of science and societal issues on the local, national, and global levels.
- *History and Nature of Science,* which helps learners to use historical events to inform the present, predict likely scientific changes in the future, and appreciate that science is not absolute but may be influenced by human nature and culture.

New questions often arise during a lesson's expansion and these questions lead to opportunities to select or design new lessons with concepts that are linked. This "setting up a new cycle" is a natural outcome of a learning cycle and provides authentic opportunities for discerning the connections children are able to make about their learning.

*Let's show what we know and can do!* EVALUATION provides numerous and authentic opportunities for learners to demonstrate what they know and can do. Figures 1.1 and 1.2 illustrate the central role that evaluation plays in a learning cycle; it is not something put off to the end of a lesson. Evaluation can be informal, such as observations of a child's use of science tools and responses to questions during learning activities, or can be formal such as special set-aside times for performing a task, including traditional-appearing measures. We encourage that evaluation be used continually and that your discoveries about learners be used to improve the learning experience. We offer many ideas for evaluation in our lessons. However, you may wish to use these guiding questions to help you to customize your own evaluations:

- What appropriate learning outcomes do you expect from your learners?
- What types of hands-on evaluation techniques can the learners do to demonstrate the basic skills of science observation, classification, communication, measurement, prediction, and inference?
- What techniques are appropriate for learners to demonstrate the integrated science process skills of identifying and controlling variables, defining operationally, forming hypotheses, experimenting, interpreting data, and forming models?
- How can pictures be used to help a learner demonstrate how well she or he can think through problems that require understanding fundamental concepts and the integration of ideas?
- What types of questions help learners reflect and measure how well they recall and understand what has been taught?

# Safe Science

Our lessons provide safety guidelines, management tips, and recommendations about grade-level appropriateness. However, location, circumstances, and understanding safe science practices can influence the extent to which a lesson is safe and appropriate for your learners. We encourage you to develop a safe-science outlook, an attitude and set of behaviors that proactively anticipate and avoid complications before you place a child (or yourself) at risk. Table 1.2 offers an easy reference that considers some safety essentials for the types of items pictured in this chapter, but it is not a substitute for knowing and following the laws, policies, and rules of your state, district, or school. Check your state and region's department of education website and look for specific safety requirements. If none is available to you, we recommend *The Total Science Safety System* at www.netins.net/showcase/jakel for a rather thorough list of requirements that fit most school science safety needs. We also recommend that you visit the National Science Teachers Association website at (www.nsta.org) and consider their several fine publications, including "Safety in the Elementary Science Classroom," a quick reference flip chart. Also, if you visit our website at www.ablongman.com/martin4e, there are brief videos that demonstrate many of the recommendations listed in Table 1.2. Our website also provides a list of reputable suppliers of science supplies and safety equipment.

## *Chapter Summary*

Science has seen many reform efforts since the Russians launched their Sputnik satellite in 1957. Past efforts have offered changes for science programs in the United States, and several of those efforts worked well, but we have a distance to travel before we can help all learners become scientifically literate. When constructing the lessons for this book, we used the National Science Education Standards (NSES) and National Educational Technology Standards (NETS). As teachers, we cannot meet all of the standards by ourselves, but we can focus our efforts on those content standards that fall within our responsibility. This book helps you focus these efforts through meaningful science lessons. While understanding fundamental science content concepts is important, some may think that the standards apply only to physical, life, and earth/space science concepts and learning activities for children. This is not true, and to focus only on these topics shortchanges students, depriving them of additional essential experiences.

The physical, life, and earth/space science content is an important context for developing scientific literacy. The NSES require four new dimensions of science learning to assure that real progress is made toward helping our students achieve literacy in science. These new dimensions challenge us to help students understand science as a process of inquiry, to understand the interrelationships between science and technology, to benefit from science personally and understand the social perspective of science, and to understand and appreciate the history and nature of science. These new dimensions predictably overlap and complement natural learning. The NETS are used strategically to bring the benefits of technology to our lessons and are discussed in greater detail in Chapter 2.

As educators, our challenge is to find a way to link all of these dimensions of science learning, literacy, and technology to the content context. Our book helps you to do

**TABLE 1.2** Criteria for Selecting and Maintaining Safety Equipment

| Item | Safety Essentials |
| --- | --- |
| Ground Fault Circuit Interrupters (GFCI) | Called GFCIs or GFIs, these microchip-controlled electrical outlets sense a disruption in the flow of electricity (such as a faulty ground) and open the circuit, shutting off the appliance and limiting serious shock. Code requires their use in bathrooms, kitchens, basements, etc., and must be installed where classroom sinks are near reachable outlets. Push the "test" button monthly and determine if a plugged-in appliance becomes "turned off." Replace with a new GFCI, approved by the Underwriter Laboratory. Covering outlets with safety caps when not in use helps to discourage children from sticking items into the outlet. |
| Goggles or Eye Protection  | Check state and local laws that govern selection of appropriate face and eye protection. Goggles or eye protective devices must meet the American National Standards Institute (ANSI) safety standard Z87, which is visible on the face plate. Select a proper size for the user. Goggles should fit securely around the eye. Side vents minimize fogging and prevent fumes from building up inside the goggles. Clean with hot soapy water and air dry or clean with sterile alcohol pads immediately before use. Store in a box or cabinet. Discard when face plate is scratched or cracked. |
| Eyewash  | Use for washing chemical splashes from eyes. A fountain fixture is an inexpensive alternative to a permanent eyewash station. Water supply must provide at least 15 minutes of aerated running water between 60–90 degrees F. Should be accessible to students and available for emergency use at all times. Bottled eye washers can become contaminated and are best considered as a last alternative or for use during field trips when there is no permanent equipment available. |
| Hot Plates | Preferred when an open flame is not needed. Should have an on-off indicator light and temperature adjustment that is easily visible to the teacher. Purposely comes with a short cord to avoid tripping hazard; do not use with extension cords. Keep out of students' reach. Touch only when cool. Unplug when not in use. Monitor on-off indicator light and temperature control; discard when neither properly controls the hot plate. |
| Alcohol Lamps  | Select a lamp with a broad base to limit tipping; place slender lamps in a clay base to avoid tipping hazard. Wicks should be trimmed to ¼ inch or less to reduce smoke and soot; wicks are replaceable. Place lamp in aluminum pie pan with damp sand to contain spills. Use alcohol made for lamps. Pure alcohol burns with a barely visible blue flame. Make flame visible by adding a few grains of table salt to alcohol (turns the flame orange). Use alcohol containers of 1 liter or less in the classroom. Store larger quantities of alcohol in approved safety containers. Label all containers. Pure alcohol has very little odor and can be mistaken for water—a potentially lethal hazard. |
| Fire Blanket  | Use blanket to smother fires. Must be safety approved and made of fire retardant wool. Select size that can be easily handled. Remove shrinkwrap from new blankets. Mount storage container in easy to reach location. Avoid using for torso fires. Wrapping the torso can create a chimney effect where flames and fumes fly up under the blanket and across the face. Practice the stop-drop-and-roll method with students as an alternative. |

*(continued)*

**TABLE 1.2** (Continued)

| Item | Safety Essentials |
|---|---|
| Fire Extinguishers  | The most versatile extinguisher is the ABC tri-class dry powder type. Works on three types of fires: wood/paper, liquids and grease, and electrical. Store in conspicuous, easy-to-access location. Regularly check the pressure gauge and recharge or replace when a full charge is not shown. Review usage directions and teach to children. Do not use on humans and animals; can irritate eyes, nose, mouth, and ears, and stimulate asthmatic symptoms. See "Fire Blanket" as an alternative. |
| First Aid Kit | Select a physician-approved kit and examine to determine if all needs are met, e.g., does it contain items such as cold pack, scissors, gloves, mouth-to-mouth apparatus, sanitary wipes, etc.? Select for portability if to be used for field trips. Review usage instructions. Replace consumables. Heed instructions relating to HIV and hepatitis prevention. Insert special items, such as permission forms, emergency medical contact forms, and student prescription medications when traveling on field trips. |
| Animals in the Classroom | Check school policies and prevailing laws before bringing animals into the classroom. Treat all living organisms humanely and train children to do the same. Assure animals have proper, clean, and safe living quarters; well-ventilated and properly fed. Arrange reliable care for weekends and holidays. Do not permit children to bring live or dead animals. Visiting pets should be handled only by their owners. Obtain all animals from a reputable supply house. Visiting animals should be accompanied by a properly trained caretaker. No poisonous animals should be brought to the school. |
| Plants in the Classroom | Many plants have not been researched for toxicity; therefore, teach children to follow these general rules:<br>• Never eat a plant part unless teacher approves. Teachers: Please distinguish between edible and non-edible parts.<br>• Never allow sap or juice to penetrate your skin.<br>• Never inhale or expose skin to the smoke of burning plants.<br>• Never pick unknown wildflowers, seeds, berries, or cultivated plants.<br>• Wash hands after handling plants and especially before eating food |
| Storage and Labeling | Select a secure area to store materials and label equipment, especially liquids and chemicals (this helps substitute teachers and volunteers). Try to use less potent common household chemicals when possible. When chemicals are necessary, keep only a one-year supply on hand (old chemicals can become unstable). Keep material safety data sheets (MSDS) on hand. Store chemicals, large heavy objects, and glassware on lower shelves, but not accessible to students. Use a stable step stool or ladder to reach higher shelves. Store non-toxic materials in labeled, stackable, sturdy boxes or sealable containers. Store chemicals in small, easy-to-handle containers, such as glass or plastic. Label chemicals with common name, scientific name, formula, precautions for use and antidote. Discard unknown or old chemicals according to school district policy or call the local fire department for correct disposal information. |

this through the lessons we have provided, and to do so safely and effectively. We hope that our lessons provide a model that you will choose to use as you construct your own cycles of learning. However, please exercise caution as you do. Safety, proper supervision, and effective management are as important as helping children to think and choose to behave safely as it is to shield them from potential hazards. This chapter offers some simple safety recommendations, but please check your local policies and laws and explore the suggested sources to deepen your own understanding of safe science.

### chapter 2

# Does Educational Technology Make a Difference?

## Using Educational Technology to Enrich Your Science Lessons

### What Is Educational Technology?

It is not uncommon when discussing the use of educational technology tools in the classroom to hear a veteran teacher say, "I don't need computers in my classroom, my students have always learned this material without them and they still can," or to hear a parent say, "My child spends too much time in front of the television already; I don't want them to spend their time at school in front of a computer monitor." Statements like these often arise out of the misconception the only educational technology tool is the computer and the only use of the computer is word processing or software games. Computers are just one component in an array of tools that are called "educational technology." Consider the following scenario, and see if you can list the variety of educational technology tools the students use as they prepare to share their understanding of science concepts related to water quality.

### Scenario

A small group of Ms. Ramirez's fifth-grade students were sprawled on the floor, pouring over several pages of data they had just pulled off the Internet from a centralized database on stream quality. Another group was off in the corner near the sink, doing a separation test on a soil sample they took from the bottom of their local stream. A third group was at the computer entering new data into a student-generated spreadsheet and creating colored bar graphs from the data, while a fourth group was transferring digital images of the stream in question from the digital camera to the computer. A fifth group was hot syncing their Palm® to download the data they collected on water pH from different stream pools in their study area. After 40 minutes had passed, Ms. Ramirez pulled the group together.

"Okay students, I'd like to spend a few moments having each team give me a status report. Kevin, how far along is your team on their stream study project?"

"We just need to check one more source on the Internet to verify these figures and we'll be ready to put our electronic presentation together. We'd like to go to Mr. Hill's room after school some day this week so he can help us edit our video and put it into our presentation. Can you find out from him which night he can work with us?"

"I'm happy to hear how much progress your team has made during the past two weeks. I'll check with Mr. Hill to determine when he's available to work with you. Are there any other groups that need to work with Mr. Hill?"

"Oh, Ms. Ramirez," said Carla, "our team also needs to edit its video. We still need to scan in some still images we took with Sam's camera and add those to our presentation. Our group worked on graphing the data we collected and made graphs that compared our data to data we pulled from that national database you identified for us on the Internet. We're starting to see some interesting comparisons."

"That's great, Carla. What about your group, Renaldo? How much work does your team have left to complete?"

"We'll probably need a few more days before all of our work is ready to share with everyone. Our team just scheduled a videoconference with an aquatic biologist from the university. We're going to use the desktop conferencing equipment in the library tomorrow afternoon and link to the scientist right at his desk. Mrs. Harp from the library set that up for us and taught us how to make the video phone call at 2 P.M. tomorrow. We're still figuring out how to videotape that session, we want to use some of that tape in our group presentation."

"Ms. Ramirez," Sally piped up, "our group's been busy as the others. We're just struggling with one problem. We have some data that seems like it's wrong. We're not sure if it was the pH meter that didn't work right, if the meter wasn't hooked to the Palm® interface correctly to give us an accurate reading, or if those of us that collected the data messed up. I know when we were at the field site we were able to see the results of our pH analysis on the PDA instantly. We knew we had some errors and corrected for those. Now I think we just can't find where we stored that data. Do you think if we went out today and got another pH reading, we could just plug that number into our data, or would we have to collect all the other data we're using to make our conclusions as well?"

"Well, you've raised an interesting problem, Sally. I'd like to pose that to the entire class. What do you think about this team's problem? To help them come up with a solution, I'd like all of you to think about that article we pulled off the Internet last week. Remember the article about the scientists at three different labs, assuming they were doing exactly the same thing with rats in their study and still got different results. What kind of conclusions would they draw from their data if one of the scientists decided to just change one number because it didn't look right? Especially if they didn't inform the others."

A lively discussion ensued. The debate ranged from e-mailing several scientists to get their ideas, doing an Internet search on the use of accurate data, to having the students

demonstrate to the class exactly how they used the pH meter complete with the Palm®
connection, just in case they did it right and their original data were correct.

Now let's look at the educational technology tools the students were using and how
the students were applying it to their learning. The first group used the Internet as a research tool to go to a national database so they could process data and report results.
The national database gave them the ability to compare local data to nationally collected data. They could search for data about streams with characteristics similar to
their local stream to draw conclusions and make decisions about their stream as compared to streams throughout the nation with similar traits. The students could add their
data to the national database and use it to make an informed decision about the water
quality of the local stream. Using educational technology as a decision-making and
problem-solving tool as well as a research tool are just two of the six foundation
standards presented in the National Educational Technology Standards (NETS) for
students.

Another NETS foundation standard for students is for students to have experience
using technology as a productivity tool. As we saw in the scenario where the student
group was adding their data to their student-created spreadsheet and then using that
data for a computer-generated bar graph, this group of students demonstrated their
skill in using the technology as a productivity tool. The objective behind this standard
is not only to increase productivity and enhance learning, but also to promote creativ-
ity and collaboration among learners in constructing technology-enhanced models of
the concepts they are learning.

The fourth group, who made use of the digital camera, added a visual component
to their understanding of the topic. Communicating their understanding of stream
quality to a public audience required adding a visual component. Here the digital
camera promoted the use of educational technology as a communication tool, another
NETS foundation standard for students. Two of the student groups carried this standard
to another level with their use of videoconferencing to gather information on their
research project.

The fifth group demonstrated the use of emerging technologies; these are just beginning to be found in the K–12 classrooms and are being explored as new tools to help
students gain a better understanding of science and to improve student achievement.
Using the personal digital assistants (PDAs) out in the field gave the students the opportunity to collect and analyze data while still out in the study area. This way they
could check for errors, make the corrections, and move on to collect more accurate data
instantly. These types of emerging technologies are lightweight, portable, and have
enough memory to carry out many of the same functions available on a typical desktop computer.

The last two NETS foundation standards for students are reflected in all of the activities requiring the use of educational technology tools in Ms. Ramirez's class: basic
operations and concepts, and the social, ethical, and human issues involved in using
technology. While the students indicated they needed some assistance with video edit-
ing and videoconferencing, their use of the computer, digital still and video cameras,
personal digital assistants, and science probe ware required no teacher assistance in our

scenario. Of course, what the scenario does not tell us is that these tools, like any other tools a teacher may have students use in a science class, have to be taught. Just as an effective science teacher will spend time in the beginning of the school year teaching the students the safe use and care of traditional science equipment like microscopes or hot plates, so too must a teacher who values the effective use of educational technology in the classroom take the time to teach the students the basic skills and responsible use of the technology.

## Why Use Educational Technology?

Chances are that in a school rich in educational technology, a teacher like Ms. Ramirez is given more opportunities to enhance her technology skills so that she incorporates more of the available technology into her students' classroom experiences. Even in a setting in which access to educational technology is difficult, the choice of applying technology is often driven by the task at hand, not the available technology. It can be seamlessly incorporated into a classroom regardless of how proficient the teacher is with all of the technology tools available. Teachers must overcome the notion that they must be experts with all educational technology before their students are given a chance to use it. As Ediger's (1994) studies on *Technology in the Elementary Classroom* have revealed, applying technology in the classroom does several things to student learning: (1) it increases interest even in rote tasks; (2) it provides purpose for learning; (3) it can attach meaning to an ongoing lesson; (4) it provides opportunities to perceive knowledge as being related, not isolated bits; (5) it allows for individual student differences; and (6) it can impact student attitudes toward learning.

The International Society for Technology in Education (ISTE) has taken the lead in creating student and teacher standards for educational technology. These are detailed on the ISTE website at http://cnets.iste.org. As shared in the scenario discussion, the six student standards identify the foundation all students can build upon as they become more proficient in the use of educational technology tools. It is important to note that this is not a linear list of step-by-step skills a student must have. Rather, it is a thoughtful way of looking at educational technology as a powerful tool for learning.

Applying these standards within the context of a science lesson can strengthen the understanding of the science concepts if we recognize and value the experiences students bring with them and then use the technology to clarify any misconceptions and stimulate proper concept formation (Nickerson, 1995). Conceptual understanding will come about when student interaction between the educational technology and the science content is purposeful. Choosing software that promotes active mental processing and student discoveries is vital and must ensure a state of mindfulness for students while they interact with the technology, and motivate and engage the students to enable them to form appropriate conceptualizations. Computer software, be it instructional software such as the multitude of titles created to address a specific science topic, or application software designed to create a document or draw a picture, is no substitute for active teaching and learning. The software can, however, become an essential part of that teaching and learning, a means for creating student products of the concepts studied.

## Levels of Use

Utilizing a computer in a science classroom seems like a contradiction to a constructivist teacher, one dedicated to engaging students in the processes of science. When appropriately used as a learning tool, educational technology tools can help learners to construct an understanding of complex concepts. At the most basic or novice level, software applications can be used to observe scientific phenomena directly. The software can provide a concrete example of an object, provide facts, or recall basic information. Beginning users of educational technology can easily use drill-and-practice software. As Berger's (1994) study notes, rarely is there mindfulness associated with this type of computer-assisted instruction.

A beginner when applying the ISTE technology standards would be capable of using software applications that supply scientific information. Information provided in CD-ROM encyclopedias and atlases or software applications that evaluate student performance, keep records, or guide students to resources rarely require anything more than novice-level skills to use them successfully.

As students are given more opportunities to apply the technology in their regular classroom activities, through practice they become more proficient in various computer tools and advance to another technology level. Many of the productivity tools that assist in the creation of multimedia productions require students to have more than a simple working knowledge of the software application. Software simulations typically require more than beginner-level skills as well. Although computer simulations are no replacement for actual experimentation, simulations are valuable conceptual tools that bring value to learning when used along with real classroom experiments.

Not all simulations require advanced technology skills, however. Software such as *Amazon Trail 3rd Edition, Bring the Rainforest to Life* (MECC, 2001), for students from fourth grade on, can participate in a virtual journey to the Amazon rain forest in South America. Many dialogue guides with text and audio conversations support the interaction along the journey. Any simulation software that does not allow for student-created models of unidentified phenomena do not require advanced technology skills. These simulations are considered *attribute mapped;* that is, they are given attributes already defined by the software with little room for manipulation of variables. Some software designed to simulate frog dissection fall into this type. This may be an insufficient substitute for a certain level of dissection.

As students become more proficient in the use of educational technology tools, they may reach a level of technological literacy in which they use software applications that simulate experiments in which variables may be manipulated and extended beyond ordinary phenomena. At this level, computer models can be created that lead to explorations of unidentified phenomena. This metaconceptual level is one in which a student uses models to explain reality, reflects on those models, and then suggests a manipulation of variables that projects far beyond what can be created in the laboratory. This type of software is *structure mapped.* This means that a code is built into the software that allows it to search for laws that govern the behavior of objects (Snir, Smith, & Grosslight,

1995). One such computer application is *Thinkin' Science* (Edmark, 2001). When using this software, students have an opportunity to explore a model of the Earth, sun, and moon as well as creating astronomical events, such as solar eclipses or phases of the moon. Simulations involve examinations of Newton's Laws of Motion and the relationship between momentum and acceleration. The simulations help the student arrive at a more complete understanding of Newton's Laws of Motion, phenomena that cannot be accurately observed or understood in the environment of a typical school laboratory.

Microworlds are computer-based laboratory experiences that simulate real-world phenomena. Students can explore undefined phenomena when given proper guidance and intervention by the teacher. Students can be given "what if" predictive situations in order to evaluate and reflect on scientific theories, pose problems that can be solved only through computer-enhanced simulations, and construct the meaning of concepts based on computer-simulated evidence. An inquiring science educator can bring the use of computers to their highest level of application by using microworld environments to give students opportunities to explore and discover scientific theories by using problem-solving strategies that ask, "What is the real problem?" "How do we know it's a problem?" "How can we go about solving the problem?" Microworlds truly embody the spirit of constructivism in its application.

Computer-based laboratories, which effectively integrate numerical and graphical data as quickly as a probe attached to the computer can record it, often require technology skills beyond the novice level. By attaching sensors and timing devices to a computer or a personal digital assistant (PDA), students can monitor heart rate, detect strength and direction of external forces, determine the strength of magnetic fields, record temperature, record pH of liquids, measure amplitudes of audio sources, sense and record humidity changes in pressure, and use an ultrasonic motion detector to measure distance, velocity, and acceleration (Arbor Scientific, 1996).

## The Networked Classroom—Removing the Walls

Using a wide area network (WAN) widens the boundaries of classroom walls and creates a virtual classroom with schools across the globe. For teachers, a network provides increased opportunities to collaborate with other educators about daily instruction or educational reform. Teachers have greater access to additional information, knowledge, and points of view by eliminating barriers of time and place. Networked teachers may discuss issues and access varied resources, including other teachers and resource agencies. A network encourages the development of professional skills: deliberation, collegial consensus building, and development and sharing of ideas related to the profession of teaching.

Future teachers may find that skills for using networked resources such as the World Wide Web (WWW), can provide opportunities to link with practicing teachers through Internet sites such as the *Global Learning Co-op* and the *GLOBE Project* (www.globe.gov/globe_flash.html). The WWW can provide teachers access to standards for science instruction for every state; often an understanding of local standards is expected during job interviews. It can also expose them to grant competitions for teachers and competitions for students, and it can introduce them to various science education associations.

Various national databases exist to support science teaching. Some national services include the National Science Teachers Association (NSTA—www.nsta.org), the National Consortium for Environmental Education and Training (NCEET—www.nceet.snre.umich.edu/), the National Aeronautics and Space Administration (NASA—www.nasa.org), and the National Park Service (NPS—www.nps.gov). These sources provide websites filled with lessons, resources, and various science topics. The Eisenhower National Clearinghouse for Mathematics and Science Education (ENC—www.enc.org) supports a national database. Like other sites it provides lessons and lists of resources as well as identifying which print, video, or computer software is available for teaching science and mathematics.

One should always review any electronically accessed lesson critically, no matter which website is accessed to acquire the resources. Just because a source is published on the Internet does not necessarily mean it is a worthwhile lesson to use. Table 2.1 suggests evaluation criteria for judging the worthiness of electronically accessed lessons. Use this table to help sort and separate the safest and most promising resources.

For students, networked learning environments provide real-world applications of science concepts. Collecting data that will be shared in a nationwide database such as the *Everglades Information Network and Digital Library* (www.nps.gov/ever/ed/index.htm) or the *GLOBE Project* (http://globe.fsl.noaa.gov/) encourages students to be more careful in applying proper scientific procedures when they collect data on a local level to be shared nationally.

*Parks as Classrooms* (www.nps.gov/interp/parkclass.html), an interactive computer-based project funded primarily by the National Park Service, is designed to promote greater understanding and appreciation of the natural and cultural heritage of the United States and to develop sustainable partnerships among parks, schools, and communities. Through this network, data are collected to monitor air, water, and land resources on park lands. This interactive project can simulate land-form changes and cycles in populations within the parks.

The National Geographic Society offers *National Geographic Explorer* (www.nationalgeographic.com), a combination of software designed to meet curricular needs, telecommunications access to classrooms around the world, teacher guides and lesson plans, homework support, and access to unit scientists (National Geographic Society, 2003). There are various problem-based links to join.

Although national projects can be accessed and joined, having access to a wide area network (WAN) within the classroom can encourage students and teachers to start their own science research projects and to invite schools throughout the nation to join the research effort. Collaborative projects can be designed to explore bodies of water, landfills, groundwater movement, seasonal changes per latitude, or any local problem or issue that may have global impact.

Using educational technology as a communication tool goes beyond transporting graphics and text. Depending on the connectivity, students can participate in networks that transport voice, video, and data. Schools throughout the nation are linking together to share in scientific explorations with full motion video and voice interface. From the primary level through college, students are linking with content providers to enrich and enhance their classroom lessons. Zoos, museums, and cultural institutions are revamping the way they present their content to take advantage of the visual medium offered

**TABLE 2.1    Is This a Worthy Task?**

Is the task based on sound and significant content?

- Identify the concepts and/or skills.
- Is the content accurate?

Is the task based on knowledge of students' understandings, interests, experiences, and the range of ways that diverse students learn?

- Identify why the task might appeal to your students.

Are all safety measures properly addressed and followed in any lessons provided? If not, can appropriate safety measures be easily applied to the given task? If you answer no to this second question, do not use this lesson.

| In your opinion to what extent would the task: | a lot | | | | not at all |
|---|---|---|---|---|---|
| engage students' intellect? | 4 | 3 | 2 | 1 | 0 |
| actively involve students? | 4 | 3 | 2 | 1 | 0 |
| develop students' understandings and skills? | 4 | 3 | 2 | 1 | 0 |
| stimulate students to make connections to other disciplines? | 4 | 3 | 2 | 1 | 0 |
| stimulate students to make connections to the real world? | 4 | 3 | 2 | 1 | 0 |
| call for problem formation, problem solving, and reasoning? | 4 | 3 | 2 | 1 | 0 |
| promote communication/interaction among students? | 4 | 3 | 2 | 1 | 0 |

through interactive video networks. Linkages like these promote greater student interaction and discussion of concepts. Providing students with as many opportunities as possible to talk about their understanding of concepts will promote greater conceptual construction and retention. Advancing technologies offer students opportunities on an ever-increasing basis.

# How Can Educational Technology Be Applied in the Context of Science Teaching?

The National Science Education Content Standards (NSES) provide a list of concept statements for three science divisions: Physical Science, Life Science, and Earth and Space Science. The intention is not to have students memorize the statements but rather to actively explore and construct an understanding of the science concepts. The lessons provided in Chapter 3 serve as examples of how the standards can be explored through student-centered inquiry activities presented in a learning cycle lesson format.

Just as the developers of the National Science Education Standards make recommendations for how a science concept may best be learned, the developers of the NET standards also make recommendations for how they are best learned. The International Society for Technology in Education (ISTE) strongly suggests that the teaching of the NET standards should not take place void of context. In the companion website (www.ablongman.com/martin4e) for the textbook *Teaching Science for All Children* (Martin, et. al., 2005), the tables found in Chapter 10 create a profile of the technology standards within the context of a science lesson. The National Science Education Content Standards for a grade-level range are found across the top of each table along with the title of each lesson included in Chapter 3. Down the side are the six National Educational Technology standards. Each table is completed by offering a suggestion of how that particular NET standard could be applied while teaching the lesson presented in Chapter 3. The tables are intended to demonstrate how you could apply the NET standards for a given grade range to a given science lesson to create experiences for students to develop their technology skills as they are learning a particular science concept. Remember, although they are found in a list, the NETS are not linear. For instance, you can use technology as a problem-solving tool without using it as a communication tool first. If you do not access the website, we suggest you look at the six areas included in the NET standards for students and using a science lesson you created, identify an activity you could include with your lesson that incorporates those six standards. For example, if you were to use the first Life Science Lesson in Chapter 3—*Plant Parts and Needs,* Table 2.2 shows how you could effectively integrate the NETS into that lesson.

The lessons included in Chapter 3 can be accomplished without the use of educational technology tools. However, as you can see in Table 2.2 and recall in Ediger's findings on what educational technology can do to enhance learning, you will discover that by applying a few of these suggestions, educational technology can truly enrich the learning experience.

As the previous example demonstrated, teachers can use many methods of integrating the ISTE and National Educational Technology Standards for Students into science lessons. Some additional strategies for incorporating the use of educational technology tools into your science lessons include:

✦ Using a digital camera to take pictures each week of a plant's growth which are placed on a bulletin board with measurements of the plant's growth,
✦ Classification activities to help students increase their vocabulary, observation skills, and critical thinking. Some activities include:
  • Creating a chart (spreadsheet activity) that shows the characteristics of pets that students in the class have in their homes,
  • Using websites (Internet activity) to locate different animals found around the world and identify their characteristics compared to the students' pets,
  • Creating a chart (spreadsheet) that shows the number and characteristics of trees on the playground.

**TABLE 2.2** How to Integrate the National Educational Technology Standards into a Lesson

| National Technology Standards for Grades K–2 | Characteristics of Organisms |
| --- | --- |
| Lesson name | Plant Parts and Needs |
| Basic operations | Students use a laserdisc such as *The Wonderful World of Plants,* part of the series "Science Alive Interactive Multimedia," for up-close views of plants and their parts. |
| Social, ethical and human issues | Students demonstrate respect and care for their environment as they work together collecting plant samples. |
| Productivity tools | Students use *Kispiration* or *Inspiration* software to make a concept map on plant parts. |
| Communication tools | Contact local universities, flower shops, state naturalists, and the like to ask permission for students to e-mail questions to the experts on how their profession makes use of plants. Be sure the responses are age appropriate. |
| Research tools | Students go to the American Horticultural Society's web site (AHS): www.ahs.org/nonmembers/hotlinks.htm to get information on plant care. |
| Problem-solving and decision-making tools | The teacher can create a spreadsheet with pictures and names of plant parts such as a beet or spinach across the top of the spreadsheet and the students' names down the side. The students will then enter into the spreadsheet their prediction as to whether the picture of the plant across the top is a stem, root, or leaf. |

✦ Keeping a scientist's journal about local habitats that includes:
  • Drawings created in *KidPix* and other drawing software,
  • Images from the web or scanned free from copyright pictures,
  • Journal entries that describe observations concerning their particular habitat and the interaction of organisms in that habitat,
  • Recording activities of organisms in the habitat with a video recorder or digital video camera to share with the class and parents,
  • Comparing and contrasting the observations in the video at different times of the day.

Young scientists enjoy investigating the world around them. Digital cameras and digital video cameras can help improve observation skills and help students become more aware of the world in which they live.

## Chapter Summary

Some time in the future, you and your students may pick up a newspaper and read a headline, such as "Genetic Engineering Unravels the Aging Process" or "Ozone Hole Increases." The stories that follow these headlines will be important to both you and your students. They will deal with important quality-of-life issues that you, as citizens, may need in order to form opinions or make decisions about your future. Understanding the consequences of your choices is important to you and to your students.

As a teacher, you will need to ask yourself whether you have done your best to provide your students with the skills they need to make these future decisions. Emphasis on student inquiry through questioning, research, issue resolution, and higher-order thinking skills must be constantly practiced as much as consistent use of educational technology to create the end products that demonstrate the students' ability to perform such skills.

Scientific and technological knowledge are changing so rapidly that it is becoming more difficult to prepare students for this complicated task. Textbooks cannot keep pace with the new discoveries in science; however, as a classroom teacher, you can supplement your textbook and your program with experiences and opportunities that are not available through print materials.

Teachers stimulate learning by serving as the bridge between the resources that are relevant and available to your students. Appropriate applications of educational technology tools can extend the learning environment beyond the confines of the classroom. Only your imagination and energy limit your uses of educational technology, which can provide inquiry-based learning opportunities that stimulate your students and provide a learning environment ripe for scientific discovery.

# Inquiry Lessons for Constructing Understanding

The next three sections contain examples of commercial and public domain supplementary materials as they are *modified* to meet the content standards for elementary and middle school science. Section I is devoted to life science lessons, Section II includes physical science lessons, and Section III contains earth and space science lessons. Our intention is to show the techniques for modification, planning, and methods of teaching. Chapter 3 is a resource for ideas and an exemplar of modification techniques.

More than 150 life, physical, and earth science activities are found within sixty-five lessons designed to fit the 4–E science learning cycle format suggested in the text. A clearly written *concept statement* can be found at the beginning of each lesson. Any concepts that may be important to the lesson expansion are also identified in the beginning of the lesson. Each lesson also has an *inquiry question*—used to pique the interest of the learner and give the lesson a *real-world context*.

The student outcomes or objectives are included in the evaluation phase of each lesson. Those of you who expect to see objectives or *learner outcomes* listed first in an activity are encouraged to look carefully at the evaluation phase of each lesson before starting the exploration phase.

*Grade levels* are suggested in the beginning of each lesson. Each teacher best knows his or her students' limitations. If, upon reading the lesson, you find the activities too difficult or too easy for your students, then by all means find a lesson more suitable for your students' ability levels.

You will not find a *time limit* on the lessons. Lessons using a science learning cycle format may take one class period or several class meetings. One lesson may represent a unit or just one piece of that unit. The length of time for each lesson will depend on the ability level of your students and the amount of detail for each activity. Generally, the lessons are organized so that the *exploration* and *expansion phases* take one or two class meetings, and the *explanation phase* one class meeting. Questions designed to meet the goals of science in personal and social perspectives, science and technology, science as inquiry, and the history and the nature of science from the National Science Education Standards may be asked at any time during the lesson. Just because they are listed after the expansion phase does not mean they have to wait until after expansion to be asked. The *evaluation phase* may also be given in parts, during or after the exploration phase, as part of the explanation phase, and during or after the expansion phase.

These lessons are designed to give your students a chance to explore a science concept thoroughly. Collect materials and try each activity before you present it to your students to make sure everything works according to the plan, to make you aware of any potential problem areas, to ensure that you have foreseen all safety requirements, and to give you an opportunity to correct problems before you are with the students.

Make sure that each student is aware of any *safety precautions* before engaging in the science activity. If certain skills are required before the students can engage in an activity, then spend the time teaching those skills before starting the new activity. Advance work will ensure the success of a lesson presented in a science learning cycle.

# Life Science Lessons

| LESSON NAME | NSE CONTENT STANDARDS FOR LIFE SCIENCE | GRADE LEVEL | ACTIVITIES |
|---|---|---|---|
| **Plants** | | | |
| Plant Parts and Needs | Characteristics of Organisms | K–4 | Plant Dig • Eggshell Planters • Food Storage |
| Osmosis and Capillary Action | Regulation and Behavior | 5–8 | Colored Carnations • Three-Way Split |
| Plant Photosynthesis | Population and Ecosystems | 5–8 | Radish Growth: Light versus Dark in a Bag • Radish Growth: Light versus Dark in Soil |
| Impact of Light in the Forest | Population and Ecosystems | 5–8 | Bean Growth: High versus Low Light • Vegetation Field Study |
| Starch Exploration | Diversity and Adaptations | 5–8 | Microscopic Starch • Beans and Starch Grains |
| **Animals** | | | |
| Colors of Wildlife | Organisms and Environments | K–4 | Animal Similarities and Differences • Create a Rainbow Animal |
| Bird Life | Life Cycles of Organisms | K–2 | What Comes First—the Bird or the Egg? • The Developing Chick |
| Wildlife and Domesticated Animals | Organisms and Environments | K–4 | Animal Needs • Domestic versus Wild Charades |
| A Bug's Life | Life Cycles of Organisms | 3–4 | Ordering Life Cycle Stages • Growing Mealworms |
| Crickets: Basic Needs of an Organism | Regulation and Behavior | 5–8 | Cricket Needs • Cricket Behavior |
| Animal Adaptations | Diversity and Adaptation | 5–8 | Mitten and Tweezer Beaks • Fish Adaptations |
| Owl Pellets | Populations and Ecosystems | 5–8 | Owl Pellet Dissection • Owl Research or Field Trip |
| **Environment** | | | |
| Humans and Trash | Organisms and Environment | K–4 | Trash and Animals • Classroom Landfill and Recycling |
| Pollution Search | Environment | 3–4 | Local Pollution Search |
| Useful Waste | Populations and Ecosystems | 5–8 | Rating Garbage • Litter-Eating Critter • Making Paper |
| Litter in Our Waterways | Populations and Ecosystems | 5–8 | Sink-or-Float Litter • Plastic Food |
| **Human** | | | |
| Sense of Taste | Characteristics of Organisms | K–4 | Buds and Tasters • Supertasters |
| Skeleton | Characteristics of Organisms | 1–4 | Bones Assembly Line • Newsprint Bone Bodies |
| Temperature Receptors on Skin | Structure and Function | 5–8 | Soaking Hands • Hot/Cold Receptor Mapping |
| Building Microscope Skills | Structure and Function | 5–8 | Microscope Use and Crystal Comparisons • Charcoal Crystals |
| Sex-Linked Genes | Reproduction and Heredity | 5–6 | Family Traits • Sex-Linked Traits |
| Passing of Traits | Reproduction and Heredity | 7–8 | What Traits Do You Share? • Inherited or Environmentally Altered? |

# Plant Parts and Needs

**Inquiry Question:** What are the basic parts of a plant?

**Concept to Be Invented:** Main idea—The basic parts of a plant are roots, stems, and leaves.

**Concepts Important to Expansion:** Soil or some nutrient-containing medium, air, water, and light are necessary for plant growth.

## Materials Needed

*For Exploration*

large paper or large plastic bags    resource books on plants    crayons
spoons for digging, or a spade or shovel    poster paint    markers
white paper    art paper

*For Expansion*

eggshells (halves or larger)    water
potting soil    sunlight or artificial light
mung beans    colored markers

 **Safety Precautions:** Always have the proper adult:student ratio when taking the students away from the school campus. Make sure that the students are buddied up and that they are able to cross streets safely and know enough not to talk to strangers while walking to the dig site or while on the site.

Make sure all students can identify any poisonous plants at the dig site, such as poison ivy or poison oak. If large amounts of poisonous plants are in the area, it may be better to choose a different site.

Demonstrate to the students a safe method for digging up the plants and make sure they practice what was demonstrated. Remind the students never to put anything in their mouths unless the teacher gives prior approval. Do not eat the plants!

## *Exploration*   *Which process skills will be used?*

Observing, identifying, comparing

### What will the students do?

Take the students on a walking field trip to an area near the school where plants can be dug up without harming the environment. Identify the plants the students may dig up, and then allow them time to dig, making sure they get most of the root systems. Instruct the students to put their plants in bags and bring them back to school. Once back in class, ask the students to choose one of their plants and spread it out on a piece of white paper. Ask them to use the materials provided to draw pictures of their plants.

• *Plant Dig*

## Explanation/Concept Invention  *What is the main idea? How will the main idea be constructed?*

*Concept:* The basic parts of a plant are roots, stems, and leaves.

Once the students have drawn their pictures, provide them with resource books that identify other plants. Ask the students the following questions:

✦ How are these plants different from the plant in front of you?

✦ How are they the same?

✦ What do all of our plants have in common?

✦ Continue with this line of questioning until the students understand that the basic parts of a plant are roots, stems, and leaves. You may choose to use a sentence starter such as: The part of the plant anchoring it to the soil is called the _____ (root). The part of the plant growing up from the ground is call the _____ (stem). The part of the plant growing off of the stem, and used most often to identify the plant is called the _____ (leaf).

✦ Ask the students to return to the drawings they created of their plants. Ask them to label the roots, stems, and leaves in their drawings. At this time the teacher may provide the students with the common names for their plants, or ask the students if they already know what they dug up, or ask them to look through the resource books to identify their plants.

## Expansion of the Idea  *Which process skills will be used?*

Observing, gathering data, recording data, interpreting data, manipulating materials

### How will the idea be expanded?

• *Eggshell Planters*

Help the students collect eggshells (halves or larger). Ask the students to draw two eyes and a nose on their eggshells with colored markers. Provide potting soil so that the students can fill the shells with soil and sprinkle mung beans on top. Have them put a little more soil on top of the seeds. Sprinkle a small amount of water on the soil. Place the filled shells near the window. Challenge the students to observe the shells each day. When they discover bean sprouts appearing, have them draw a smile on the shell to complete the face.

Once the beans are well grown, ask the students to pull one of the sprouts out. Can you identify its root, stem, and leaves? Ask the students to describe what they did to help the plant grow from the bean seed to the sprout. What things were necessary for plant growth? Make a list on the board. Review with them why the items they identified are necessary for plant growth. Discuss the fact that leaves are necessary to plants because they are the place in the plant where food is created. The water and minerals are taken from the soil through the roots and brought up to the leaves. Gases from the air enter the plant through the leaf, and with the help of sunlight the leaves make food for the plant.

### What additional ideas can be used for expansion?

• *Food Storage*

The teacher can share with the students ways in which plants store food and what humans do with this knowledge. For instance, when food is stored, such as in nuts and

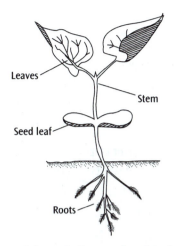

Leaves

Stem

Seed leaf

Roots

seeds, the leaves drop off because they are no longer needed. Also, food is stored in various parts of plants. Provide the students with actual fruits, vegetables, and seeds (or pictures of them) to classify. Make a bulletin board of drawings done by students of roots, stems, leaves, flowers, fruits, and seeds eaten by humans. Hang the pictures near the appropriate term. Some possibilities are roots (beets, carrots, radishes, sweet potatoes), stems (asparagus, celery, green onions), underground stems (onions, potatoes), leaves (lettuce, spinach, cabbage), flowers (artichokes, broccoli, cauliflower), fruits (apples, pears, tomatoes, peaches, plums, apricots), seeds (nuts, peas, beans).

### Science in Personal and Social Perspectives

✦ What would your life be like without plants? Why do you need to take care of plants?
✦ How might taking care of plants help you to develop responsibility?
✦ Ask the students if any of their parents or grandparents have a garden or grow plants indoors. Discuss the special care these plants need. Discuss how large fields of plants can be watered.

### Science and Technology

✦ Why do plants sometimes need to be fertilized?
✦ Do all plants have to be in soil in order to grow? Hydroponic farming does not use soil. Can you think of what it uses instead of soil to grow plants?

### Science as Inquiry

✦ Why do you need to know what plants need to grow?
✦ Why is research done on growing plants?
✦ What must we do to keep the plants healthy?
✦ During what part of a plant's life cycle can it grow without sunlight? Why?

### History and Nature of Science

✦ Discuss with the students jobs or professions that involve caring for plants, such as gardening, working as a forest ranger, selling vegetables in a grocery store, or working in a nursery or flower shop.
✦ Growing and caring for plants takes a lot of work; some of the people who do this are agronomists, horticulturists, florists, botanists, and nutritionists.
✦ Ask the students to have their parents help them discover what Luther Burbank and Gregor Mendel did to help us understand plant growth better.

## Evaluation  *How will the students show what they have learned?*

Upon completing the activities, the students will be able to:

✦ identify the root, stem, and leaf on a complete plant;
✦ name the four things most plants need to live;

◆ when given potting soil, sunflower seeds, water, and a cup, demonstrate the steps necessary to grow and care for a plant;

◆ when given a beet, spinach, and a piece of asparagus, identify which is a root, which a stem, and which a leaf.

# Osmosis and Capillary Action

GRADE LEVEL: 5–8

DISCIPLINE: **Life Science**

**Inquiry Question:** How does water move through a plant?

**Concept to Be Invented:** Main idea—Fluid is drawn up the stem of a plant by osmosis and capillary action.

**Concepts Important to Expansion:** Fiber membranes run throughout a flower from the roots to the petals.

## Materials Needed

*For Exploration (per student group)*
2 to 3 white, long-stem carnations      water
food coloring                                      knife or sharp blade
2 clear cups or glass beakers

**Safety Precautions:** Remind students to take care not to drop glass or beakers, thus increasing the likelihood of cuts and to use caution if using the knife or sharp blade.

## Exploration  *Which process skills will be used?*

Observing, predicting, reasoning, inferring, recording data

### What will the students do?

• *Colored Carnations*

Separate the class into groups of four to six students. Give each group two carnations and two beakers or clear cups. Fill the cups or beakers with water. Dissolve one color of food coloring in one cup and a different color in the other. Dark colors like red or blue work well. Take one of the carnations and cut a fresh end on the stem (this may be done by the teacher with students in each group assisting). After this cut, split the stem in half, starting a cut with the knife and further splitting it along the fibers without breaking them. Place each half of the stem in each beaker and observe the white flower. Record your observations over 3-minute time periods for a total of 30 minutes.

## Explanation/Concept Invention  *What is the main idea? How will the main idea be constructed?*

*Concept:* Fluid is drawn up the stem of a plant by osmosis and capillary action.

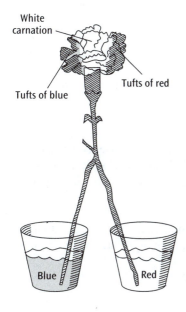

White carnation

Tufts of blue

Tufts of red

Blue

Red

Ask the students questions such as the following to help invent this concept:

✦ What did you observe during the first 3 minutes of this experiment?
✦ How long did it take before you observed any changes in your flower?
✦ What were these changes? Why do you think they happened?

The stems of green plants support the plants and hold up the leaves and flowers. Some plants, like this carnation, have thin, green stems. Other plants, such as trees, have thick wooden stems. The trunk of an oak tree is its stem. It holds heavy branches and thousands of leaves. Water and food move up and down the plant through the stem. Water moves through special tubes in the stem. The water goes from the roots to the leaves and other parts of the plant. Other tubes carry food from the leaves to the roots and other plant parts. The colored water in our experiment is drawn up the stem of the carnation by osmosis and capillary action. The water molecules diffuse through the fiber membranes from a lesser to a larger concentration of plant sap (osmosis). The fibers are so tiny that the adhesive force of the water molecules to the fiber walls becomes very great. This capillary force in combination with the osmotic pressure pulls the water up the flower.

Ask the students to summarize their understanding of capillary action by completing this sentence starter:

Capillary action is the process whereby _____.

## Expansion of the Idea  *Which process skills will be used?*

Communicating, problem solving, experimenting, recording data

### How will the idea be expanded?

When the stem is split three ways, it is very likely that the flower will be three colored. Ask the students to design an experiment to demonstrate this. This will show that the fibers must somehow run all the way from the stem to the petals of the flower. Encourage the students to experiment with how many ways they can get the stem to split to create as multicolored a flower as possible.

• *Three-Way Split*

Ask the students to think about the following: What would happen if the stem were cut irregularly, such as diagonally? What if a cut was made that was jagged and cut across the fibers? How many other types of plants can be used to demonstrate this same phenomenon? Demonstrate this.

### Science in Personal and Social Perspectives

- ✦ If you wanted to give someone a bouquet of carnations to celebrate the Fourth of July and could find only white ones, what can you do to those to get red and blue ones too? Do you think the same thing is done by florists?
- ✦ If you were to receive a bouquet of flowers and you wanted them to stay fresh for a long time, what should you do for them, and why?

### Science and Technology

- ✦ How has knowledge of capillary action been used to create more efficient car engines?
- ✦ Artificial hearts and other organs are continuously being developed. How will osmosis and capillary action of blood affect the function of these artificial organs?

### Science as Inquiry

- ✦ What force is pulling the colored solution up the stem of the carnation in this activity?
- ✦ What if the flower were placed in *clear* water? Would the liquid still be drawn up the stem? How could you tell?
- ✦ Could a plant live without a stem? Why or why not?

### History and Nature of Science

- ✦ Can you name some people who work with plants?
- ✦ Why do you think it might be important for a farmer to understand plant growth? A florist? A grocer?
- ✦ Would you like to work in any of these occupations? Why or why not?
- ✦ How did the tradition of giving flowers on special occasions get started? Can you trace the history of this tradition? Can you trace the history of when flowers were artificially colored?

## Evaluation   *How will the students show what they have learned?*

Upon completing the activities, the students will be able to:

- ✦ explain the purpose of splitting the stem in two during this lesson;
- ✦ demonstrate their knowledge of capillary action by explaining the process using a piece of celery, food coloring, a beaker, and water;
- ✦ observe several plants in various stages of watering (underwatered, overwatered, just right) and explain why the plant looks as it does.

## Plant Photosynthesis

**GRADE LEVEL:** 5–8

**DISCIPLINE:** Life Science

**Inquiry Question:**  How do plants feed themselves?

**Concept to Be Invented:**  Main idea—Plants are capable of making their own food by a process called *photosynthesis.*

**Concepts Important to Expansion:** Seeds, moisture, chlorophyll, designing investigations

**Materials Needed**

*For Each Student Group*

Radish seeds
2 Ziploc bags (large storage size)
2 paper towels

1 piece of aluminum foil
paper towels
metric ruler

 **Safety Precautions:** Remind students not to put anything in their mouth and to avoid eating leaves or seeds of plants. Do not play with plastic bags and keep them away from the face.

## Exploration *Which process skills will be used?*

Predicting, observing, inferring, controlling variables, experimenting, reducing experimental error, analyzing

### What will the students do?

Provide each group of students with some radish seeds, 2 Ziploc bags, 2 paper towels, and 1 piece of aluminum foil. Challenge the students to design a way in which they could use these materials to compare the growth of radish seeds. Explain to them that the variable to be manipulated in this experiment is light. All other factors must remain constant. The students must write up the method they plan to use; do not be concerned if the students change too many variables. This will be a valuable lesson to them, as they will soon discover by their experimental results. Once they have designed and written up their experimental methods, including predictions of potential outcomes, give them time to act on their design. Check their uncovered bags each day. When leaves begin to grow in the uncovered bag, uncover the covered bag and compare the two environments.

* *Radish Growth: Light versus Dark in a Bag*

## Explanation/Concept Invention *What is the main idea? How will the main idea be constructed?*

*Concept:* Photosynthesis is a process in which chlorophyll-bearing plant cells, using light energy, produce carbohydrates and oxygen from carbon dioxide and water. Simply put, it is a way in which green plants use the sun's energy to make their own food.

Have the students share the data they collected. Ask the following questions:

✦ Where did you place your bags in the room?
✦ Were they both put in the same place?
✦ Why is it important to make sure the bags were in the same area?

Uncovered bag
(radish begins growing)

Covered bag
(with aluminum foil)

- What about the number of seeds you used? Was that kept constant?
- Is it important to keep the number of seeds the same? Why or why not?
- What happened inside both of your bags? Was it as you predicted?
- If so, can you explain why? If not, why not?
- Did the seeds sprout leaves in both the covered and uncovered environments? What color were they?
- Which environment appears more successful?
- What gives your skin color? (Pigment.) Do plants have pigment?
- Where did the green leaves come from? Does anyone know the name of the pigment that gives plants their green color? (Chlorophyll.)
- Do you think, based on your experimental results, you can determine what the chlorophyll does for the plant? (It makes food for the plant.)
- Complete this sentence: The process whereby the chlorophyll makes use of light energy to make food for the plant is called _____ (Photosynthesis).

## Expansion of the Idea  *Which process skills will be used?*

Experimenting, hypothesizing, predicting, observing, analyzing, controlling variables, inferring, recording data

### How will the idea be expanded?

• *Radish Growth: Light versus Dark in Soil*

Challenge the students to design another experiment, this time planting the seeds in soil instead of bags. Once again make light the manipulated variable. Predict the outcome, plan and record the methods, and act on your design. Once the seeds in the light begin to sprout, compare these results to the bag experiment. Were your predictions accurate? Why do you think you obtained the results you did? Did photosynthesis occur in the covered pot? the uncovered pot? Why? Continue to grow the plants and measure and record the results for one month.

### Science in Personal and Social Perspectives

- How do plants help people survive on this planet?
- What would your life be like without plants?

### Science and Technology

- Because they need land to live and grow things on, some people in Brazil are cutting down the tropical rain forests. Should this concern you? Do you think there is a technological solution to the problem of vanishing rain forests? Share your ideas.
- Of what advantage has hydroponic farming been to the people of the world?

### Science as Inquiry

- New concepts for further inquiry include growth rates, leaf shapes, deciduous versus coniferous, and so on.
- Can photosynthesis occur if a plant does not contain chlorophyll?

+ Does photosynthesis take place in plants that grow on the ocean floor?

### History and Nature of Science
+ What impact has the farming industry had on our daily lives? On the lives of people throughout the world today and in the past 100 years?
+ Who was Gregor Mendel (1822–1884)? How did his knowledge of photosynthesis open up an entirely new field of genetics?
+ Can anyone become a landscape architect? What kind of background knowledge does a person in this field need?

## Evaluation  *How will the students show what they have learned?*

Upon completing the activities, the students will be able to:

+ when provided with two examples of the same plant, one grown in a shady environment and the other in a sunny one, identify which was grown where;
+ observe plants growing around the classroom and accurately predict what will happen to the leaves if a small piece of paper is clipped over part of a leaf for one week;
+ read a problem about a science exploration and accurately determine which variable should be manipulated and which should be controlled.

---

# Impact of Light in the Forest

GRADE LEVEL: **5–8**
DISCIPLINE: **Life Science**

**Inquiry Question:** Does light intensity affect the type of vegetation found in an area?

**Concept to Be Invented:** Light is a necessary factor for life by way of photosynthesis. The intensity of light varies throughout canopy levels within a forest.

**National Science Education Standards:** Grades 5–8—NSE Life Science Populations and Ecosystem Concepts:

+ For ecosystems, the major source for energy is sunlight. Energy entering ecosystems as sunlight is converted by producers into chemical energy through photosynthesis. Energy then passes from organisms in food webs.

NSE Science as Inquiry Concepts:

+ Activities that investigate and analyze science questions.
+ Groups of students analyzing and synthesizing data after defending conclusions.

### National Educational Technology Standards Met Through Lesson

1. Basic operations and concepts
   a. Use of the Palm® with the ImagiWorks or Vernier Interface to collect light intensity data

2. Social, ethical and human issues
   a. What were the advantages and disadvantages of using the Palm® to collect and analyze data?
3. Technology communications tools
   a. How did you use the Palm® to communicate the results of your field study?

**Science Attitudes to Nurture:** Open-mindedness, cooperation with others, tolerance for other opinions

**Materials Needed:** *For each group of 4–5 students:* 1 Palm®, Vernier Light Sensor, ImagiWorks Interface and one-prong interface to sensor adaptor. A computer to download and analyze Palm® data. The software needed on the computer should be LOGGER Pro, Microsoft Word and Excel, and Internet Explorer.

**Safety Precautions:** Handle all equipment with care. If any equipment is broken, contact teacher immediately. Do not take equipment near water. Use caution when working in a poorly lighted area. Always walk, do not run, in the classroom and out in field study area.

**Exploration** *Which process skills will be used?*

Observing, collecting, and recording data, interpreting data, hypothesizing, designing an experiment

Put students into groups and give them Vernier probes and Palm® and ask them to measure the amount of light in different areas of the room with the lights off and only one window with open curtains. Give students three specific areas to measure light in and three areas to choose themselves. Students will collect and analyze data. Results will be portrayed in a model to be put on the chalkboard for whole class review.

As the students maneuver through the introduction activity, they will find that areas away from the window have less light. Wave properties of light will be seen where light is detected even behind obstacles.

+ Where is the intensity of light the greatest and the least?
+ Why is the intensity of light the greatest, the least in these particular areas?
+ How does light get around obstacles?
+ How does light move? (Straight lines? Curves?)
+ Does light bend? Explain.

• *Bean Growth: High versus Low Light*

Begin the next activity once students demonstrate they can use the light probes with the Palm® to collect light intensity data. Divide the students into research groups and provide each team with three growing, potted bean plants. Ask the teams to think about the results of light intensity data they collected while becoming familiar with the probes. Based on the analysis of their data, ask them to select three study areas in which to place their growing plants—(1) the area where they found the light intensity to be the greatest, (2) where they found the light intensity to be the least, and (3) an area where they found the light intensity to be between the greatest and the least. Before they place the plants in the three study areas, ask them to create a data sheet to record the condition of their plants. Allow the teams to pick which variables they will record regarding the *condition* of their plants. Remind them they are manipulating the variable of light only through placement in three different areas. Since they are manipulating the amount of light—all other variables should remain constant, e.g., amount of water provided to each plant, how each plant will be watered, amount of nutrients given to each plant (if any), conditions of the plant that will be recorded (e.g., height, number of leaves, sturdiness of stem). Ask them to record light intensity on their plants and record the condition of their plants on a daily basis. After two weeks, ask the student teams to create a graph that compares the conditions of their three plants over time. Ask them to draw conclusions on the relationship between light intensity and the condition of their plants. They should be able to share their results with the entire class.

## Explanation/Concept Invention   *What is the main idea? How will the main idea be constructed?*

Ask the student teams to share the results of their data analysis. Ask students to reflect on their exploration activity to answer the following:

✦ Was there a difference between the plants grown where the light intensity was the greatest and the plants grown where the light intensity was the least?
✦ What did you observe about the growth of the plants in the "in-between" area?
✦ Based on the data you collected, what could you conclude about the relationship between light intensity and plant growth? (Students should conclude that too much or too little light intensity would stunt plant growth.)
✦ Once the students can articulate that plant growth depends upon light intensity, then explain to them that light is necessary for plant growth in that it stimulates food production, a process that is called photosynthesis. At this point the teacher can develop a presentation on photosynthesis explaining how light energy is converted to food energy for the plant. Background knowledge on photosynthesis will help the students respond to the inquiry question posed in the beginning of the lesson and explored in the Expansion phase of the lesson.

## Expansion   *Which process skills will be used?*

Experimenting, hypothesizing, observing, recording data and analyzing data, cognitive thinking, drawing conclusions

*• Vegetation
Field Study*

The student groups will be assigned to a field study area within the forested school land lab, in the open prairie area, and in an area right next to the school void of vegetation. On day 1, as a team, the students will go to all three of their assigned study areas and record the type and amount of vegetation found within each area. It is up to the student teams to develop a data table to collect and record this data. A schedule will be set up so that at specific times during the school day, different students within the group will be responsible for going to these three study areas and collecting data on light intensity using the light probes. They will record the light intensity data on their record sheets. (Note: this can be created on the Palm® through Excel or even using the ImagiProbe software on the Palm®.) They will record this data at the same times throughout the day for 5 consecutive days. The inquiry question behind this study is: "Does light intensity affect the type of vegetation found in an area?" Once the students have collected and analyzed this data, the teacher will use that information to get into a discussion on photosynthesis, asking how they think varying levels of light affect the rate of photosynthesis, and how light intensity affects the types of plants found in the study areas.

### Science in Personal and Social Perspectives

+ How will your understanding of light intensity affect where you place the plants you have growing in your homes?
+ When you see a house plant with yellowed leaves, what do you think the plant is telling you?

### Science and Technology

+ What is the benefit of using the probes with the Palm® in the field or the lab?
+ Can you come up with any other uses for the light intensity probe other than collecting information on plant growth?

### Science as Inquiry

+ Why do we need plants?
+ Can we live without plants?

### History and Nature of Science

Why is it important when conducting an experiment to manipulate one variable and control all of the others?

## Evaluation   *How will the students show what they have learned?*

Upon completing these activities, the students will be able to:

+ explain the importance of light in the process of photosynthesis;
+ explain why plants found on a deciduous forest floor grow earlier in the spring compared to the trees of the forest;
+ design an experiment that shows the relationship between light intensity and plant growth.

# Starch Exploration

**Inquiry Question:** Are all starches the same?

**Concept to Be Invented:** Main idea—Starches have a structure that is unique for each type of vegetable.

**Concepts Important to Expansion:** Starch grain, hilum, slide preparation, microscope use

## Materials Needed

*For Each Student Group*

| | |
|---|---|
| microscope | rice that was soaked in water |
| 5 slides | for at least 4 hours |
| 1 scalpel | kidney beans |
| cover slips | corn kernels |
| tapioca | potatoes |

**Safety Precautions:** Although the starches are edible, the students should be discouraged from tasting them. Caution should be used around electrical outlets for the electric microscopes. The bulb for the microscope will get hot. Students should be reminded of safety techniques when using the scalpel.

## Exploration  *Which process skills will be used?*

Observing, predicting, comparing, manipulating materials, recording data

### What will the students do?

The students will prepare slides of each of the given vegetables by using the scalpel to gently scrape a newly cut surface on the vegetable. A very small speck of each should be placed on each slide with a drop of water. A cover slip should be applied. The students should make predictions before observing the different starch grains. Will all of them look alike, since they are all starches? What do you think? Record this prediction. The students should observe each prepared slide under the microscope and draw their observations of the starch from each vegetable.

• *Microscopic Starch*

## Explanation/Concept Invention  *What is the main idea? How will the main idea be constructed?*

*Concept:* Starches have a structure that is unique for each type of vegetable.

Key questions to ask the students to help them come to these conclusions are:

- What did you observe as you looked at the potato grains?
- How were they different from the corn or rice?
- What did the bean and tapioca starch look like?
- Ask the students to compare their drawings to actual pictures of the various grains. Were you able to observe the detail these pictures show?
- Can you differentiate between parts of the grain?
- Ask the students to complete this concluding statement: While potatoes, rice, and beans are all considered starches, they differ in their _____ (structure).

### What additional information will help develop the concept?

The students should find countless oval, ellipsoidal, or even triangular shaped, almost transparent bodies that look like miniature oyster shells when they observe the potato

Corn starch

Rice starch

Bean starch

Tapioca starch

starch grains. Since the grains are not flat, it may help if the students slowly rotate the fine adjustment on the microscope back and forth to get all the parts in focus. Usually on the narrower end the students will find a tiny dark spot that is not in the center of the grain. This is called the *hilum,* the oldest part of the starch grain, around which the remainder of the shell has grown layer by layer until fully formed. If you focus up and down at this point, you will find concentric lines or rings called *striations,* which indicate the layers where the grain has grown larger and larger.

Corn starch is different from potato. The grains may have an irregular globular shape or a very distinct polygonal shape. The shape will vary depending on the part of the kernel the students take their samples from—the horny or the floury portion. Corn starch has a central hilum that is usually a point but sometimes shows two, three, or four radiating clefts.

Rice starch grains are very small and many sided. They may be square, triangular, or pentagonal in shape. The hilum is not distinct, but in some grains a central portion appears brighter. This difference may be due to the drying of the grain. Ovoid or spherical shapes are usually due to a number of grains being compacted together.

Bean starch grains are usually ellipsoidal or kidney shaped. They have an irregular branching cleft running out from the center that appears black because of enclosed air.

Tapioca grains are usually circular or loaf shaped, depending on whether they sit on their flat surfaces or on their sides. The hilum is centrally located, usually coming to a point or small cleft. When students view the flattened surface, the hilum may appear triangular.

# Expansion of the Idea  *Which process skills will be used?*

Observing, predicting, comparing, manipulating materials, recording data, hypothesizing

### How will the idea be expanded?

- ✦ The students may brainstorm a list of other starch-containing foods. Obtain these foods, prepare slides, and check students' predictions by looking for evidence of starch grains. Are they similar to any of the grains previously identified? Are they different? What kind of starch do you think this food contains?
- ✦ The students may obtain several different kinds of beans. Pose a question: Will all beans contain the same kind of starch grains, no matter the type of bean? Allow the students to design an experiment to answer that question.

• *Beans and Starch Grains*

### Science in Personal and Social Perspectives

- ✦ Do you think the differences in the starch grain will affect your ability to digest that starch? Why or why not?
- ✦ Are there any other kinds of plants that contain starch grains that humans do not eat? What are these? Why do you think we do not eat them?
- ✦ Why are starches important in a person's diet?

### Science and Technology

- ✦ Why does the United States send starchy foods to underdeveloped countries? What kinds of conditions are necessary to grow starch-containing foods? Can modern technology do anything to help these underdeveloped nations to grow starches on their own?
- ✦ What kinds of products have modern industries created that make use of starches? How have these helped modern society? How have these hindered modern society?

### Science as Inquiry

- ✦ Are all starch grains, no matter the plant they come from, the same? Will starch grains from many different varieties of potatoes look the same? Why or why not?
- ✦ What is the name of the oldest part of the starch grain? Does finding this structure under the microscope help in identifying the type of plant the starch grain came from?
- ✦ Did the process skills the students had to engage in to do these activities (predicting, manipulating materials, forming hypotheses, solving problems, recording data, making careful observations) enhance their overall academic growth?

### History and Nature of Science

- ✦ Why do you think a person responsible for creating frozen dinners should understand that different vegetables have different starch structures?

◆ What kinds of jobs entail making careful observations and accurately recording what was observed?

◆ Do you think an insurance adjuster could benefit by learning the skills you utilized while participating in this lesson?

## Evaluation  *How will the students show what they have learned?*

Upon completing the activities, the students will be able to:

◆ prepare a slide of starch grains;
◆ accurately draw starch grains observed under a microscope;
◆ identify with 80 percent accuracy the various starch grains and their sources;
◆ explain in writing or orally why certain starches can be digested by humans while other starches cannot.

## Colors of Wildlife

GRADE LEVEL:  **K–4**
DISCIPLINE:  **Life Science**

**Inquiry Question:**  Are animals all the same color? Why or why not?

**Concept to Be Invented:**  Main idea—Wildlife occurs in a wide variety of colors.

**Concepts Important to Expansion:**  Camouflage allows an organism to blend in or hide in its environment.

### Materials Needed

*For The Entire Class*
Magazines that have a wide variety of animal pictures, such as *National Geographic, Ranger Rick, National and International Wildlife, Audubon.* Try to have magazines that can be cut up.

Construction paper, crayons or markers, scissors, glue, felt, cotton balls, natural materials from outdoors (acorns, leaves, grass); an appropriate storybook with a wide variety of different-colored animals in it will also help introduce the topic. Richard Buckley and Eric Carle's *The Greedy Python* (New York: Scholastic Books, 1992) is a good selection.

**Safety Precautions:**  Remind students not to poke each other with the scissors and to use them only while seated.

# Exploration  *Which process skills will be used?*

Observing, comparing, generalizing

### What will the students do?

Introduce the lesson by reading the students a book like *The Greedy Python.* Encourage the students to make note of the color of the python and of all the other animals it comes across. You will return to the ideas provided by the story later.

*•  Animal Similarities and Differences*

After the story and brief discussion about it, provide each student group with several wildlife magazines to look at. Ask the students to find pictures of animals, make observations about the animals, and compare the animals to one another. Create two lists on the board. Title one list *similarities,* the other *differences.* Ask the students to share their observations about the animals they found by providing information about the similarities and differences of the animals. Ask each student to cut out three different animals.

# Explanation/Concept Invention  *What is the main idea? How will the main idea be constructed?*

*Concept:* Wildlife occurs in a wide variety of colors.

Refer back to the story you read. For instance, if *The Greedy Python* was used, you might ask the following questions to help invent the concept:

+ What animals did you see in the book?
+ What colors were they?
+ Why do you think the python was so successful in eating all the animals?
+ Could a green python hide easily in a jungle?
+ Hold up a variety of different-colored pieces of construction paper. Ask the students to identify the colors. Then ask the students to raise their hands if they cut out animals that match the color of the paper you are holding. Assist them to complete this statement about animals: Animals appear in a _____ (variety) of colors.
+ Let the students help in gluing the animals on to the construction paper that matches the animal's color. Hang these animal pages around the room.
+ Ask the student farthest from each picture if it is difficult to identify the animal on the page, that is, a red animal on a red piece of paper. Ask why he or she thinks it is difficult.
+ How would this coloration help it survive in the wild? Draw the students to the conclusion that camouflage allows an organism to blend in or hide in its environment.

# Expansion of the Idea  *Which process skills will be used?*

Observing, manipulating materials, generalizing, comparing, communicating

• *Create a Rainbow Animal*

## How will the idea be expanded?

Use the materials from the material list to have the students create their own animal. The animals may be real, or they can make them up. Encourage the generalization that wild animals appear in a wide variety of colors and that the animals' colors and markings help them survive. Encourage the students to look for rainbow animals—those that have three or more distinct colors on their bodies. Ask the students to share their creations with one another. Get them to communicate to one another how their animal can hide in its environment.

### Science in Personal and Social Perspectives

✦ Where would you find _____? (Insert an animal name.)
✦ Do you think it is as important for a pet to blend in with its surroundings as it is for wild animals? Why or why not?
✦ Do we need to protect the environment where some animals live? Why?
✦ What are some things society can do to protect animal environments?

### Science and Technology

✦ Hunters used to wear only clothing that blended into the environment when they hunted. Today we see hunters wearing bright orange vests and bright orange hats. Why do you think the design of their clothing changed?

### Science as Inquiry

✦ Where could you learn more about a particular animal?
✦ What are some ways that color helps animals survive?
✦ Besides color, what other kinds of things can animals use for camouflage?

### History and Nature of Science

✦ Can you think of any jobs in which people work with or study animals?
✦ Can you think of any jobs in which people work with aquatic animals?
✦ Can you think of any animals that work? (Police dogs, seeing-eye dogs, sled dogs, horses, pigeons, animals that help on a farm.) How are these animals trained?

## Evaluation *How will the students show what they have learned?*

Upon completing the activities, the students will be able to:

✦ construct an animal using a variety of colors when given materials;
✦ explain how a cartoon animal relates to a real animal;
✦ make a graph of animals that have one, two, or more colors.

# Bird Life

**Inquiry Question:** What is a life cycle?

**Concept to Be Invented:** Animals have a life cycle that includes being born, developing into an adult, reproducing, and eventually dying.

**Concepts Important to Expansion:** The details of a life cycle are different for different animals.

## Materials Needed

*For Exploration*

reproducible pictures of birds at various stages of their life cycle, that is, egg, 1–2 days old, two weeks old, month old, adult. Enough copies to supply student groups of 4–5 students per group with a set.

computer software such as *Birds and How They Grow* or a video that shows birds as they develop in the nest

poster paper

crayons or markers

glue

*For Expansion*

access to an incubator with developing chicken or duck eggs and the ability to make daily observations

journal or computer-generated log to record observations

**Safety Precautions:** Stress the importance to students of respecting the developing bird and not banging on the sides of the incubator or creating excessive noise while making observations.

## *Exploration* *Which process skills will be used?*

Observing, comparing, predicting

### *What will students do?*

Provide each student group with a stack of bird development pages. Have the students work in teams to color the various pictures of the bird in different stages of its life cycle. After they complete that task, ask them to lay out each of the pictures in front of the team. Ask them to describe what is different in each picture. (The children should be identifying differences such as in one picture it was an egg and in the next it is a chick with little to no feathers, and then in the next it has a feathers but mostly soft fluffy ones, then in the adult picture it has a full set of feathers.)

If the students are capable of writing, ask them to record these differences on the poster paper under a heading titled "Differences." Ask them to then describe anything the pictures may have in common. (The children should be able to identify that once past the egg stage, each of the chickens has two legs, wings, a beak, etc.) Record those on the poster paper under the heading "Same." Then ask the students to decide as a

• *Which Comes First— the Bird or the Egg?*

group what picture comes first, then second, then third, and so on. Ask the students to arrange them in order on a sheet of poster paper.

## Explanation/Concept Invention  *What is the main idea? How will the main idea be constructed?*

*Concept:* Animals have a life cycle that includes being born, developing into an adult, reproducing, and eventually dying.

Ask the student teams to share items from their list labeled "Differences." Did each of the student teams come up with similar lists? Ask them to explain any observations that did not show up on all of the student team "Differences" lists.

Then ask the student teams to share items from their list labeled "Same." Did each of the student teams come up with similar lists? Ask them to explain any observations that did not show up on all of the student team "Same" lists.

Hang up the team posters with the ordered pictures in the front of the room. Ask the students to look at the posters and check for similar or different orders. Have them share their observations. Ask them to predict why some teams pasted the pictures in one order and other teams in another if differences exist among the posters.

Some sample questions to ask the students as they make their observations are:

- ✦ How are the birds in the various pictures similar? How are they different?
- ✦ Why do you think this team put the picture of the egg first? Or the picture of the adult bird, or the small bird?
- ✦ Which picture represents the bird before it is hatched?
- ✦ Which picture shows the bird just after it has hatched?
- ✦ Which picture shows the bird as an adult?

After the students respond to your questions, explain to them that these pictures represent various stages in the bird's life. Ask them to think about their own life. Do they remember seeing pictures of themselves as a baby? Have they changed since they were babies? Just as they have changed, the pictures that they placed in order show how the bird will change as it gets older. You can use one of the posters to add labels to the pictures such as: egg, one day old, two weeks old, one month old, and adult. Give the student teams an opportunity to rearrange their posters in the order from egg to adult if theirs was out of order.

Ask the students to complete this sentence starter: A life cycle is a process that starts with _____ (being born), developing into an _____ (adult), then making more of you or _____ (reproducing) and then eventually _____ (dying).

## Expansion of the Idea  *Which process skills will be used?*

Observing, predicting, recording data, drawing conclusions

### How will the idea be expanded?

• The Developing Chick (or Duck)

This expansion activity can take place in your classroom if you have access to the materials and space permits, or if your school has one central area for containing live animals that is more conducive to this type of activity. Do not do this activity if you do not feel comfortable growing live chicks or ducks or if your building does not have the facilities to accommodate growing birds. You may want to do this activity in conjunction with a teacher from a higher grade level, where older students could be responsible for making sure the needs of the birds are met as they hatch.

Another possibility is finding a website that has a live camera trained on an incubator with developing chicks or ducks. Several schools throughout the United States have made this service available. Search the Internet for such a site. This activity is often done during the spring of the year.

Still another possibility is for the teacher to create a "virtual bird" via a computer-generated draw package. "Grow" the bird over a period of days. Provide the students with its weight and height to enter into a database. Ask them to make predictions about changes in the bird's height and weight, amount of feather cover, beak size, and so forth over time.

Once you have established a source for observations, have your students engage in the following activity:

+ Visit the incubator site the day the eggs are placed in the incubator. Have them record their observations in a journal. Start with "day 1" and continue beyond hatching. If space and time permit, allow the students to make observations throughout the rest of the year.
+ Assign student teams different times during the day to go to the incubator to record their observations on a daily basis. Remind them not to tap on the incubator or to disturb the eggs in any way.

Throughout the time that the students are making their observations, bring the students together as a class on a weekly basis to discuss what they have observed. Have them make predictions about what they could expect to see happen next. If all of the eggs do not hatch, be prepared to discuss why. Offer possible reasons such as improper development, lack of essential needs such as heat to foster egg development, or even the possibility that the egg was not fertilized. If some of the chicks die, be prepared to have a conversation about this as a natural part of a life cycle. You will have to judge if all of your students at this grade level are prepared for this.

Another possible activity to expand on the concept of animals having a life cycle that includes being born, developing into an adult, reproducing, and eventually dying— without going through the expense and time needed to hatch live chicks or ducks—is to show a variety of videotapes that take students through the life cycle of different animals. Conversations about the videotape should lead students to conclude that the details of a life cycle are different for different animals.

### Science in Personal and Social Perspectives

+ Could someone have expected you to stay the same as when you were born? Why is this a silly idea?
+ If you live in a tiny house or apartment and you have an opportunity to get a puppy, would you choose one who had a mother that was a large dog? What do you know about the life cycle of a dog that might lead you to believe this is not a good idea?

### Science and Technology

✦ How can an incubator help us hatch an egg if a mother bird is not around?

✦ If you don't see an animal in every stage of its life cycle, how do you know it went through different stages? What evidence do we use to prove that it did? Think about the evidence we used in our class activities to answer this question.

### Science as Inquiry

✦ The observations and predictions the students make about the developing bird and conclusions that they draw provide them with early science inquiry skills. Gathering and organizing data extend their inquiry skills.

### History and Nature of Science

✦ What do you think your doctor needs to know about the human life cycle to help you as you grow? Invite a pediatrician into your class to share ideas with your students.

✦ Visit a pet store. Have the students prepare questions to ask the shopkeepers about what they know about the life cycles of the different pets in their store and how that information helps them keep their pets healthy.

## Evaluation   How will the students show what they have learned?

Upon completing the activities, the students will be able to:

✦ describe what a life cycle is and use it in the context of the life of a bird and the life of a human;

✦ order pictures in the proper sequence for the life cycle of an animal other than a bird or human;

✦ label the stages of growth of a given animal from birth to adult.

## Wildlife and Domesticated Animals

GRADE LEVEL:  K–4

DISCIPLINE:  Life Science

**Inquiry Question:**  What is wild?

**Concept to Be Invented:**  Main idea—Wildlife includes animals that are not tamed or domesticated.

**Concepts Important to Expansion:**  Endangered animals, extinct, threatened, safe

**Materials Needed**

*For Exploration*
Pictures of both wild and domesticated animals, attribute blocks

**Safety Precautions:**  Tell students not to throw attribute blocks, and to use care when acting out animals in expansion activity so as to not hit another student.

# Exploration  *Which process skills will be used?*

Observing, hypothesizing, inferring, categorizing, recording data

### What will the students do?

Using attribute blocks, ask the students to place these blocks into two different groups. This activity will ensure that the students understand the concept of grouping. Next, ask the students to look around the room at the pictures hanging up. What do you observe in the pictures? (Animals.) Divide the class into groups of four to six. Provide them with pictures of both wild and domesticated animals (at least as many pictures as there are students in a group). Each student in the group will pick up an animal and record characteristics of the animal that make it different from any other. Some prompting questions could be: Where do they live? How do they get their food? Are they dependent on humans for their survival? Once each child in the group has listed the characteristics of the animal he or she chose, ask the students to decide how they could put their animals into two different groups. Once they make that decision, then divide the animals.

• *Animal Needs*

# Explanation/Concept Invention  *What is the main idea? How will the main idea be constructed?*

*Concept:* Wildlife includes animals that are not tamed or domesticated.

Ask the students questions such as the following to help invent this concept:

+ How did your group decide to divide your animals?
+ What characteristics of your animals led you to this decision?
+ How do the animals in one of your groups get their food?
+ How do the animals in your other group get their food?
+ Do either of your groupings separate the animals into whether they rely on humans for their survival?
+ Based on the students responses to the questions above, ask them to complete these statements: Animals that do not rely on humans for survival and that are neither tame or owned are called _____ (wild). Animals that rely on humans for their survival are called _____ (domesticated).

# Expansion of the Idea  *Which process skills will be used?*

Observing, classifying, analyzing, inferring, communicating

### How will the idea be expanded?

Ask the students to choose an animal, and without telling anyone else in the class, write down the name of that animal. The students may choose one from a picture in the room or think of one on their own. Divide the class in half, and collect their listed animals in two groups. Explain to the students how the game of charades is played. Have students from one half of the class pick from a pile of animals that came from the other

• *Domestic versus Wild Charades*

| Wild | Domestic |
|------|----------|

half of the room, and vice versa. Ask the students to look at the name of the animal on the card, and without saying what is written on the card, act out the behaviors of that animal for the students on your side of the room to guess. Write the words *domestic* and *wild* on the board. Once the students guess which animal was acted out, ask the student who just acted out the animal to decide whether that animal should be listed as domestic or wild. Make sure all of the students agree on the listing before acting out the next animal.

### Science in Personal and Social Perspectives

+ Name some domesticated animals that we could find in your neighborhood. What would the neighborhood be like if these animals were wild?
+ What do you think life would be like if any of the wild animals we acted out no longer existed, that is, they became extinct?
+ What do you think would happen if you tried to tame a wild animal?
+ Why is a wildlife preserve important to our society?
+ Can the study of wildlife give us any ideas about how people behave?

### Science and Technology

+ Propose a method to change an animal from wild to domestic.

### Science as Inquiry

+ What important facts must we remember when dealing with wildlife?
+ What things are important to remember when taking care of pets?
+ What is the difference between a wild and a domesticated animal?

### History and Nature of Science

+ What type of job requires knowledge of wildlife or requires someone to work with wild animals?
+ Interview a zookeeper. What special skills does someone in this line of work need?
+ What kind of jobs would have to be created if wildlife started taking over our community?
+ Choose a domesticated animal. Search throughout history to determine when it first became domesticated and why.

Upon completing the activities, the students will be able to:

- ✦ give two examples of a wild animal;
- ✦ give two examples of a domestic animal;
- ✦ list the characteristics of a wild and a domestic animal;
- ✦ draw a picture of an animal and identify it as wild or domestic by drawing an appropriate habitat for it.

## A Bug's Life

GRADE LEVEL: 3–4

DISCIPLINE: Life Science

**Inquiry Question:** Are the life cycles of *all* animals the same?

**Concept to Be Invented:** Animals have a life cycle that includes being born, developing into an adult, reproducing, and eventually dying. The details of a life cycle are different for different animals.

**Concepts Important to Expansion:** Plants and animals closely resemble their parents.

### Materials Needed

*For Exploration*

a set of reproducible images of a black beetle's life cycle from egg, larva (the mealworm), pupa, and adult (the black beetle)

a set of reproducible images of a dog's life cycle from birth to adult

a set of reproducible images of a butterfly's life cycle from egg larva (the caterpillar), pupa, and adult (the butterfly)

*For Expansion*

mealworms to raise as part of the expansion activity; available at a pet shop or bait store

materials to raise the mealworm in, such as a large container with a lid and food like bran, flour, dried bread, cracker crumbs and oatmeal; a slice

of apple or carrot will be needed to provide humidity

journal or computer-generated logs to record observations and other data student teams identify as important to collect

**Safety Precautions:** Tell students that care should be used in handling the mealworms and to avoid placing hands in their mouth after working with the insects. Remind them to wash hands immediately after handling any insects.

## Exploration  *Which process skills will be used?*

Observing, comparing, drawing conclusions, recording data, making hypotheses

### What will students do?

- *Ordering Life Cycle Stages*

Have the students work in teams of two or three. First, give the student teams the pictures that represent the life cycle of a black beetle. Do not give them in order from birth to adult. Just ask the student teams to arrange them in that order, if indeed they think they all belong together. Time how long it takes them to put these in order. Stop this activity once each team has recorded how long it took them to come to an agreement as to the proper placement.

Then without explanation ask the students to set those pictures aside. Now provide them with the pictures that represent the life cycle of the butterfly. Once again, do not give them to the students in any kind of order. Again ask the student teams to arrange them in order from birth to adult, if indeed they think all of the pictures belong together. Again time how long it takes for the student teams to put these in order from birth to adult.

Do this same activity a third time, making use of the pictures that represent the life cycle of a dog.

Which took the longest, arranging the life cycle of the black beetle, the butterfly, or the dog? Ask the students to discuss within their groups possible reasons for the time differences.

## Explanation/Concept Invention  *What is the main idea? How will the main idea be constructed?*

*Concept:* Animals have a life cycle that includes being born, developing into an adult, reproducing, and eventually dying. The details of a life cycle are different for different animals.

Ask the students as a class to share their reasons for why it may have taken them longer to order one animal's life cycle than another. Ask questions such as:

- ✦ Did each of these animals start its life cycle in a similar form?
- ✦ At what stage or stages of the life cycle do these animals look different?
- ✦ Why was it easier to arrange the life cycle of one animal than another?

The students will be sharing responses such as the animals they are more familiar with are easier to arrange in order from birth to adult. Animals that have basically the same form from birth to adult are easier to arrange. After the students discuss their observations, ask them to summarize what they have learned by completing this statement: The life cycles of bugs are similar to dogs in that they _____ (include being born, developing into an adult, reproducing and die). The life cycles of bugs are different from dogs in that _____ (as they move from being born to an adult their bodies change in that what they start out as and what they look like as an adult are totally different).

## *Expansion of the Idea* *Which process skills will be used?*

Observing, predicting, recording data, drawing conclusions

### How will the idea be expanded?

Provide each student team with the materials you assembled for the expansion phase of this activity. Give the students ample time to make observations of the mealworm. Ask them to recall the exploration activity and to predict what the mealworm will look like as it becomes an adult. Once their observations of the mealworm are complete, guide them in constructing a growth chamber for their mealworms. This is done by placing in a large container with a lid (like a 2-lb coffee can or a plastic shoe storage container with lid) the food mixture of bran, flour, dried bread, cracker crumbs, and oatmeal. By placing an apple slice or carrot in the container, humidity will be added to the environment. Place several mealworms into the container and store in a warm area (between 75° and 80° F). Have students record the number of mealworms placed into the container. Light is not needed for growth, so a warm, dark cabinet or storage area in the classroom will be an ideal growth area. Students should check the container every few days, adding more food and apple or carrot.

* *Growing Mealworms*

Ask the students to collect information on changes in the mealworm over time. Have any begun to change body form? What do they now look like? How many mealworms are now in the container? Are there other stages in the black beetle's life cycle present? Count and record how many of each.

Since a mealworm will stay in the larval stage for about six months, chances are that the container may eventually contain a form of the black beetle in each stage of its life cycle. It will depend upon the ages of the mealworms when obtained from the supplier. Ideally you'd like to find that within the growth chambers there are black beetles as larvae, pupae, and adults within a few weeks.

Ask the students to explain why their mealworm counts changed. What happened to those mealworms? Do all of the adults look alike? Could you tell one adult from another? Is that an easy thing to do? Ask the students to find within their growth chamber an example of the black beetle in each stage of the beetle's life cycle. Help them to conclude that each larval mealworm ended up looking like its parent, and that each generation of black beetles that follow will look just like their parents in the adult stage of their life cycle.

### Science in Personal and Social Perspectives

✦ How does having an understanding of the life cycle of an insect help protect your home from being overrun with insects?

✦ What "bug" problems do you commonly face? During what stage of the bug's life cycle does that "bug" "bug" you?

### Science and Technology

✦ What kinds of things have cities done to control insect populations like flies or mosquitoes? At what stage of their life cycle are they easier to control?

✦ Do you think it is a good idea to use chemicals to control insect populations? Why or why not? What kind of an impact will continued use of chemicals have on future insect populations?

### Science as Inquiry

✦ Design an experiment to determine at which stage in an insect's life cycle they feed and at which stage they reproduce. Use the mealworms and black beetles to carry out your planned experiments. Be sure to apply proper scientific methods such as controlling variables, making consistent observations, and accurately recording data for later analysis.

### History and Nature of Science

✦ In the late 19th century growers in California brought the ladybug over from Australia to help battle tiny insects that threatened orange groves. The ladybugs fed on the smaller insects to control their population. Today there are several beneficial insects used by gardeners. These include ladybugs, mealworms, parasitic nematodes, parasitic wasps, praying mantises, green lacewings, and predatory mites. Identify at what stage of the insect's life cycle they are most beneficial. Using an electronic resource such as a website or CD-ROM, find pictures of these insects in the most beneficial stage of their life cycle and prepare a multimedia presentation that describes how they benefit gardeners.

## *Evaluation*  *How will the students show what they have learned?*

Upon completing the activities, the students will be able to:

✦ describe the life cycle stages of an insect and explain how these differ from the life cycle stages of a mammal;

✦ accurately predict what the offspring will look like when given a picture of an early stage in the life cycle of a given organism (Do the things you learned about animals and their life cycles hold true for plants? Why or why not?);

✦ design an experiment to show how plants go through a life cycle and demonstrate that each new plant will look like its parent.

---

## Crickets: Basic Needs of an Organism

GRADE LEVEL: 5–8
DISCIPLINE: Life Science

**Inquiry Question:** What are the basic needs of all living things?

**Concept to Be Invented:** All organisms, no matter the size, have a basic need for food, water, shelter, and space in a suitable arrangement.

**Concepts Important to Expansion:** Living organisms respond to stimuli from their environment. Animals in captivity must be able to adapt to their environment in order to survive.

**Materials Needed**

*For Each Group of Students*

1 terrarium
1 plastic pint container with
   screen top
1 hand lens

1 piece of black construction paper
seeds (6 each of clover, grass,
   wheat, radish, and bean)

*For the Entire Class*

Eric Carle's *The Very Quiet Cricket* (New York: Philomel Books, 1990); 4 plastic bags, each containing eighteen crickets; felt pen, paper clips, tape or staples, chart paper.

 **Safety Precautions:** Remind the students to wash their hands after handling the crickets, and not to eat the seeds or put them in their mouth, or to poke each other with the staples or paper clips.

## Exploration *Which process skills will be used?*

Observing, recording data, experimenting, drawing conclusions

### What will the students do?

Begin the lesson by doing something that students of this age level would never expect. Read very animatedly *The Very Quiet Cricket,* by Eric Carle. Although not age appropriate, the story is very effective in getting students to think about the task to come. Divide the class into research groups of four. Allow library time for the students to find answers to the following questions: What is necessary for the survival of a cricket? Are their needs similar to human needs? What requirements do they have for food, water, and shelter? Can many crickets live in a small space? How many can live comfortably together?

* Cricket
  Needs

## Explanation/Concept Invention *What is the main idea? How will the main idea be constructed?*

*Concept:* All organisms, no matter the size, have a basic need for food, water, shelter, and space in a suitable arrangement.

Ask the student groups to report on the results of their inquiries. Through their reporting, continue to question them to clarify the results of their research efforts. Questions for clarification may include:

+ What did you discover about the crickets' eating habits?
+ What kind of habitat does a cricket survive in best?
+ Does a cricket need water?
+ Help the students to draw the conclusion that all organisms, no matter the size, have a basic need for food, water, shelter, and space in a suitable arrangement by asking them to complete this sentence starter: An animal's habitat will provide it with its basic needs of _____ (food, water, shelter and space in a suitable arrangement).

## *Expansion of the Idea*  *Which process skills will be used?*

Observing, communicating, problem solving, formulating models, classifying, questioning, hypothesizing

### How will the idea be expanded?

• *Cricket Behavior*

Set up a terrarium with a few crickets living in it. Encourage the students to make observations about the crickets in the terrarium as they are collecting their data. Assign each of the different research groups from the exploration phase of this lesson one of the following tasks so that they will understand the behavior of a cricket:

◆ Take a cricket from the terrarium. Place it on a smooth surface and then on a rough surface. Watch the cricket for 3 to 5 minutes on each surface. Record your observations. Which surface causes the greater obstacle to movement? Why do you think this is so? Try manipulating the environment in other ways: hot versus cold surface or light versus dark conditions. Return the cricket to the terrarium.

◆ Obtain a shoebox. Cut a hole on one side about the size of a small flashlight. Cut a hole on the other side just big enough for your eye to peep inside. Take a cricket from the terrarium. Place the cricket in the dark end of the shoebox (opposite end from the flashlight hole) and put on the lid. Cover the flashlight hole with your hand in an effort to make the box as dark as possible inside. Watch the cricket's behavior for 5 minutes. Record your observations. Now place a small flashlight in the hole and turn it on. Observe the cricket for another 5 minutes. Record your observations. Were there any differences in the cricket's behavior when the light was on versus when it was off? If so, why do you think this occurred? Return the cricket to the terrarium.

◆ Take a cricket from the terrarium and place it in a shoebox. As a group, decide on three different kinds of food you think a cricket might like to eat. Place the three types in front of the cricket. Make sure you keep accurate records about the amount of food placed in the box. It may be important to weigh each food choice. Put the lid back on the box. Place the box in a dark, quiet place in the classroom. Ask the group members to make predictions about which food type they think the cricket will choose. Make and record observations every 30 minutes for one school day. Did the cricket choose the food you predicted? Why or why not? Do you think more than one cricket should be used in this experiment? Why or why not? Return the cricket to the terrarium.

Ask each of the different research groups to report on their findings. Encourage all the students to communicate to one another exactly what they did, why they did it, and what they discovered as a result. Help them in their discussion to come to the following conclusions: Living organisms respond to stimuli from their environment. Animals in captivity must be able to adapt to their environment in order to survive.

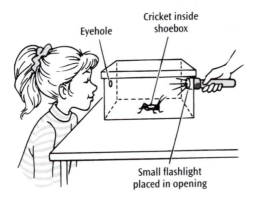

Eyehole

Cricket inside shoebox

Small flashlight placed in opening

### Science in Personal and Social Perspectives

- What legends exist about crickets? How and why have these been handed down through generations?
- What could you do for an animal if it has lost its mother? How could you help it survive without removing it from its environment?
- Why would it be important for you to know how to care for an animal in a situation like that?

### Science and Technology

- Do you think fluctuations in cricket populations could tell us something about what people are doing to their environment? How would you design an experiment to determine what humans are doing to their environment?
- Do you think it is important that humans understand something about other animals no matter what their size? Why or why not?

### Science as Inquiry

- Why does a terrarium need to have soil in it?
- Can a cricket drink water out of a bowl? Why does a cricket rub its wings?
- What are the basic needs of a cricket?

### History and Nature of Science

- What kinds of occupations deal with a variety of animal species? (Game wardens, zookeepers, wildlife officers.)
- What would it be like if there was no one who understood the basic needs of certain animals? Was there ever a time in history when our lack of understanding affected the life of an animal? Provide an example.
- What does an entomologist do?

## Evaluation  *How will the students show what they have learned?*

Upon completing the activities, the students will be able to:

- design and build their own terrarium for a cricket, making sure that it is designed to meet all of the cricket's basic needs;
- pick one animal and determine its basic needs for food, shelter, water, and space;
- pick a domesticated animal such as a chicken, dog, or hamster and describe the adaptations necessary for that animal to survive in the wild;
- participate in a discussion of how humans would have to adapt in order to survive in the wild.

# Animal Adaptations

**GRADE LEVEL:** 5–8

**DISCIPLINE:** Life Science

**Inquiry Question:** What is so good about an adaptation?

**Concepts to Be Invented:** Main idea—The shape of a bird's beak determines the type of food it will eat. This is one form of an adaptation.

**Concepts Important to Expansion:** Many animals have developed specialized adaptations in order to survive in their environments. Fish utilize adaptive coloration, body shape, and mouth placement to help them survive in different aquatic environments.

## Materials Needed

*For Exploration*

Enough tweezers and mittens so that each student in the class has one or the other of these. Numerous pipe cleaners, paper wads, and strips of construction paper to serve as "food" for the birds. Place pictures of various kinds of birds with different feeding habits all around the classroom.

*For Expansion*

Pictures of various kinds of fish placed around the room. The fish should demonstrate such differences in coloration as light-colored belly, dark upper side, mottling, vertical stripes, or horizontal stripes. Differences in body shape could be flat bellied, torpedo shaped, horizontal disc, vertical disc, or hump-backed. The mouth shapes may be an elongated upper jaw, duckbill jaws, an elongated lower jaw, an extremely large jaw, or a sucker-shaped jaw. A fish tank with fish that live at different levels of the tank would also serve to

emphasize the secondary concept. Art materials like crayons, markers, scissors, scrap material, construction paper, chalk, old buttons, yarn, pieces of felt, and so on are also needed.

**Safety Precautions:** Remind the students to walk, not run, while participating in the bird-feeding activity. Use caution with scissors in the expansion activity.

## Exploration   *Which process skills will be used?*

Observing, inferring, experimenting, analyzing

### What will the students do?

Distribute the pipe cleaners, paper wads, and paper strips throughout the room. Place some on the floor and some of them in harder-to-get-to places. Each student will choose the type of "beak" (mitten or tweezers) that he or she wants to use. The students will explore a bird's eating habit by trying to pick up the different types of food using the beak they chose.

• *Mitten and Tweezer Beaks*

## Explanation/Concept Invention   *What is the main idea? How will the main idea be constructed?*

*Concept:* The shape of a bird's beak determines the type of food it will eat. This is one form of adaptation.

Ask the students questions such as the following to help invent this concept:

✦ Choose two students that used different kinds of beaks (i.e. mitten and tweezer). Why was it easier for _____ (student's name) to pick up the paper strips than _____ (a different student's name)?

✦ What kind of beak did each have?

✦ Do you see any pictures of birds in this room with a beak that would work like the tweezers? Can you think of any others?

✦ What do you think they use these beaks for?

✦ What types of food can a bird with a beak like a pair of mittens eat?

✦ Why do you think some birds eat one kind of food and others a different type? Do you think it would be to a bird's advantage if it could eat a different kind of food than another type of bird? For instance a robin will eat worms, but it won't eat nectar like a hummingbird, yet you can find both of them living in the same area.

✦ Ask the students to complete this summary statement: Many varieties of birds can survive in one area because they eat different kinds of food. Their ability to eat different foods has to do with the shape of the _____ (beak). Having a different beak shape is an example of an _____ (adaptation).

## Expansion   *Which process skills will be used?*

Hypothesizing, observing, questioning, classifying, analyzing, inferring, manipulating materials, communicating

*How will the idea be expanded?*

The students will look at pictures of different types of fish and try to categorize them in three different ways: coloration, mouth shape, and body shape. A discussion should ensue on how these three classifications are important adaptations to ensure the fish's survival in its environment. After the discussion, the teacher should assign each student or group of students a particular combination of adaptations from each of the three groups, such as mottled coloration, torpedo body shape, and sucker-shaped jaw. Ask the students to use the art materials provided to create fish with those three types of adaptations. Ask them to create environments in which fish with those adaptations could survive. Have the students share their creations.

### Science in Personal and Social Perspectives

+ What are some ways in which people have adapted to their environment?
+ What are some ways in which we share our environment with the birds? Fish?
+ What has society done to improve the lives of animals in their habitat?

### Science and Technology

+ If you were to make a hummingbird feeder, would it be useful to know the type of beak this bird has? Why?
+ What are some disadvantages of taking an animal out of its natural habitat?
+ Could an animal adapt quickly enough to survive in a new environment? Why or why not?
+ Choose an animal. Outline all of the problems that would need to be overcome for that animal to survive in a different habitat.

### Science as Inquiry

+ Can an animal's inability to adapt to rapid changes in its environment lead to its extinction? What other events may lead to the extinction of an animal?
+ Is there any one species of bird that has a beak that allows it to winter in an area with a relatively cold climate? What advantage does this beak shape have over any other?
+ If you were to buy a fish from a pet store and wanted one that would clean the food off the gravel in the bottom of your fish tank, what kind of a mouth shape would it have?

### History and Nature of Science

+ How important is it for a zookeeper to understand the special feeding adaptations many animals have developed? Why?
+ If you were working at a nature center and were responsible for creating an aquarium that made use of fish found at a local lake, what would you need to know about the local fish to make your display enjoyable for center visitors?

## Evaluation *How will the students show what they have learned?*

Upon completing the activities, the students will be able to:

◆ identify bird beak adaptations and explain how these contribute to the survival of the bird;

◆ design an ideal habitat for an animal of their choice, emphasizing that animal's special adaptations for survival in its environment;

◆ explain why several species of fish can live together in one lake without competing with one another for food.

---

# Owl Pellets

**Inquiry Question:** What is an owl pellet?

**Concept to Be Invented:** Main idea—The owl coughs up, or regurgitates, owl pellets, which contain the undigested parts of animals eaten by the owl, such as hair and bones.

**Concepts Important to Expansion:** Digestion, eating habits

### Materials Needed

*For Each Student Group*
One owl pellet, which may be obtained through a local division of your state department of natural resources or wildlife. Sterilized pellets can be ordered through a supplier. One dissecting kit, glue, handouts of the skeleton of a vole, mouse, or rat.

**Safety Precautions:** Remind the students to use caution when handling the sharp dissecting tools.

## Exploration *Which process skills will be used?*

Observing, predicting, inferring, hypothesizing

### What will the students do?

Provide each pair of students with an owl pellet and a dissecting kit. Ask the students what they think the pellet is. How was it created? What do they think they will find as they carefully pick the matted hair away from the owl pellets? After student predictions are shared, instruct the students to keep everything they find as they pick away carefully at the pellets. Try to reconstruct a skeleton of a rodent, using the picture as a guide.

• *Owl Pellet Dissection*

## Explanation/Concept Invention  *What is the main idea? How will the main idea be constructed?*

*Concept:* The owl coughs up, or regurgitates, owl pellets, which contain the undigested parts of animals eaten by the owl, such as hair and bones.

Ask the students questions such as the following to help invent this concept:

+ What kind of rodent do you think your owl ate?
+ Did you find the remains of more than one kind of rodent?
+ What do these findings tell you about the type of food an owl eats?
+ What is an owl capable of digesting?
+ Based on your dissection of the owl pellet, tell me what an owl pellet is. An owl pellet is _____ (coughed up or regurgitated by the owl. It contains the undigested parts of the animals eaten by the owl).

## Expansion of the Idea  *Which process skills will be used?*

Observing, communicating, problem solving, formulating models, recording data

### How will the idea be expanded?

+ *Owl Research or Field Trip*

+ Take the students on a field trip to an area where owls are known to nest. Look carefully on the ground around the area. What do you expect to find to indicate to you that owls may be in the area? How are pellets different from owl scats?
+ Invite a wildlife specialist to bring an owl to visit your classroom to discuss its characteristics and habitat. Ask your class to prepare in advance sound questions to ask the visitor about the owl.
+ Assign each student team to write a report about a different species of owl. This report should include such things as where it is found and its life span, habitat, and food preferences.

### Science in Personal and Social Perspectives

+ What might happen to owls if humans disrupt their habitats?
+ What are some ways that owls are adapted to their environment?
+ How are we adapted to our environment?
+ What has technology done to improve the lives of animals in their habitats? What could society do?

### Science and Technology

+ What are some disadvantages of taking an animal out of its natural habitat and placing it in another environment?
+ If you came across some bones of an animal, how could you go about identifying which animal they came from?

### Science as Inquiry

+ What special needs does an owl have in order to survive in any habitat?
+ Why were the bones and hair of the rodents not digested by the owls?

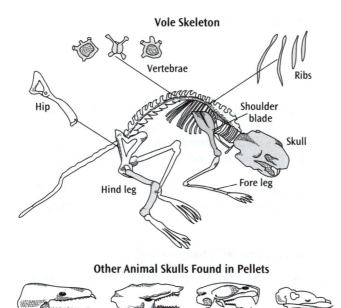

**Vole Skeleton**

Vertebrae

Ribs

Hip

Shoulder blade

Skull

Hind leg

Fore leg

**Other Animal Skulls Found in Pellets**

Shrew          Mole          Rat          Sparrow

## History and Nature of Science

✦ What kinds of professions are dedicated to ensuring animal safety? What kinds of careers endanger animals?

✦ In this activity you found the bones of a rodent and reconstructed them to determine which rodent it was. Do any other careers expect you to take evidence and reconstruct it to find answers? Which ones?

## *Evaluation*   *How will the students show what they have learned?*

Upon completing the activities, the students will be able to:

✦ construct a food chain, placing the owl at the highest level;

✦ dissect an owl pellet and use the bones found to reconstruct the skeleton of a rodent;

✦ speculate on how information provided through owl pellet dissection can assist people in raising the survival rate of many owl species.

# Humans and Trash

GRADE LEVEL: K–4

DISCIPLINE: Life Science

**Inquiry Question:** What *harm* does my trash cause?

**Concept to Be Invented:** Human-made trash affects all living matter.

**Concepts Important to Expansion:** Recycling can decrease the amount of waste created by humans.

### Materials Needed

*For Exploration*

Selected (clean) trash, drawing paper, crayons, glue, stapler. Enough of these materials should be collected so that each child in the class can actively participate in the lesson. One large box filled with a piece of trash for each child, five or six medium-sized boxes that can be labeled for glass, paper, plastic, aluminum, tin, and so on.

**Safety Precautions:** Remind the students to use caution when handling trash, not to put fingers in mouth, and to wash hands thoroughly after handling trash.

## Exploration *Which process skills will be used?*

Questioning, inferring, predicting, hypothesizing, communicating, manipulating materials

### What will the students do?

• *Trash and Animals*

Before doing this lesson with the class, collect enough trash so that each child in the class may have several pieces to choose from. Be sure that any trash chosen is free of rough edges, broken glass, or sharp points so that the children will not be harmed during the lesson. Wash out any plastic bags and cans used as trash.

Ask each student to think of an animal and draw a picture of it.

Supply the students with a large selection of trash. Ask the students to choose one piece that particularly intrigues them. Ask the students to draw a picture of how that piece of trash would hurt their animal if the animal came across that piece of trash while outside. Ask the students to attach the piece of litter to their picture. Each student should be allowed to share the picture with the class, explaining how their animal was harmed by the piece of trash they chose. Encourage the students to act out how the animal moved both before and after the trash affected them.

## Explanation/Concept Invention *What is the main idea? How will the main idea be constructed?*

*Concept:* Human-made trash affects all living matter.

Ask the students questions such as the following to help invent this concept:

✦ What is wrong with leaving our garbage just anywhere?

✦ How do you think trash can hurt animals besides the ways each of you just shared? The teacher can give such examples as: How many of you have been fishing? What happens when your line gets stuck? Just as it tangles up in the weeds, if you simply cut the line and leave it in the water, it can get tangled on ducks' necks, legs, and beaks. It can keep them from walking, flying, and swimming. Sometimes it may become wrapped around their beak, and they starve to death.

- ✦ Hold up a ring from a six-pack of pop cans. Could this hurt an animal? How? Explain how fish or birds can get tangled up in it. Check the local wildlife office for pictures of tragedies like these. Show the students how to break up the plastic rings before they place them in the garbage. Explain to them that even though they put them in the garbage, eventually that garbage bag will break down and that plastic ring will be left to cause possible harm to some animal. If they cut it up before placing it in the trash, there is less of a chance of it harming an animal.
- ✦ In what ways do people get rid of their trash? Do you think the way in which we get rid of our trash harms animals?
- ✦ How do you think our trash harms plants?
- ✦ What can you conclude about human-made trash? Complete this sentence: All human-made trash affects _____ (all living things).
- ✦ What do you think we can do to get rid of trash? (Pick up trash alongside the road, reduce our use of materials in excessive packaging, recycle, and so on.)

## *Expansion of the Idea*   *Which process skills will be used?*

Observing, communicating, problem solving, formulating models, classifying, questioning, hypothesizing

### How will the idea be expanded?

Refer back to the explanation phase of this lesson. Remind the students of the conversation they had in which you asked about the ways people get rid of their trash. Perhaps some students mentioned that their garbage is hauled away by a service. Ask them to think about where that trash goes after hauling. Introduce the term *landfill* (the place where trash gets hauled to be buried in the ground) if they are not already familiar with it. Ask them to suggest alternatives to taking trash to a landfill. As they make suggestions, list them on the board.

• *Classroom Landfill and Recycling*

After the students have created a list, show them a large box in the front of the room labeled *landfill*. (Note: The teacher should have filled this box with a piece of trash for every child in the class.) Have each child pick out one item. Ask them if they think it can be recycled. If so, they should place it in the appropriately labeled medium-sized box. Sum up this activity by getting the children to surmise that recycling can decrease the amount of waste created by people.

### Science in Personal and Social Perspectives

- ✦ What can you do to help eliminate excessive trash?
- ✦ Do you know what to do with recyclable materials where you live? If not, why not ask your parents to help you work on recycling some of your trash?
- ✦ What are some ways businesses can cut down on their trash?
- ✦ How can companies that make different products help the environment?
- ✦ Do you think businesses have a responsibility to reduce the amount of trash they create?

### Science and Technology

✦ Do you think twice about buying a toy that is not only boxed but then wrapped in paper and then in plastic? Do you think the practice of excessive packaging affects our environment?

✦ Create a map of what happens to a toy's packaging from the time the toy is packaged until the packaging no longer exists.

### Science as Inquiry

✦ What kinds of household items can be recycled?

✦ How does trash harm animals?

✦ How does trash harm plants?

✦ It has sometimes been said that one person's trash is another person's treasure. After doing these activities, how true do you think that statement is?

### History and Nature of Science

✦ Who is responsible for making sure that animals are not harmed by human trash?

✦ Who is responsible for making sure that plants are not harmed by human trash?

✦ Do you think you could make a career out of collecting recycled trash? Can people make money from recycling?

## Evaluation   *How will the students show what they have learned?*

Upon completing the activities, the students will be able to:

✦ separate recyclables into appropriate groups;

✦ state three ways in which trash harms animals;

✦ draw pictures of our environment before trash was recycled and after it was recycled. The students will be able to explain the difference between the two drawings.

## Pollution Search

**Inquiry Question:** Does our school neighborhood have a pollution problem?

**Concept to Be Invented:** Pollution is considered any contamination of the air, water, or land that affects the environment in an unwanted way.

**Science Attitudes to Nurture:** Curiosity, open-mindedness, cooperation with others

GRADE LEVEL: 3–4
DISCIPLINE: Life Science
Mathematics
Language Arts
Social Studies and
National Educational
Technology Standards
(NETS) for Students

## Materials Needed

### For Exploration (Whole Class)
Dr. Seuss's, *The Cat in the Hat Comes Back* (New York: Random House, 1958)
large poster paper, white board, or chalkboard to record class observation while reading the story

### For Expansion (for Each Student Team of 4–5 Students)
clipboard with paper, computer with spreadsheet software, graphing software such as *Graph Master* by Tom Snyder Productions (optional), word processing software (optional).

**Safety Precautions:** Remind students to sit quietly, keeping hands to themselves during the reading of the story. Be sure proper student-to-adult ratio is followed when taking students on a pollution search in the neighborhood around the school. Remind students to always walk, not run, in classroom and outside in field study area.

## Exploration *Which process skills will be used?*

Observing, predicting, communicating, problem solving, designing an experiment

Ask the students to gather around you as you read *The Cat in The Hat Comes Back* by Dr. Seuss. As you read the story, use the poster paper or white board to write the story's events. Ask the children to summarize what happens at each stage of the story.

1. The cat shows up at the house.
2. The cat takes a bath and leaves a bathtub ring of pink stuff.
3. The cat uses a dress to get the pink stuff off the tub and ends up getting it all over the dress.
4. The cat gets the pink stuff on the wall and uses shoes to clean it off.
5. And so on.

## Explanation/Concept Invention *What is the main idea? How will the main idea be constructed?*

Use the sequence of story events to have a discussion about how a story like this might be real. Be sure to refer to the list of events as you ask the students questions such as:

+ Out in the playground when people just throw their trash around, we consider that behavior polluting our environment. What in the story might represent pollution?
+ Where did the pollution come from?
+ How did the cat deal with the pollution?
+ Did that help solve the pollution problem?
+ What did the little cats do? Did they help with the pollution problem?
+ Who finally cleaned up the pollution and how did that happen?

Use the students' answers to make a summary statement about pollution. Ask the students to complete this sentence starter: When we put things into the air, water, or land, which affect our environment in an unwanted way, this is considered _____ (pollution); or Pollution is _____.

## Expansion of the Idea  *Which process skills will be used?*

Observing, planning an investigation, recording and analyzing data, comparing and contrasting, problem solving, drawing conclusions, communicating findings

• *Local Pollution Search*

Prepare the class to go on a *local pollution sources search.* As a class, the teacher will remind the students about the story and how the "pink stuff" spread, making a mess of the house. Ask them if the pink stuff was pollution, contaminating the house. What might that look like if it contaminated the water? The air? Ask the students that since we don't have to worry about a *Cat in the Hat,* what other ways might *we* pollute our surroundings? Collect a list of these suggestions. Draw two intersecting circles on the board. Label the *inside* circle and the *outside* circle, and label the intersecting area of the two circles, *both.* Ask the children to predict where each of the suggested pollutants may be found—inside, outside, or both—and have a student write that pollutant(s) in the appropriate circle.

Tell the students that this is a Venn diagram and ask them to look at the diagram again. Ask them if there is another way they could group pollution besides inside, outside, and both? Lead them toward these three groups: air, water, and land. Make three new intersecting circles. Label them Air, Water, and Land (see Figure A). Ask the students to take the items from their previous list and now place them in the appropriate new circles. Tell them they will use these categories to search for evidence of pollution—called pollutants—as they work in teams in the neighborhood around the school.

Assign student teams to a field study area within the neighborhood around the school. Have adults supervise each student team. Assign cooperative roles to each of the students (i.e., reporter, recorder, etc.). Direct the student teams to walk around the school neighborhood looking for pollution or pollutants and to record what they see on a data sheet. Figure B is a data sheet to record the field data. When the students encounter litter that can be collected in their neighborhood, instruct them to first record the data, then using rubber gloves and garbage bags, collect the litter for disposal once they return to school.

When the students return to the classroom have them work in the same teams at the computers to record their data into a spreadsheet. The students should be able to graph the data they collect. Figure C (page 70) provides an example of how that data could be organized for graphing and a sample graph.

Provide the student teams time to log their data into the spreadsheets. If the class is familiar with graphing software such as *Graph Master,* have them use their data to create a bar graph of the pollution types. If no software is available, provide them time to create a bar graph of the pollution types versus number of examples of pollution. Use the individual team data to create a bar graph of the entire class data. Discuss with the

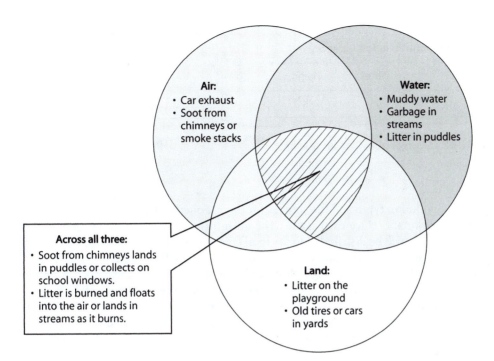

Across all three:
- Soot from chimneys lands in puddles or collects on school windows.
- Litter is burned and floats into the air or lands in streams as it burns.

Air:
- Car exhaust
- Soot from chimneys or smoke stacks

Water:
- Muddy water
- Garbage in streams
- Litter in puddles

Land:
- Litter on the playground
- Old tires or cars in yards

**FIGURE A**  Venn Diagram

### Field Data

| Name of Pollution Source | Where It Was Found | Size or Amount | Type |
|---|---|---|---|
| Fast-food wrapper | In playground by swing set | 1 wrapper | Land |
| Soot from chimney | Coming from house on Elm Street | Watched chimney for 5 minutes and soot was coming out entire time. | Air |
| Oil slick | Floating on the surface of a puddle on Grant Street | Since it was an irregular size, we estimated the area of the oil slick to be about 15 cm x 22 cm. | Water |
| Candy wrappers | In front of house on Lee Place | 5 wrappers | Land |

**FIGURE B**  Field Data

**Amount/Pollution Category**

| Air | Water | Land |
|-----|-------|------|
| 1 | 1 | 6 |

**FIGURE C**  Organizing Data for Graphing

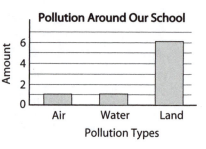

class the pollution types and the sources for them. Solicit potential solutions to eliminate the pollutant. Have each team write an informational story to be shared in a newsletter that will be distributed to the local community about the data they collected and the results of the data analysis. Be sure each team includes data to back up their story. Ask each team to offer suggestions on what the students in the school can do to reduce pollution and what members of the local community can do as well.

Once the public display of the results of the pollution search in the school neighborhood have been completed, reconvene the class and ask the students to reflect on all of their experiences. Suggested questions to ask students to make the connection to each of the disciplines addressed in the lesson include:

- What is pollution? *(Designed to address the science concept.)*
- What math skill did you need to communicate or show what you found? *(Looks for an understanding that data can be communicated using a bar graph.)*
- What did you learn about pollution by listening to the story *The Cat in the Hat Comes Back*? Who was your audience when writing about the results of your pollution search around the school neighborhoods? Why was it important to keep your audience in mind? *(Designed to address the identified language arts concept.)*
- In our social studies class we learned that throughout time people will endure great hardships to bring about a social change, such as the pilgrims coming to America to start a new society that would allow them to practice freedoms they did not have while living in Europe. How do you think the activities we just completed show that you can become an advocate for social change? How do you think you might have started some changes in the local community? *(Designed to address the identified social studies concept.)*

### Science in Personal and Social Perspectives

- What suggestions can you provide members of the local community to reduce the amount of pollution your team found around the school?
- What kinds of things can you do to eliminate a pollution source around the school? Around your home?

### Science and Technology

+ Did you identify any pollution sources that were originally made to make a person's life easier? If so, what were they?
+ Do you think we can live without this technology? If not, do you have any suggestions as to how it can be changed to make less pollution?

### Science as Inquiry

+ What other things or events in our life can we collect data on to make informed decisions?
+ Does it help to follow a sequence of events to figure out how to solve problems? Why?

### History and Nature of Science

+ Are scientists the only people that collect data and make informed decisions based on the analysis of that data? In what other careers is the ability to collect and analyze data important?

## Evaluation  *How will the students show what they have learned?*

Upon completing these activities, the students will be able to:

+ describe a source of pollution and provide a plan for how that source could be eliminated or at least reduced.
+ identify the pollution sources when given a picture of an area with obvious problems due to pollution, or speculate as to possible sources if none are found within the picture.
+ create and distribute a news story to the local school community explaining the various sources of pollution found around the school and what all members of the community can do to reduce the amount of pollution; use graphs and charts that identify the location, the types, amounts, and size of the pollutants found from their *local pollution search* to backup the information in their story.

## Useful Waste

GRADE LEVEL:  5–8
DISCIPLINE:  Life Science

**Inquiry Question:**  Is one man's trash another man's treasure?

**Concept to Be Invented:**  Main idea—A great majority of human-made waste can be recycled or reused.

**Concepts Important to Expansion:**  Recycle, reuse, water, litter, useful and non-reusable waste, landfill, hazardous waste

## Materials Needed

*For Exploration*

aluminum can          plastic soda bottle          rope
bottle cap            tin can                      bug-spray can
glass bottle          cigarette butt               orange peel
newspaper

*For Expansion*

art supplies—crayons, markers,          old piece of screen
   scissors, construction paper, glue          rolling pin
food blender          water
strips of scrap paper

**Safety Precautions:** Remind students to be careful of the sharp edges and glass, and to exercise care when carrying and using the scissors and blender.

## Exploration *Which process skills will be used?*

Observing, questioning, hypothesizing, predicting, reasoning, recording data

### What will the students do?

• *Rating Garbage*

Separate the class into groups of four to six students. Give each group the materials listed above for exploration concealed in a brown grocery bag. Ask the students to remove the items from the bag, make observations, and rate or arrange the items in order from the most usable to the least usable. The students' reasoning behind their rating scheme should be recorded.

## Explanation/Concept Invention *What is the main idea? How will the main idea be constructed?*

*Concept:* A great majority of human-made waste can be recycled or reused.

Ask the students questions such as the following to help invent this concept:

◆ What did you find in your bags?
◆ How did you rank these items from most usable to least usable?
◆ Why did you put _____ (name item) as the most usable?
◆ Why did you put _____ (name item) as the least usable?
◆ Refuse is often regarded as useless waste and ends up in landfills and pollutes our environment. Although not all human-made materials can be recycled, they can be reused in a number of ways not originally intended. Why is it important for us to recycle and reuse?
◆ What is the difference between recycling and reusing?
◆ What can you do to see that materials such as those found in your bags are recycled or, if possible, reused?
◆ So what do you think it means when someone says "One man's trash is another man's treasure"?

## **Expansion of the Idea** *Which process skills will be used?*

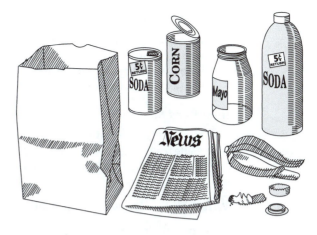

Communicating, problem solving, interpreting data, classifying, making assumptions, drawing conclusions, manipulating materials

*How will the idea be expanded?*

Ask the groups of students to decide what kind of litter-eating creature they could create using the materials found in their grocery bags and the art supplies you make available. After they create plans for their creatures, allow them sufficient time to make and explain to the class just how their litter-eating creatures function.

• Litter-Eating Critter

Hold up the bug-spray can in order to introduce hazardous wastes that are found in the home. Ask the students if they can think of any household items that cannot be disposed of in a regular fashion. Some examples of items that are dangerous and need to be disposed of properly are paint thinners, paints, and motor oils. Ask the students if they are aware why these items cannot be dumped in regular landfills. Explain in detail the impact these items have on the environment.

Encourage the students to learn how to recycle paper by doing the following activity with them: Collect different types of paper scraps, and using a blender, cut the paper into very small pieces. Mix the fine paper to a pulp mixture with water. Pour out of the blender and roll flat. This can be done on an old piece of screen using a rolling pin. Place an old towel over the pulp as you roll it flat to help squeeze out some of the excess water. Allow the new piece of paper to dry before use.

• Making Paper

### *Science in Personal and Social Perspectives*

✦ Do you think you have a responsibility to future generations to reduce the amount of waste you create? Why or why not? Do you think your parents and grandparents thought about the amount of waste they generated in the past and how it would affect the quality of your life?

✦ How can reducing, reusing, and recycling our resources ensure that future generations will have a lifestyle comparable to or better than ours?

### *Science and Technology*

✦ How does a landfill function? Who is responsible for selecting a site for the landfill? How long can we continue dumping our waste into the same landfill?

✦ What technological advances have decreased the amount of waste we put into our landfills? What technological advances have added to the problem of overflowing landfills?

✦ What things can you do to reduce litter in your home? What plans do you have for reducing, reusing, and recycling waste materials you generate?

### Science as Inquiry

✦ How can a product be recycled or reused?
✦ Can all waste products be recycled? If not, is there anything else that can be done with a waste product first before you throw it away?
✦ Should cost factors prohibit you from recycling waste products? Why or why not?

### History and Nature of Science

✦ How many different jobs are involved in the recycling of any product?
✦ Aside from using natural resources, what other sources can manufacturers go to in order to obtain materials to create their products?

## *E*valuation *How will the students show what they have learned?*

Upon completing the activities, the students will be able to:

✦ differentiate between litter and waste in terms of definitions and usefulness;
✦ rank a pile of materials according to which are the most to least recyclable and which are the most to least reusable;
✦ identify and collect from home one clean waste item, one clean recyclable item, and one clean reusable item;
✦ start a recycling project for the entire school.

---

## Litter in Our Waterways

GRADE LEVEL: 5–8
DISCIPLINE: Life Science

**Inquiry Question:** Should I worry about litter in the river if I can't see it?

**Concept to Be Invented:** Main idea—Irresponsible actions by people are causing the earth's waterways to become littered. This upsets the ecological balance of the water.

**Concepts Important to Expansion:** Beaches, floating, lakes, litter, oceans, recycling, rivers

### Materials Needed

*For Exploration*
aquarium
plastic six-pack holder
empty tin can
empty plastic 2-liter soda bottle
metal bottle cap

water to fill aquarium three-fourths full
empty aluminum soda can
empty glass soda bottle
metal can opener

**Safety Precautions:** Remind students to be careful of the sharp edges and glass, and to keep hands away from the aquarium.

## $\bullet$ Exploration  *Which process skills will be used?*

Observing, questioning, hypothesizing, predicting, experimenting, recording data

### What will the students do?

◆ Display the seven litter items specified in the materials list above. Ask the students to predict which items will sink when placed in the water. Record their predictions. Allow student volunteers to place each item in the water (one at a time) and observe what happens. Record the results and compare with the initial predictions made by the students.

*• Sink-or-Float Litter*

◆ Ask the students if they think any of the items that floated could sink eventually. After soliciting several answers, point out that some empty containers may fill with water and sink. The time they take to sink may vary based on certain conditions, such as rough water or human manipulation.

◆ Ask the students to generate a list of litter they think may be underwater in lakes and rivers. Ask the students how they think it got there.

## $\bullet$ Explanation/Concept Invention  *What is the main idea? How will the main idea be constructed?*

*Concept:* Irresponsible actions by people are causing the Earth's waterways to become littered. This upsets the ecological balance of the water.

Ask the students questions, such as the following, to help invent this concept:

◆ What types of litter sank to the bottom of the aquarium? What types of litter floated on top?

◆ Do you think that those that floated may eventually sink?

◆ What do you think happens to the litter after it sinks?

◆ How do you think this affects water life, such as aquatic plants and animals?

◆ What do you think will happen to an aquatic animal if it eats a piece of litter, such as a plastic bag?

◆ Litter that floats is easily mistaken for food by many aquatic animals. It is not uncommon for sea turtles to mistake plastic bags for jellyfish and eat them. When this happens, the sea turtle thinks it is full because the plastic bag is stuck in its stomach. It eventually starves to death. Ducks and some fish get their beaks or bodies tangled in six-pack rings. This prevents them from eating, and they starve to death.

◆ Litter that sinks is not always considered a nuisance. Some sunken ships become places for coral reefs to grow upon.

+ How do you think litter such as this could end up in a lake or river? Help the students to make a summary statement about the actions of irresponsible people when it comes to littering our waterways. Ask them to now answer the inquiry question—Should I worry about litter in the river if I can't see it?

## Expansion of the Idea   *Which process skills will be used?*

Communicating, problem solving, interpreting data, classifying, making assumptions, drawing conclusions

### How will the idea be expanded?

• *Plastic Food*

Ask the students to collect and save every piece of plastic waste used in their homes for one week, clean the waste, and bring it to school. Divide the class into groups of four to six. Ask them to pool their plastic collection. Ask the students to classify the waste according to how an aquatic animal might look at that plastic as a source of food. The categories might be definitely, somewhat likely, unlikely. List some animals that would go for the "food" in each of the categories. Share these divisions with the class. Once they have discussed their divisions, ask the students to divide the plastic waste according to whether an animal could get tangled up in it. Again, discuss the classification scheme the students developed and why. Ask the students as a summary activity to state one positive thing they could do to prevent further pollution of a waterway.

### Science in Personal and Social Perspectives

+ Does litter affect your everyday life? If so, how?
+ What could you do to cut down on litter?
+ Why should someone who lives far from a major waterway be concerned with litter in our waters?
+ Do you and your family recycle? If so, what and how?
+ Who in our community should be responsible for cleaning up our waters?
+ What are some projects in your neighborhood that deal with litter control?
+ What are some different litter control agencies operating in your community?

### Science and Technology

+ Contact a local hospital. Determine how its medical waste is disposed of. Do you think its disposal methods will keep that waste out of our waterways? Why or why not?

### Science as Inquiry

+ Are pollutants that float in a waterway just as dangerous as pollutants that sink? Why or why not?
+ Are people in danger if they play on beaches near polluted water? Why or why not?
+ Can a sunken ship ever be beneficial to aquatic organisms?

### History and Nature of Science

+ Are there any special precautions one must take if his or her job is to clean up a waterway?

+ How could an oceanographer use his or her knowledge of ocean currents to help the Coast Guard to identify businesses or cruise ship lines that pollute the waterways?
+ Do health care workers have a responsibility to the rest of us to know exactly where their garbage will be disposed? How can they prevent it from ending up in the nation's waterways?

## *Evaluation* *How will the students show what they have learned?*

Upon completing the activities, the students will be able to:

+ explain how plastic bags could cause the death of a sea turtle;
+ give an example of a piece of plastic litter that can be harmful to aquatic life and propose a solution about how this product could be eliminated from the environment without harming wildlife;
+ write a letter of concern to a product manufacturer that they believe uses excessive amounts of plastic packaging on its products.

# Sense of Taste

GRADE LEVEL: K–4
DISCIPLINE: Life Science

**Inquiry Question:**  What is a taste bud?

**Concept to Be Invented:**  Main idea—A person can taste sweet, sour, salty, and bitter on every single area of the tongue that has taste buds.

**Concepts Important to Expansion:**  People with more taste buds taste things more strongly than those with fewer taste buds.

### Materials Needed

*For Each Pair of Students*

| | | |
|---|---|---|
| lemon juice | 4 paper cups | blue food coloring |
| cocoa powder | wax paper | 10 cotton-tipped swabs |
| brown sugar | magnifying glass | hole puncher |
| salt | | |

*Preparation*

For each pair of students, label four cups A, B, C, and D. Fill three of the paper cups with water. Dissolve in cup A the salt, cup B the cocoa, and brown sugar in cup C (corn syrup may be used instead of brown sugar). Pour some lemon juice in cup D. Create an outline of a tongue on a sheet of paper, and duplicate it for each pair of students.

 **Safety Precautions:**  Before distributing the cotton-tipped swabs, remind the students that they are to be used carefully and cautiously to avoid eye injury. Also, to avoid contamination of the unknowns and to inhibit the spread of germs, students should be reminded not to put used cotton-tipped swabs back into the cups after they place them on their tongue.

## Exploration  *Which process skills will be used?*

Observing, predicting, experimenting, evaluating, generalizing, inferring, recording data

### What will the students do?

• *Buds and Tasters*

Ask the students to choose partners or assign partners yourself. Each set of partners should be provided with four paper cups labeled A through D, each filled with a different liquid. Ask the students to make predictions as to what kinds of tastes they think they have and where on the tongue they think they will taste them. Once predictions are recorded, have one student dip a clean cotton swab into the paper cup labeled A, then touch the cotton swab to the tip of his or her partner's tongue. He or she will then touch the back and the sides of the tongue. Record how your partner thought liquid A tasted. Was it as predicted? Mark on the tongue map the places on the tongue where liquid A was tasted. Repeat this procedure for liquids B and C. Do the same for each partner. Remember that a *clean swab* should be used for each cup and by each student.

## Explanation/Concept Invention  *What is the main idea? How will the main idea be constructed?*

*Concept:* A person can taste sweet, sour, salty, and bitter on every area of the tongue that has taste buds.

Ask the students questions such as the following to help invent this concept:

◆ How did your partner think each liquid tasted?

◆ Did you agree with your partner?

◆ Did you find any special places on the tongue where these tastes could be detected? Why or why not? Have the students share their findings. They should conclude that there is no single area on the tongue where each of these tastes can be detected more so than another. Your tongue is the organ that gives you your sense of taste. If you observe it closely starting at the tip, you will notice thousands of tiny bumps that make you tongue look rough. The tiny bumps are called *filiform papillae*. They are responsible for grabbing onto your food as you chew. The roundish *buttons* you find interspersed within the filiform papillae are called *fungiform papillae*. Anywhere from five to seven taste buds can be found on each fungiform papilla. The *taste buds* are made up of a bundle of cells, each containing special sensors or receptors that can pick out the four basic tastes of sweet, sour, bitter, and salty. The *circumvallate papillae*, found on the back of your tongue, are larger than the other papillae. Found within deep furrows of the circumvallate papillae are taste buds that also can detect the four basic tastes.

◆ In order to taste your food, you must chew it. Chewing grinds up your food. It also wets the food by mixing it with saliva, the liquid made by small organs in your mouth. When your food is well mixed with saliva, your taste buds can pick up messages about its flavor. Nerves take these messages to taste centers in each side of your brain. Your brain then decides what you are tasting.

+ Your senses of taste and smell work closely together. The taste of many foods is really a mixture of taste and smell. Food often seems to have no taste when you have a cold. The cold stops up your nose and dulls your sense of smell. When you cannot smell the food, a part of its taste seem to be missing.

+ Ask the students to complete this statement: Taste buds for sweet, sour, salty and bitter can be found _____ (all over or in every part of) the tongue.

## Expansion of the Idea  *Which process skills will be used?*

Observing, problem solving, recording data, inferring

### How will the idea be expanded?

Ask the students to go back with their partners to perform the following task:

• *Supertasters*

+ Cut a piece of wax paper 1 inch square. Punch a hole using the paper puncher in the middle of the 1-inch-square piece of wax paper.
+ Place the piece of wax paper on the tip of your partner's tongue just slightly off center. Be sure the tongue is slightly wet so the paper will stick.
+ Using a cotton-tipped swab, dab blue food coloring where the hole is. Be careful not to use too much coloring. For accurate data collection, you want just the dot of tongue exposed to be dyed.
+ Use the magnifying glass to count the number of larger, raised dots that did not turn blue. These will be the *fungiform papillae.*
+ Take the number of fungiform papillae you discover and multiply by six. This will give you an estimate of the number of taste buds your partner has.
+ Repeat this procedure for the other partner.

Were you able to find the same number of fungiform papillae on your partner as your partner found on you? Did everyone have the same number of taste buds?

You will discover that the fewer the raised dots, the less likely the person tasted the four basics tastes all over his or her tongue. Some people are *supertasters* because they have a large number of fungiform papillae, whereas those with just a few are considered *nontasters.*

### Science in Personal and Social Perspectives

+ Where on the tongue did your partner taste the sweet liquid, the sour, salty, and bitter? Was it the same place as yours?
+ Why do you think many adults tolerate flavorings like hot pepper sauce that a baby cannot?

### Science and Technology

+ Do you think that people from countries other than your own have different amounts of taste buds on their tongue? How do you explain that many cultures

tolerate food much spicier than typical American fare? Does the number of taste buds have anything to do with it? How might you design an experiment to determine the answers to these questions?

### Science as Inquiry

+ How do the filiform papillae differ from the fungiform papillae or the circumvallate papillae?
+ What do the fungiform papillae and the circumvallate papillae have in common?
+ Where on the tongue can the circumvallate papillae be found?

### History and Nature of Science

+ Ask the students to generate a list of spices used in cooking. Assign each student a spice. From which country does it originate? How does it grow? How is it harvested? How important is that spice to the society of the country in which in grows? When was it first used as a spice?
+ Do you think someone with permanent damage to his or her nose resulting in the loss of the sense of smell would have a promising career as a professional chef? Why or why not?

## Evaluation  *How will the students show what they have learned?*

Upon completing the activities, the students will be able to:

+ list the four major tastes that can be picked out by receptors on the tongue;
+ design a method for separating the class into nontasters, regular tasters, and supertasters;
+ describe the role of the filiform papillae, fungiform papillae, and the circumvallate papillae.

## Skeleton

**GRADE LEVEL:** 1–4
**DISCIPLINE:** Life Science

**Inquiry Question:**  What does my skeleton do for me?

**Concepts to Be Invented:**  Main idea—The internal support system for muscles in mammals is the bones. All the bones arranged together make up the skeleton.

**Concepts Important to Expansion:**  Joints help skeletons move.

### Materials Needed

*For Each Student*
One large sheet of newsprint, markers, crayons, several brass paper fasteners, a packet of paper bones that when put together will create a replica of a human skeleton.

**Safety Precautions:**  Explain to the students how to use the brass fasteners. Remind them that they could hurt themselves if they poke themselves or others with the pointed edge.

## Exploration *Which process skills will be used?*

Observing, questioning, manipulating materials, analyzing

### What will the students do?

Introduce the lesson by reading two poems from *A Light in the Attic*, by Shel Silverstein. The poems are "Day After Halloween" and "It's Hot!" Begin a discussion with the students about the ideas behind the poems. Ask questions such as: What would it be like if we didn't have a skeleton? Why do we need bones in our bodies?

Give each child several brass fasteners and a packet containing paper bones cut into the different major bones of the body using the figure on page 82. Ask the students to empty the packets and to manipulate the materials in any way they wish in an effort to determine what they can create with all the bones. Encourage them to use the brass fasteners to assemble the bones. Walk around the room asking questions like: What do you think all of these different parts make up? Do you think you know where all the parts go? What could the brass fasteners represent in a real body that helps us to move? How do the bones in our body connect for real?

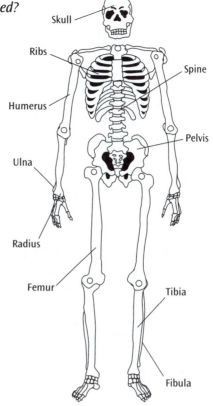

• *Bones Assembly Line*

## Explanation/Concept Invention *What is the main idea? How will the main idea be constructed?*

*Concept:* The internal support system for muscles in mammals is the bones. All the bones arranged together make up the skeleton.

Using a picture of a skeleton and a life-size skeleton, ask the children if they know the nonscientific names of the bones. Write these on the board. If students offer the scientific names, list those as well; compare them to the common name, e.g. scapula for collar bone. Show a picture of the muscle system of the human body. Explain to the students how the bones help give the muscles support.

Walk around the classroom very stiffly. Encourage some or all of the students to do the same. Really play it up. Tell them they cannot bend their elbows or knees. Remind the students that they used brass fasteners to connect the bones in their skeleton. Ask the students:

✦ Do you think brass fasteners are used in our bodies? Of course not; what do we have? (Joints.)

◆ Ask the children to demonstrate what would happen to them when they are standing up if they did not have bones in their body. The students should drop to the floor.

◆ Ask the students to complete this sentence about our skeleton: Our skeleton supports our _____ (muscles).

## *Expansion of the Idea* *Which process skills will be used?*

Observing, classifying, recording, manipulating materials

### How will the idea be expanded?

• *Newsprint Bone Bodies*

Pair up the students and provide each child with a large sheet of newsprint and a pencil. Ask the students to spread the paper out on the floor. The paired children should take turns. One child should lie flat on the paper with his or her face down. The other child should outline the body. Let each child switch roles. After they have created their outlines, have each child fill in the outline with the bones of the body.

### Science in Personal and Social Perspectives

◆ Do you think it is good to know what is inside our body? Why?

◆ How do joints help us move?

◆ Could you do the same activities you do on a daily basis if you didn't have a skeleton?

### Science and Technology

◆ What do you think scientists do with bones found in nature?

◆ Do you think bones found by scientists tell them anything about the organism and the environment it lived in?

◆ How do you think we see our bones inside our body? What is that picture called?

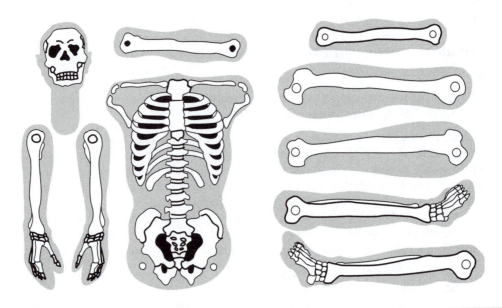

### Science as Inquiry

+ How do bones connect together?
+ Why do you think it is good to understand how our bodies move?
+ Why do you think we have two bones in our forearms and lower legs?

### History and Nature of Science

+ What is the name of the person who shows you pictures of your bones inside you?
+ If you had some back problems and you wanted your spine readjusted, what type of professional would you go to?
+ What would you call a person who went to different locations to dig up buried bones and artifacts?
+ What does a doctor do if you have a broken bone? How do you think the first doctors figured out how to mend broken bones?

## Evaluation  *How will the students show what they have learned?*

Upon completing the activities, the students will be able to:

+ assemble a paper skeleton;
+ identify at least five bones in the body with common names;
+ understand why we need joints in our bodies and explain what they do;
+ play Hokey-Pokey Skeleton; that is, do the Hokey-Pokey, but use the common names of bones rather than body parts.

## Temperature Receptors on Skin

GRADE LEVEL: **5–8**
DISCIPLINE: **Life Science**

**Inquiry Question:**  What is it about skin that allows me to feel changes in temperature?

**Concept to Be Invented:**  Main idea—Skin has spots, called receptors, for feeling temperatures that are hotter or colder than body temperatures.

**Concepts Important to Expansion:**  Water can feel hot and cold to our bodies at the same time.

### Materials Needed

*For Each Student Group*

a source of hot and cold water
3 bowls
6 nails

2 fine-tipped pens, each a different color
paper towels

**Safety Precautions:**  Ask students not to poke each other with the nails and to use care around the water: If it is knocked over, be sure to clean it up immediately. Make sure hot water is not so hot that it will scald.

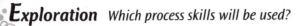

## Exploration   Which process skills will be used?

Observing, questioning, designing an experiment, recording data, predicting, generalizing

### What will the students do?

• Soaking Hands

Divide the students into cooperative working groups of four. Ask the materials manager to obtain three small bowls. Fill one with hot water, one with cold water, and the third with warm water. The groups' mission is to find out how hands feel when placed in water of different temperatures. Encourage the groups to design an experiment to solve this problem. Ask them to record their data. Their experimental designs may look something like this: Each student in the group will take turns placing one hand in hot water and the other in cold. Hands should be left for several minutes in the water. Remove hands from those bowls and immediately immerse them in the warm water. Students should be able to describe what happens next. There may be some variations to this plan. Teachers may find that some groups first put both hands in cold and then in hot. They all should be able to help invent the concept, no matter the experimental design.

## Explanation/Concept Invention   What is the main idea? How will the main idea be constructed?

*Concept:* Skin has spots, called receptors, for feeling temperatures that are hotter or colder than body temperatures.

To help invent this concept, ask each of the student groups to report on the experiment they designed. Ask the following questions:

- ✦ What did you do? What results did you get?
- ✦ Did the water feel hot and cold at the same time? How can that be?
- ✦ Do the results have to do with the temperature of the water your hand was in first or just the temperature of your hand?
- ✦ Lead the students to conclude that the temperature of the water their hand was in first will determine how hot or cold their hand felt. Share with them that on their skin are receptors that sense temperatures different from normal body temperature.
- ✦ Ask them to now respond to the inquiry question: What is it about skin that allows me to feel changes in temperature?

## Expansion of the Idea   Which process skills will be used?

Observing, classifying, recording, predicting

### How will the idea be expanded?

• Hot/Cold Receptor Mapping

Ask each student to use one of the pens provided to the groups to draw a square on the back of his or her hand. Place one nail in the bowl of cold water and another in the bowl of hot water. Ask the group members to pair up. Ask one student from each pair to take the nail from the cold water and touch the tip of the nail to any spot in the square of his or her partner's hand. If it feels cold, mark that spot with the pen (marking all the cold ones in the same color). Now switch so that each partner has cold receptors marked. Other student pairs in each cooperative group can be doing the same thing with the hot water and a nail. Be sure to use a different color pen for hot spots. Now exchange bowls and make marks for the opposite water type. Are you surprised at where you find the hot and cold receptors?

### Science in Personal and Social Perspectives

+ People say that to test bathwater you should use your elbow, or to test a baby's bottle you should use your wrist. Why do you think they chose those particular body parts?
+ How would you test your bathwater, with your hand or your toes? Why?

### Science and Technology

+ On a hot summer day it is nice to enter an air-conditioned building. After you've been in the building for an hour, you begin to think the air-conditioning has been shut off. Why do you think you feel this way?
+ How has technology allowed us to exist comfortably in the winter and the summer? Can you design a way to keep cool during hot weather without using an air-conditioner or fan?

### Science as Inquiry

+ Could you find a way to pick up a snowball and not feel the cold?
+ Which part of your hand is most sensitive to hot things?
+ What is a receptor?

### History and Nature of Science

+ Why do people who work in meat lockers wear gloves?
+ Do you think it is important for someone involved in child care to make sure that his or her heat receptors are not damaged? Why or why not?
+ In 1853 Georg Meissner described a corpuscle that became known as *Meissner's corpuscle*. What is this, and what did Meissner do to discover it?

## *E*valuation  *How will the students show what they have learned?*

Upon completing the activities, the students will be able to:

+ identify the different hot and cold receptors on each hand;
+ explain how water can feel hot and cold at the same time;
+ identify the child with the cold hands when looking at a picture of children involved in building a snow fort (the one without gloves);
+ view a picture of working firefighters with and without fire coats and identify which ones will feel hot. Why is this not the same as pictures of children in the winter with and without coats?

# Building Microscope Skills

GRADE LEVEL: 5–8
DISCIPLINE: Life Science

**Inquiry Question:** What is the advantage of using a microscope?

**Concept to Be Invented:** Main idea—A microscope is used to identify objects not visible to the naked eye.

**Concepts Important to Expansion:** Identifying a compound by its characteristic crystal shape, slide preparation

## Materials Needed

*For Exploration*

| | | |
|---|---|---|
| noniodized salt | water | microscope |
| iodized salt | eye droppers | scale |
| sugar | cups | graduated cylinder |
| alum | slides | pictures of crystals |
| borax | slide covers | |

*For Expansion*

| | |
|---|---|
| water | laundry bluing |
| noniodized salt | household ammonia |

**Safety Precautions:** Ask students to avoid placing hands near eyes or mouth while working with materials to prepare slides. When using an electric microscope, be sure to use proper safety measures near electrical outlets. The microscope lamp may be hot to touch. Apply the usual safety standards when working with such chemicals as bluing and ammonia.

## Exploration — Which process skills will be used?

Observing, classifying, recording data, diagramming, comparing, manipulating instruments

### What will the students do?

• *Microscope Use and Crystal Comparisons*

Measure out 5 grams of each solid. Dissolve each in a separate cup containing 25 ml of water. Be sure to label the cup with the name of the material dissolved in the water. As the solution is forming, label a slide for each solute. Place a drop of each solution on its assigned slide. Allow the water to evaporate. Carefully place the cover slip over the remaining crystals on the slide. Focus each slide under the microscope and record your observations for each at low power. Focus under a higher power and again record observations.

## **Explanation/Concept Invention** *What is the main idea? How will the main idea be constructed?*

*Concept:* A microscope is used to identify objects not visible to the naked eye.

Key questions to ask students to help them come to this conclusion are:

+ What shapes did you observe on the slide?
+ How does it compare to a drawing of the crystal shape?
+ Can you share a diagram of those shapes with the class? How are these shapes similar? How are they different?
+ How did the microscope help you to observe the crystal?
+ What advantage do you see in using a microscope over just using your eye? The students should be able to conclude that a microscope can be used to identify objects not visible to the naked eye.

## **Expansion of the Idea** *Which process skills will be used?*

Graphing, classifying, experimenting

### *How will the idea be expanded?*

+ Use the results of the previous crystal comparison activity to graph the crystal shapes versus the number of substances that have that particular shape.
+ The students should be encouraged to brainstorm a list of other possible substances that contain crystals. Observe these under the microscope.
+ The students will grow a crystal garden in a Styrofoam egg carton by first placing pieces of charcoal into the egg sockets. In a separate container, mix the following substances:

> 6 tablespoons of water        6 tablespoons of laundry bluing
> 6 tablespoons of noniodized salt   2 teaspoons of household ammonia

*• Charcoal Crystals*

Once this solution is prepared, the students should carefully pour it over the pieces of charcoal in the egg container. The students can then place these in an area in the classroom where they will not be hit or bumped. The crystals will grow for several days. If the students want colored crystals, they may place a few drops of food coloring on the charcoal after the solution is poured on them. The students may wish to make each egg socket a different color. Once the crystals have grown, the students may safely carry them home in their egg cartons. If the crystals do get bumped in transit, sometimes they can be revived by putting a little water on them.

### *Science in Personal and Social Perspectives*

+ While rummaging through your kitchen for a salt shaker, you come across a container you think will work. After placing the salt into the container, you find that no salt comes out of the holes when you shake the container. Why do you think this happened? Will the size of the salt crystals determine the size of the holes that should be on top of a shaker?

✦ Do you think there are any other areas of your life where the skills you learned in this lesson can be applied? If so, where?

✦ How do you think your increased knowledge of crystal shapes will help you become a better consumer? Would you buy ice cream that contained frost crystals? Why or why not?

### Science and Technology

✦ Knowing that salt or sugar can be placed in solution allowed past generations to preserve foods more easily, thus ensuring their survival. How have our present-day technologies expanded on these early ideas?

✦ Think about the frozen food industry. How does it make use of their knowledge of crystal formation?

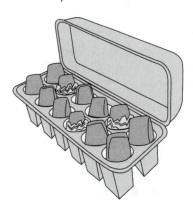

### Science as Inquiry

✦ What scientific concepts did you discover while participating in these activities?

✦ What problem-solving techniques did you employ?

✦ What procedures were used with the microscope?

### History and Nature of Science

✦ How important is it for a gemologist to understand the differences between crystal shapes? Why?

✦ In addition to knowledge about crystals, what other kinds of skills would a geologist need? A gemologist? A hospital laboratory technician?

✦ Anton van Leeuwenhoek is credited with creating one of the earliest microscopes. What kind of discoveries was he able to make with his primitive microscope?

## Evaluation  *How will the students show what they have learned?*

Upon completing these activities, the students will be able to:

✦ demonstrate proper slide preparation techniques,

✦ prepare a slide of a crystal and focus it under a microscope,

✦ identify on a diagram the basic crystal shapes,

✦ state why different compounds may have different crystal shapes.

# Sex-Linked Genes

**Inquiry Question:** Who do I get my genetic traits from?

**Concept to Be Invented:** Traits are passed from parent to offspring.

**Concepts Important to Expansion:** Sex-linked traits are carried through sex chromosomes. Heredity information is contained in genes, located in the chromosomes of each cell.

## Materials Needed

*For Exploration*

pictures of several generations of a family where the resemblance over the generations is easy to see, and pictures of family members where the relationship is not so obvious

or arrange to have a family come into your class or have a video of a family showing multiple generations

or have students bring in family pictures of themselves and a sibling or adult family member, or bring in a picture of a family

poster paper or chalkboard to collect class observations

*For Expansion*

50 drinking straws (this is for a class of 25 @ 2 per student)

0.5-cm × 2-cm strips of light and dark blue construction paper (37 total)

0.5-cm × 2-cm strips of light and dark green construction paper (37 total)

0.5-cm × 2-cm strips of light and dark red construction paper (13 total)

 **Safety Precautions:** None needed

# Exploration  *Which process skills will be used?*

Observing, comparing, recording data, making hypotheses

## What will students do?

If you have enough pictures of various families throughout the generations, the students can work in groups of 4–6; if you have a small number of pictures or videotape of a family, then work together as a class. Either way, ask the students to look at the family members closely for similarities. If the students are having trouble or looking confused, encourage them to look for similar traits like hair or eye color, freckles, skin coloration, height, etc. Ask students to record the things they find that the family members have in common. Tell them to be prepared to share their observations and to draw some conclusions about their observations and those of the class.

• *Family Traits*

# Explanation/Concept Invention *What is the main idea? How will the main idea be constructed?*

*Concept:* Traits are passed from parent to offspring.

If the students worked as separate teams, ask the student teams to share with the class the pictures they used to make their observations. If they made their observations from videotape, this will not be necessary. As the students share their observations, record commonly recurring ideas for all to see. For example, if one group talks about all family members having green eyes and another group talks about all family members having brown eyes, then record "eye color" for all to see. Continue with the sharing until all students or student groups have had an opportunity to share their observations and until you have a list of observations that includes a variety of traits, i.e., skin, eye, and hair color; body shape and height.

Ask the students leading questions to invent the concept of a trait, such as:

+ Did all the siblings in the picture have the same color of eyes? Or hair?
+ Did you see much resemblance between the mother and her daughter? Or between the parent and the child?
+ Share with the students that the list of observations they made are of characteristics we get passed on to us from our parents. Those characteristics are called *traits.* These traits are given direction by genes that are carried on our chromosomes. We inherit or receive the genes from one or both of our parents. For instance, some of you may have found that a child looked just like one of the parents in the pictures. Others of you may have found that the child looked like a combination of both parents. Thus, traits are passed from parent to offspring. What a person looks like on the outside is called the person's *phenotype.* The inherited traits that make a person look like that (what's in the inside) is called the person's *genotype.*
+ Ask the students to answer the inquiry question: Who do I get my genetic traits from?

# Expansion *Which process skills will be used?*

Observing, predicting, recording data, drawing conclusions

### What preactivity preparation is necessary?

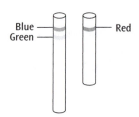

Before the activity the teacher should cut the straws into 10- and 7-cm lengths. These will be representing X and Y chromosomes respectively. To demonstrate the naturally occurring distribution you will need three times as many 10-cm lengths (X chromosomes) as 7-cm lengths (Y chromosomes). For a class of 25 students you need 37 long and 13 shorter-length straws. To the long straws, tape a strip of light- or dark-blue paper near one end; then tape a strip of light- or dark-green paper a few centimeters below the blue paper. (See diagram.) Tape a red strip to the short straw at the same distance from one end as you taped the blue strip to the long straws. (See diagram.)

Prepare the rest of the straws in the same manner, alternating the light- and dark-colored bands.

Use the following key: Long straws = X chromosomes; short straws = Y chromosomes; blue strips = color blindness gene (dark blue, the trait is not present; light blue, the trait is present); green strips = baldness gene (dark green, the trait is not present; light green, the trait is present); red strips = hairy ears gene (dark red, the trait is not present; light red, the trait is present).

### How will the idea be expanded?

Give two straws to each student so that they receive either two long or a long and a short straw. They cannot receive two short straws as you are modeling how sex chromosomes are inherited. Remind them of the earlier exploration activity. Explain to them that each straw represents one of the sex chromosomes they inherited from their parents; a long straw represents an X chromosome and a short straw represents a Y chromosome. Two X chromosomes (long straws) mean you will be female; an X and Y chromosome (1 short, 1 long straw) means you will be male.

• *Sex-Linked Traits*

Share the key to the colored bands. Have the students determine their gender and what traits they will inherit. Ask them to identify their phenotype (what they will look like on the outside) and their genotype (what traits their genes carry). For example, if they have one long straw (representing an X chromosome) and one short straw (representing a Y chromosome) they have a male phenotype and XY genotype. If the long straw has a dark blue band and a light green band and the short straw has a dark red band, then the phenotype is a colorblind male. In another example, if a student has two long straws with a dark blue band on one straw and a light blue band on the other and a light green band on both straws, then the phenotype is a colorblind female with an XX genotype.

Have the students trade a straw with another student (just don't end up with two short straws). Again have them identify the phenotype and genotype. Ask them what conclusions they can draw about the three traits—color blindness, baldness, and hairy ears. Use your questioning skills to get them to reflect on the observations they shared about the phenotypes and genotypes.

The students should be led to conclude that color blindness, specifically affecting green color vision, and baldness (premature baldness at the crown of the head) are recessive traits that are only carried by the X chromosome. The gene for hairy ears is a recessive trait carried on the Y chromosome; thus, girls don't get hairy ears. If the recessive gene for hairy ears is present, it is with increasing age that it is expressed more prominently in men carrying this trait. These traits are sex linked. Thus the concept developed is that sex-linked traits are carried through sex chromosomes, and heredity information is contained in genes, located in the chromosomes of each cell.

### Science in Personal and Social Perspectives

✦ Have you ever known a family where each of the siblings look almost exactly alike or where the child looked as if she were cloned from one of the parents? Can you now explain how this is possible?

✦ Do you think personality traits can be inherited as well? Explain your answer.

### Science and Technology

✦ Understanding how traits are inherited has led many couples to seek genetic counseling before having children. What do you think one could learn from genetic counseling?

✦ There are many products on the market designed to prevent hair loss. Do you think these are useful to someone who has inherited the sex-linked gene for baldness? Why or why not?

### Science as Inquiry

✦ What is the difference between someone's genotype and phenotype? How can these be determined?

✦ If you had a grandfather on your mother's side who was bald, will you be bald when you get older? What would your genotype have to be to show up bald if you were a female?

### History and Nature of Science

✦ Gregor Mendel is known as the "father of genetics." What observations did Mendel make that led to this branch of science? Describe his experiments.

✦ Genetic engineering is one of the fastest-growing career fields. Research the skills needed to be a genetic engineer and what industries would require the services of someone trained as a genetic engineer.

## *E*valuation   *How will the students show what they have learned?*

Upon completing the activities, the students will be able to:

✦ describe a trait and explain what it means to inherit that trait;

✦ when given a particular phenotype, predict the possible genotype for the given traits;

✦ look at the phenotypes of a given couple and predict the phenotypes of their male and female offspring;

✦ research information on sex-linked genes and identify other phenotypes that result because of a sex-linked gene other than those discovered in the expansion activity.

# Passing of Traits

**Inquiry Question:** Are personality traits inherited?

**Concept to Be Invented:** Traits are passed from parent to offspring.

**Concepts Important to Expansion:** The characteristics of an organism can be described in terms of a combination of traits. Some traits are inherited and others result from interactions with the environment.

## Materials Needed

digital cameras to loan students to take home to take pictures of family members that possess similar traits

or—students should bring in family pictures of themselves and a sibling or adult family member, or

bring a picture of a family where similar traits are obvious

poster paper

index cards (each student should have as many index cards as there are students in the class)

 **Safety Precautions:** None needed.

## *E*xploration *Which process skills will be used?*

Observing, comparing, recording data, making hypotheses

### What will students do?

Have students use digital cameras to take close-up pictures of one another. Then allow them to take the cameras home to take a picture of a family member or members with whom they share similar traits. The students should return the cameras to the class, download, and print the pictures they took. If a digital camera is not available, they should bring in a recent photo of themselves and pictures of family members (this can be an aunt, uncle, grandmother, etc. Be sure you are sensitive to the feelings of adopted students or students in step or foster families).

• *What Traits Do You Share?*

Ask the students to tape or glue the photos on the poster paper. Below the photos create a list of physical traits that the people in the photos share. Display the photo posters around the room.

Provide each student with a stack of index cards. Have students use one card for each poster they observe. On the card they will write the name of the student who prepared the poster, and then list some observable traits of that student as shown by the poster. Once students have listed the traits, instruct them to leave the index cards on the appropriate students' desks. In the end each student should have a stack of index cards with descriptions of traits that other students observed in his or her poster.

## *E*xplanation/Concept Invention: *What is the main idea? How will the main idea be constructed?*

*Concept:* Traits are passed from parent to offspring.

Using your questioning skills, encourage students to reflect on the observations their peers made about their poster. Ask questions such as:

✦ Were the observations your peers made about inherited traits similar to the ones you observed?

✦ Were you surprised that your peers noticed a trait that you did not see at first? What were some of those?

The students should be making suggestions about traits such as: the shape of the lips, nose, chin, cheekbones, eyebrows, eyes, coloring of hair and skin, height, dimples, freckles, and smile.

Encourage them to conclude that some traits are easily observable and that they are passed from parent to offspring.

## *E*xpansion of the Idea *Which process skills will be used?*

Observing, predicting, recording data, drawing conclusions

### *How will the idea be expanded?*

• Inherited or Environmentally Altered?

Have the students reuse the index cards by passing them back to the student who filled them out. Ask the students to move around the room again, looking at each student's poster. This time ask them to list on the reverse side of the appropriate card any personality traits that they may know about that student. Once completed, have the cards returned to the students to whom they apply. Ask each student to take a new index card and to complete a "personality trait" list for him- or herself as well. Not all students will feel comfortable sharing the results of this activity aloud; instead, ask them to create a data chart that lists the type of personality trait in one column and the number of times someone in the class identified that trait for them in the other. Without naming the personality trait (to eliminate student embarrassment) or by using yourself as an example, ask the students to think about the top three personality traits on their list. Ask them to determine where they think they got that trait from. Is their someone in their family who exhibits the same trait? Does more than one person in their family exhibit that same personality trait? Do you exhibit traits that are a combination of traits from your parents? The characteristics of an organism can be described in terms of a combination of traits.

Ask the students to think about these questions: Do you think this trait is inherited or was it learned by living in the family environment? How far back can you trace this personality trait in your family? To your grandparents? Your great-grandparents? Your great-great-grandparents?

Personality traits may be inherited just like a laugh or the sound of one's voice. However, some personality traits can be acquired through years of living in a certain environment. The same can happen to physical characteristics. Certain traits are inherited, but changes in the gene environment can occur during cell reproduction to alter the phenotype expressed. Thus some traits are inherited and others result from interactions with the environment.

### Science in Personal and Social Perspectives

+ What would be the advantage of thoroughly reviewing the observable traits found within your family tree? Would it be as easy to trace personality traits?
+ What observable traits do you have that you think you inherited from your male parent? From your female parent? What observable traits do you have that you believe are a combination of both parents?

### Science and Technology

+ How have some couples turned to technology to alter the outcome of some observable traits in their offspring?
+ Can genetic engineering change the personality traits of an offspring?

### Science as Inquiry

+ Choose a famous family such as that of a president, a king or queen, or a known actor. Research the family lineage to identify any inherited traits carried through the generations.
+ If you were born with red hair and each of your siblings had brown hair, but you knew of a deceased great uncle with red hair on your father's side of the family, explain how that red-hair gene showed up as your phenotype.

### History and Nature of Science

+ Gregor Mendel is known as the "father of genetics" due to his extensive experiments with pea plants. What other organisms have scientists turned to as a means of adding to the ever-increasing body of knowledge in the field of genetics? Share at least two organisms and the work done with those to explain a genetics concept.
+ How would one use the concept that some traits are inherited and others result from interactions with the environment to explain why some people have the ability to play a musical instrument and other people in the same family don't have that ability?

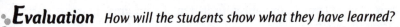

**_Evaluation_** _How will the students show what they have learned?_

Upon completing the activities, the students will be able to:

+ describe a trait and explain what it means to inherit that trait;
+ determine how a particular trait such as curly black hair can be found on a child from a family with siblings all having straight black hair and parents with straight black hair;
+ explain why when identical twins are raised apart they could exhibit identical personality traits.

# Physical Science Lessons

| LESSON NAME | NSE CONTENT STANDARDS FOR PHYSICAL SCIENCE | GRADE LEVEL | ACTIVITIES |
|---|---|---|---|
| **Waves: Sound and Light** | | | |
| Sound versus Noise | Position and Motion of Objects | K–4 | School Sound Search • Magazine Sound Search |
| Sounds Are Different | Position and Motion of Objects | 2–4 | Megaphones and Vibrating Straws • Bell Ringers |
| Vibrations Causing Sound | Position and Motion of Objects | 2–4 | Sound Makers • Waxed Paper Kazoo |
| Loudness and Pitch | Position and Motion of Objects | 2–4 | Soda Bottle Orchestra • Cigar Box Strings • Fish Line Harps • Homemade Music |
| Sound Movement as Waves | Position and Motion of Objects | 2–4 | Vibrating Fork • Striking Rod • Clapping Blocks • Sound Producers? • Tapping Tank • Paper Cup Telephone |
| Sound Waves | Position and Motion of Objects | 5–8 | Soup Can Reflectors • Slinky Waves • Sound Waves and the Ear |
| Sound Production | Properties of Matter | 5–8 | Noise and Sound Identification • Sound Movement • Sound Game: "What Is Sound?" |
| **Matter** | | | |
| Characteristics of Matter | Properties of Matter | 3–4 | Plastic Bag Chemistry • Marble Matter |
| Physical Properties of Matter | Properties of Matter | K–4 | Egg-Citing Observations • Chocolate Chip Exploration |
| Air | Properties of Matter | K–1 | Party Horn • Air Bubbles |
| Changing Matter | Properties of Matter | 5–8 | Physical and Chemical Paper Change • Polymer-Rubber Balls |
| Identification of an Unknown | Properties of Matter | 5–8 | Physical Properties of an Unknown • Chemical Properties of an Unknown |
| Bubbles | Properties of Matter | 5–8 | Detergent Bubbles • Variables |
| Using the Scientific Method to Solve Problems | Properties of Matter | 5–8 | Exploring with Efferdent Tablets • Exploring with Cornstarch |
| Heat Energy | Light, Heat, Electricity, and Magnetism | 1–4 | Liquid Birthday • Liquids to Solids |
| Magnets | Magnetism | K–2 | |
| Simple Circuits | Electricity | 3–4 | Light the Bulb • Parallel versus Series |
| **Physics** | | | |
| Structure Strength | Motion and Forces | 5–8 | Simple Construction • Triangle Construction |
| Make a Sinker Float: Clay Boats | Motion and Forces | 5–8 | Buoyancy • Clay Boats |
| Mirrors and Reflection | Transformations of Energy | 5–8 | Mirrors and Reflectors • What is a Mirror? |
| The Slinky Potential | Transformations of Energy | 7–8 | Energy Conversions with a Slinky • Energy Transfer—Having a Ball! |
| Toys in Space | Motion and Forces | 5–8 | Toy Behavior in Zero Gravity • Toys and Newton |
| Simple Machines: The Lever | Motion and Forces | 5–8 | Lever Creations • Spoons and Nuts • Lever Scavenger Hunt |

# Sound versus Noise

GRADE LEVEL: K–4
DISCIPLINE: **Physical Science**

**Inquiry Question:** When does sound become noise?

**Concept to Be Invented:** Main idea—Sound can be considered useful or simply noise.

**Concepts Important to Expansion:** Sound can be pleasant or unpleasant.

### Materials Needed

whistle
magazines for cutting up

tape recorder (if possible, one per group)
one blank audiotape per group

**Safety Precautions:** The students should be reminded of the importance of walking, not running, as they move through the school to find a place to listen to different sounds. They should use care when carrying pencils or pens to record their observations and to exercise caution when using the scissors in the expansion activity.

**Discrepant Event:** While the students are working quietly at their desks, make sure no students are looking, and then take out a whistle and blow it loudly. Ask the children what they first thought when they heard the whistle. Record some of their thoughts on the board.

## Exploration  *Which process skills will be used?*

Observing, classifying, predicting, describing, recording data, communicating

### *What will the students do?*

• School Sound Search

Divide the class into four groups. Send each group to different parts of the school building, such as the janitors' workroom, the playground, the gym or music room, their own classroom. Ask them to go to these areas quietly. Have them sit quietly in their areas for 3 minutes. Create a list of all of the sounds they hear in those areas. Return to the classroom. Instruct the students to work with the people in their group to decide if there is any way they could group the sounds. When all of the groups have analyzed their lists, share the categories of sounds with the rest of the class. Ask the students if any of the groups came up with categories their group never thought of.

## Explanation/Concept Invention  *What is the main idea? How will the main idea be constructed?*

*Concept:* Sound can be considered useful or simply noise.

Place on the board in separate columns the terms *useful, noise, pleasant,* and *unpleasant.* Ask the students if any of these terms fit the feelings they had when you blew the whistle unexpectedly. Do any of these terms fit the categories you placed your sounds under? If so, which of your sounds would go under the different headings? Encourage members of the group to write their sounds under the appropriate headings. Do all sounds fall *only*

into one classification? Fire alarms, whistles—where do they fall? Sounds can be harmful. We need ear protection from some sounds. Ask the students to summarize their findings placed in the table on the board by completing these statements: Sounds can be useful when _____. Sounds can be considered just noise when _____. Or you can ask them to answer the inquiry question: When does sound become noise?

## Expansion of the Idea  *Which process skills will be used?*

Observing, classifying, communicating, inferring, manipulating materials, interpreting data

### How will the idea be expanded?

The children will work in groups, looking through magazines, cutting out possible sources of sound. Each group will create an audiotape, mimicking the sounds that the different items they collected make. Each group will place its pictures on a poster, then play its tape to the other groups. The members of the other groups will guess which item the sound goes with and then determine if it is useful or noise, pleasant or unpleasant, or any combination of these. They must be able to explain why they would classify the item that way.

• *Magazine Sound Search*

### Science in Personal and Social Perspectives

+ When listening to a radio with headphones on, is it wise to have the volume so loud that those around you can hear it?
+ If you were asked to create a sound that would serve as a warning for some devastating disaster like a tornado, what would this sound be like? How would you categorize it? How unique would it have to be?

### Science and Technology

+ Why was it necessary for the Occupational Safety and Health Administration (OSHA) to set standards for an acceptable noise level in work areas?
+ Personal computers have changed our lives in many ways. While they have been a help, they have also created problems. How have they contributed to the problem of noise pollution, and what has the computer industry done to eliminate some of this noise?
+ Many airports near major cities were built in areas long considered migratory routes for some animals, mating habitats for others. The constant roar of jet engines affects the behavior of these animals. What have people done to eliminate some noise hazards brought upon these creatures? What must we continue to do?

### Science as Inquiry

+ How would you classify the sound best suited for quiet study time?
+ Can sounds be classified into more than one category?

### History and Nature of Science

+ Which type of work do you think would be most affected by noise pollution? Least affected? Which type of work would you choose? Why?
+ Do you think it is important for a music critic to distinguish between a useful sound or noise? A pleasant or unpleasant sound?

## *E*valuation  *How will the students show what they have learned?*

Upon completing the activities, the students will be able to:

+ listen to an audiotape of various sounds and classify them according to useful/noise and pleasant/unpleasant;

+ take one of the assigned categories—useful/pleasant; useful/unpleasant; noise/pleasant; noise/unpleasant—and over a week find some music that they think fits into their assigned category and explain why they believe it does. Encourage the students to get their families involved in their search. If they cannot find some music that fits their category, they can create their own sound.

# Sounds Are Different

**GRADE LEVEL:** 2–4

**DISCIPLINE:** **Physical Science**

**Inquiry Question:** What can I do to make a sound, sound louder or sound higher?

**Concept to Be Invented:** Main idea—Sounds vary in loudness and pitch.

**Concepts Important to Expansion:** Loudness is determined by the strength of the vibration. Pitch is determined by the length of the vibrating object. Magnification of sound is achieved by megaphones and speakers.

### Materials Needed
several large and small bells
pieces of at least 8-inch × 8-inch
   square paper

tape
paper straw
scissors

**Safety Precautions:** Remind students to be careful when using the scissors and to remember basic scissors safety. Also, be careful when placing the straws into your mouth, and during the expansion activity, do not ring a bell in anyone's ear.

**Discrepant Event:** Find a time when the students are working quietly in their seats. Take a large and a small bell and ring them at the same time. Ask the students: "Did I get your attention? Did you hear just one noise or two? Did one sound softer than the other? Higher than the other?"

## *E*xploration  *Which process skills will be used?*

Observing, communicating, inferring, predicting

• *Megaphones and Vibrating Straws*

### What will the students do?

Ask half the students to shout "hello" to you from their seats. Now ask them to cup their hands around their mouths and shout "hello" again. Ask those who did not yell if they noticed a difference in the sound produced. Now let the other half try it. Give the children pieces of paper and have them roll them into cones. Tape the sides together to maintain the cone shapes. Use the scissors to cut away about 1 inch of the pointed end of each cone. Once again have half the class shout "hello," and then shout again, holding the cut ends of the cones by their mouths. Once again, ask the listeners if they noticed a difference in the sound produced each time. Allow the other half to test their cones too.

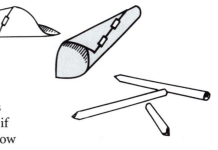

Give the students one straw each. Ask them to cut a little piece off both sides of one end so that what remains looks like an inverted V. Ask them to predict what will happen when they blow into the cut end of the straw. What do they need to do to get the cut V-shaped pieces to vibrate? As they hold the straws in their mouths, they should continue to blow into the straws and start cutting off pieces at the ends of the straws. What is happening to the sound as the straw gets shorter?

## Explanation/Concept Invention  *What is the main idea? How will the main idea be constructed?*

*Concept:* Sounds vary in loudness and pitch.

To invent the concept ask the students the following questions about their exploration activities:

- ✦ When did the "hellos" sound the loudest? Was it when you used nothing, your hand, or your school-made megaphone?
- ✦ What does a megaphone do? It magnifies sound. It increases the strength of the vibration, thus making the sound louder.
- ✦ What happened to the sound produced by the straw as you cut it?
- ✦ Was the loudness of the sound the same? What property of sound changed? The pitch got higher. *Pitch* is determined by the length of the vibrating object.
- ✦ Summarize this activity by asking the children to respond to the inquiry question: What would you do to make a sound, sound louder? What would you do to make a sound, sound higher?

## Expansion of the Idea  *Which process skills will be used?*

Predicting, designing an experiment, communicating, controlling variables, experimenting, observing, recording data, hypothesizing, inferring

### How will the idea be expanded?

Divide the students into groups. Give each group at least four different-sized bells. Before ringing each bell, ask the students to create a prediction sheet identifying the loudness and pitch of the bell. Have each group design a way that will most fairly and

• *Bell Ringers*

accurately ring the bells. Emphasize the importance of keeping all other variables constant when comparing the four bells, such as having the same person ring the bells for each trial, or having each person in the group ring each bell to see if the person doing the ringing affects the loudness or pitch. After filling out their prediction sheet and designing a way to ring the bells without letting their predictions prejudice them, they should ring the bells. Record your results. Did your results match your predictions? Is there any way you can alter the bell to magnify the sound coming from it?

### Science in Personal and Social Perspectives

✦ What harm can the earphones on headsets have on your eardrums? What does the magnification of sound do to your eardrums?

✦ Would the magnification of sound be useful at a baseball or football game? Why or why not? Would everyone at these games appreciate sound being magnified?

### Science and Technology

✦ How has knowledge of loudness, pitch, and magnification led to the creation of devices that are important for crowd control? For large group communication? For the production of music?

✦ Why do you think a baseball stadium needs to be designed differently from a concert hall? In which would you want the sound to be louder? To be magnified?

### Science as Inquiry

✦ How could you control the loudness of the sound created by a piano?

✦ How could you change the pitch of a guitar?

### History and Nature of Science

✦ In what careers would you need to understand that loud sounds could set objects vibrating, which could cause structures to collapse? (Safety engineers, contractors, civil engineers, hotel/motel managers, high-rise office building workers.)

✦ How can a cheerleader save his or her voice by knowing about sound, loudness, pitch, and magnification?

## Evaluation  *How will the students show what they have learned?*

Upon completing the activities, the students will be able to:

✦ infer, when given a set of pictures (large bell, small bell, siren, whistle), which would create a loud or soft sound;

✦ infer, when given another set of pictures (long and short guitar strings, large bell, small bell, man's voice, child's voice), which would create a high or low sound;

✦ give at least three ways in which one could magnify one's voice.

# Vibrations Causing Sound

**Inquiry Question:** What causes sound?

**Concept to Be Invented:** Main idea—Vibrations are caused by the movement of air molecules due to a disturbance.

**Concepts Important to Expansion:** There are many ways to produce sounds. You may not be able to see all vibrations.

## Materials Needed

*For Exploration*
prerecorded tape of classroom sounds, tape player, string, wire, meter stick, drum and beans, tuning forks and rubber mallet, pans of water, kitchen fork

*For Expansion*
combs and waxed paper squares

**Safety Precautions:** Remind students of the importance of using the rubber bands as instructed. Any other use may result in injury to eyes or faces. Exercise caution when carrying the kitchen forks during the exploration activity.

**Discrepant Event:** Ask the students to listen carefully as you play the tape recording of classroom sounds. Try to guess what these familiar sounds are. Can you give any descriptive terms to remember them by?

## Exploration *Which process skills will be used?*

Observing, communicating, recording data, experimenting, predicting, inferring

### What will the students do?

+ Have the students place their hands on their throats and make sounds. Record what it feels like.
+ In groups, ask the students to stretch and pluck rubber bands and strings. Record their observations.

• Sound Makers

+ Have the students place the handle end of a kitchen fork between their teeth. Quickly flick the other end of the fork. What do their teeth feel like?
+ In groups, ask the students to tap pans of water and observe.
+ In groups, have the students tap tuning forks with rubber mallets and observe. Ask them to predict what will happen if they strike a tuning fork and quickly thrust it into a pan of water. Have them check their predictions.

## Explanation/Concept Invention *What is the main idea? How will the main idea be constructed?*

*Concept:* Vibrations are caused by the movement of air molecules due to a disturbance.

To invent the concept, ask the students the following questions about their exploration activities:

+ What did it feel like when you placed your hands on your throat and made sounds? Did your hands begin to tingle?
+ What happened to the rubber bands when you stretched them out and plucked them?
+ How did your teeth feel when you flicked the kitchen fork?
+ What path did the water create when the pan was gently tapped?
+ Did the tuning fork tickle your hand when you struck it with the rubber mallet?
+ What happened when you thrust the tuning fork into the water? Was it as you predicted?
+ As the students are sharing their responses, record key terms they use to describe their observations. They may use terms such as they felt movement or it tickled or tingled. Elicit the idea that sound is produced by movement. If no one says "vibrate," introduce this term now. Ask the students to reflect on what was vibrating; in each case they might say their throat, the rubber band, the fork, etc. Ask them to think about what surrounded each of those objects—air. Summarize by asking for their ideas on the inquiry question: What causes sound?

## Expansion of the Idea *Which process skills will be used?*

Inferring, experimenting, hypothesizing, communicating

### How will the idea be expanded?

• *Waxed Paper Kazoo*

Have each student make a comb-and-waxed-paper kazoo by folding a piece of waxed paper over the teeth of a comb. Instruct the children to place their lips on the wax paper and to hum a tune. How is the sound being produced? What is vibrating?

### Science in Personal and Social Perspectives

+ How is sound made? Can you avoid sound?
+ Do sounds affect the way you feel and act?
+ Would you want to attend a concert or go to a movie where the sound kept echoing off the walls? Why or why not?

### Science and Technology

+ The quality of speakers and sound systems relies heavily on sound vibrations; how has modern technology eliminated a lot of excess vibrations?

+ How important a role does the design of a room play in carrying sound vibrations?
+ How did an understanding of sound vibrations help in the creation of the microphone, the phonograph, the telephone, underwater depth sounding, and ultrasound? How have these inventions changed the world?

### Science as Inquiry

+ Knowing that sound is produced by a vibrating object, do you think you can make a bell ring under water? Try it.
+ Some birds, like loons, can dive under water for their food and stay down for an extended period of time. Do you think they call to one another while they are under the water? Can they hear each other? What could you do to determine whether your answer is correct?

### History and Nature of Science

+ Who was John William Strutt, also known as Baron Rayleigh? What role did he play in helping us understand how sound behaves? (For second grade, the teacher could give a brief biography of Baron Rayleigh. He was born in England in 1842. While many people before him expressed opinions about the nature of sound—Pythagoras, Galileo, Mersenne, Chladni ("the founder of modern acoustics"), Colladon and Sturm, and von Helmholtz—Baron Rayleigh was the first to put it all together in a book titled *Theory of Sound,* which he published in 1877. A second edition was published in 1894. In 1904 Rayleigh won the Nobel Prize for physics, mainly for his work that led to the discovery of argon and other inert gases. Baron Rayleigh died in 1919.)
+ Sound production is important in entertainment. Develop a list of entertainment careers that utilize sound.

## *Evaluation*  How will the students show what they have learned?

Upon completing the activities, the students will be able to:

+ predict from a given set of objects which will vibrate and produce sound (Nerf ball, drum, taut rubber band, loose rubber band, ruler, feather);
+ spend one week in which they will be expected to test various wall surfaces to determine which ones allow for maximum and for minimum sound vibrations. They will share their findings with the class and, based on these findings, accurately predict which type of wall surface would be best for a movie theater or a concert hall.

## Loudness and Pitch

GRADE LEVEL: 2–4

DISCIPLINE: Physical Science

**Inquiry Question:**  If I change the loudness of a sound, do I change the pitch?

**Concept to Be Invented:**  Main idea—Sounds vary in loudness and pitch.

**Concepts Important to Expansion:** Size and strength of vibration will affect loudness and pitch.

**Materials Needed**

| | |
|---|---|
| drinking glasses | wooden board with eye hooks and fish line |
| large nail | oatmeal boxes |
| empty soda bottles | wood blocks |
| water | pan lids |
| cigar box | guitar or piano |
| rubber bands | |

**Safety Precautions:** Remind students that care should be taken when handling any of the glass containers used in many of the activities, and to protect eyes against flying rubber bands by wearing goggles!

**Discrepant Event:** Ask the students to predict what will happen to the sound as you tap an empty glass with a nail and gradually add water as you tap. Once all predictions are given, begin to tap the glass and fill it as you do so. Did the sound behave as you predicted? What happened to the sound as more water filled the glass? Do you have any ideas why this happened?

# Exploration   *Which process skills will be used?*

Observing, manipulating materials, predicting, communicating, recording data, inferring, hypothesizing

## What will the students do?

Divide the class into four groups. Have each group rotate through the following activities:

• *Soda Bottle Orchestra*    Soda bottles, glasses, water, nails: Set up a center with glasses and bottles filled with water at varying levels. Have children explore sound variation with water levels in both glasses and bottles. Ask them to record their observations, taking special note of the relationship between the sound produced and the amount of water in the different containers.

Soda bottles filled with water at varying levels

Glasses filled with varying levels of water

Rubber bands of varying widths and lengths, open cigar box: Stretch the different-sized rubber bands over the open cigar box. Pluck the rubber bands. What kinds of sounds do they make? Record the sounds made by the different-sized rubber bands.

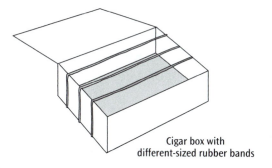

*• Cigar Box Strings*

Cigar box with different-sized rubber bands

Make a fish line harp by cutting at least eight different lengths of fish line. String each line through two eye hooks that are screwed into a foot-long piece of board (a 1 × 8 will do) the same distance apart as the string length. (The teacher can make this harp ahead of time.) Pluck the strings. What do you observe about the relationship between the string length and the sound produced? Is there a relationship between the sound produced and the tightness of the string?

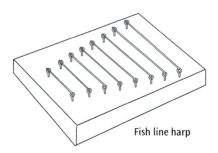

*• Fish Line Harps*

Fish line harp

Strum a guitar, or play a piano in which the guts are exposed. If you are using a guitar, what relationship do you observe between the size of the guitar string and the sound it produces? For the piano, what relationship do you observe between the size of the piano string and the sound it produces?

## *E*xplanation/Concept Invention *What is the main idea? How will the main idea be constructed?*

*Concept:* Sounds vary in loudness and pitch.

Ask the students to reflect on their exploration activities by responding to the following questions:

- ✦ What did you observe when you tapped the various glasses and bottles?
- ✦ What happened to the sound if you used a lot of force to strike the nail to the container? In which containers were the sounds higher?
- ✦ How were you able to make the rubber band sound loud when plucked?
- ✦ What types of sounds were produced with very skinny, tightly stretched rubber bands? Very fat, loosely stretched ones?
- ✦ When you played the harp, which length string gave you the highest sound? The lowest? Did you try loosening the strings? What happened to the sounds when the strings were loose?
- ✦ When you played the guitar or piano, what did you do to create a very loud sound? How were you able to get a very high sound? A low sound?

◆ Summarize all the answers by asking the students to complete these sentence starters: The strength of the vibration determines the _____ (loudness) of the sound. When you change the length of the vibrating object, you change the _____ (pitch).

## Expansion of the Idea *Which process skills will be used?*

Predicting, communicating, experimenting, interpreting data

### How will the idea be expanded?

• Homemade Music

Based on your conclusions from the previous activities, choose a song familiar to everyone in your group and try to play that simple melody on the glasses, the bottles, or any of the other instruments. Each group will take a turn performing for the other groups.

### Science in Personal and Social Perspectives

◆ The ability to produce music enriches the lives of children and can lead to a lifetime skill. The ability to control sound enhances self-concept.

◆ How could you use sound to help you determine how much soda you have left in a can? Or how much milk is left in a carton? Or how much laundry detergent is left in its container? Or if a new bottle of perfume or aftershave is totally full?

### Science and Technology

◆ Many video games use sound to heighten the suspense and action of the play. Do you think these games would be as popular if all sound were eliminated?

◆ What effect does the loudness and pitch of music have on moviegoers? Would scary movies be as effective without the sound effects?

◆ How has the computer industry made use of the loudness and pitch of sounds in personal computers?

### Science as Inquiry

◆ What properties affect the pitch of a sound? The loudness of a sound? Can you create an instrument with high pitch and soft sound? With low pitch and loud sound?

### History and Nature of Science

◆ Children enjoy music for listening and movement and may look to a future as an entertainer. Ask the students to trace the history of an instrument. Who designed it? How does it produce sound?

◆ Where do you think someone with a background in music production, sound engineering, or the creation of musical instruments could use his or her talents?

## Evaluation *How will the students show what they have learned?*

Upon completing these activities, the students will be able to:

◆ predict whether a high or low pitch will be produced by looking at pictures of various-sized strings or columns of water;

- predict loudness and softness of sound when given pictures of thick or thin strings of the same length;
- create a high-pitched sound when given a straw;
- create a low pitch with a soda bottle.

## Sound Movement as Waves

GRADE LEVEL: 2–4
DISCIPLINE: Physical Science

**Inquiry Question:** Can sound move through everything?

**Concepts to Be Invented:** Main idea—Sounds move in the form of waves through air, water, wood, and other solids.

**Concepts Important to Expansion:** Sound waves must strike your eardrum for you to hear sound; sound waves weaken with distance.

### Materials Needed

*Set Up the Following as Activity Centers*
(1) fork and string chime, (2) metal rod, (3) meter stick, wood blocks, (4) pieces of cloth, cotton balls, feathers, cork, Nerf ball, (5) 10-gallon fish tank filled with water

*Per Student Pair*
2 paper cups and 2 paper clips per student; string for telephone; tin can and fish line telephone for comparison with paper cup telephone

**Safety Precautions:** Remind students that care should be taken when handling the kitchen fork and tuning forks; keep them away from your own eyes and those of your friends. Be careful where you place your fingers as you bang the two wood blocks together; avoid crushing them between the blocks.

**Discrepant Event:** Ask the students to listen as they tap the sides of their desks. Now ask them to lay their ears on their desktops while tapping the sides of the desks with the same force as before. Have them describe the sounds they hear. Are there any differences? Why?

 **Exploration** *Which process skills will be used?*

Observing, recording data, predicting, inferring, describing, communicating, measuring, defining operationally

### What will the students do?

Divide the class into five groups. Have each group record its observations while rotating throughout the following activity centers.

Tie about a 12-inch length of string to the handle end of a fork. Allow it to bang on the side of a desk or a wall as you set it in swinging motion. Write a description of the sound

• *Vibrating Fork*

it creates. Can you manipulate the string or fork in any way to change the pitch or loudness of the sound? Can you feel the vibrating fork through the string?

- **Striking Rod**

Hold the metal rod and strike it against a wall, a book, a desk, a variety of surfaces. Is sound produced? Which striking surface will make the rod sound the loudest? The softest? Why do you think this is so?

- **Clapping Blocks**

Take turns with members of your group clapping the two wood blocks together. Use the meter stick to measure at what distance the clapping blocks sound the loudest. How far can you move away from the clapping blocks and still hear them?

- **Sound Producers?**

Using the cloth, cotton, feathers, cork, and Nerf ball, try to produce a sound. Is it possible to create a sound if you simply drop the items on your desk? What if you strike them with your hand? Are these items capable of producing sound? Why or why not?

- **Tapping Tank**

Place your ear to one end of the filled fish tank. Have another student gently tap the glass on the other side of the tank. Can you hear this sound? Did the sound travel through the glass or through the water? This time place your ear so that it is directly above the tank. Have a friend gently drop a quarter into the fish tank when you are not looking. Could you hear when the quarter hit the bottom of the tank?

## Explanation/Concept Invention  *What is the main idea? How will the main idea be constructed?*

*Concept:* Sounds move in the form of waves through air, water, wood, and other solids.

Ask the students to reflect on their exploration activites to answer the following questions:

- ✦ Were you able to make the fork sing? How did you do this?
- ✦ Did the hand that was holding the string feel anything as the fork sang?
- ✦ What about the metal rod? How did you get it to sound the loudest? Could you see the rod moving as it made sound?
- ✦ What about the wood blocks? Were they very loud? How did your hands feel as you banged the blocks together?
- ✦ What about the cloth, cotton, feathers, cork, and Nerf ball? Were you able to get them to make a sound when they were dropped? Why or why not? Do these items behave like the fork, metal rod, or wood blocks? What can those items do that the cloth items cannot? (Help students realize that objects that vibrate will set the air in motion to create a sound.)
- ✦ Could you hear sound through the water? When was it the easiest to detect?
- ✦ Why is it important that your ear be facing the source of the sound? Sound waves must strike your eardrum for you to hear sound.
- ✦ Based on your observations from our class activities, how would you answer our inquiry question—Can sound move through everything? The students should conclude that sound cannot move through everything. Sounds move in waves through air, water, wood, and other solids.

## Expansion of the Idea  *Which process skills will be used?*

Communicating, experimenting, interpreting data, reducing experimental error

### How will the idea be expanded?

Provide each student with 2 paper cups and any length of string (minimum 2 feet). Instruct the students to poke a small hole in the end of their paper cups and thread the string through them. Tie the end of the string to a paper clip to prevent the string from slipping out of the cup. Ask the students to work in pairs trying out their paper cup telephones. Experiment with loose string versus tight string, long versus short string. Compare results. Touch the string as they talk to dampen the sound. Ask each pair to try using the tin can—fish line telephone. Is there any difference between this phone and the one you made? Which telephone sets up more vibrations? What can you say about how sound travels?

• *Paper Cup Telephone*

### Science in Personal and Social Perspectives

- ✦ Where in your house would be the best place to set your stereo speakers: on a metal table or a cloth-covered bench? Or would neither of these be good? Can you suggest a good place?
- ✦ Why do you think most homes have doorbells? How are these better than just yelling for our friends?
- ✦ Do you think it is fair for people who are fishing to use a fish echolocator to determine where the fish are before they begin fishing?
- ✦ Do you think it is ethical for someone to use knowledge of sound to eavesdrop on other people for such purposes as collecting military intelligence, listening in on criminals, or listening to other people's conversations?

### Science and Technology

- ✦ What materials would you use and how would you go about building a sound-proof room? Can you create a plan that would be easy to follow that takes all variables into account in building this room? Work with your parents to create a working model of your design.

### Science as Inquiry

- ✦ A knowledge of the conductivity of sound helps develop further concepts of controlling sound loudness, quality, and usefulness.
- ✦ Do you think you could design a tin-can phone that lets three or more people use it at once? Try it. Draw a diagram of your design.

### History and Nature of Science

✦ How have marine biologists used their knowledge of sound to study the hump-backed whale? Why should we be concerned with the singing behavior of the humpbacked whale?

✦ Why would a pilot be concerned with how sound travels? If you had been a pilot of the Concorde, would you have had a problem trying to get permission to land your plane in Columbus, Ohio? Why?

✦ How did Alexander Graham Bell apply his understanding of sound? Identify one of his inventions and describe how it works.

## **E**valuation *How will the students show what they have learned?*

Upon completing the activities, the students will be able to:

✦ rank-order a given set of materials from good to poor conductors of sound: air, wood, metal rod, cotton string, wire, water, cotton balls;

✦ take an object that is capable of creating sound when struck and alter it so that when it is struck, the loudness of the sound is decreased.

## Sound Waves

**GRADE LEVEL:** 5–8

**DISCIPLINE: Physical Science**

**Inquiry Question:** What is a sound wave?

**Concepts to Be Invented:** Main idea—Sound travels in waves.
Waves consist of areas of compression and rarefaction. Waves move through the air.

**Concepts Important to Expansion:** Sound waves cause vibrations as they hit the eardrum, causing us to hear sounds.

### Materials Needed

*For Each Group of Students*

soup can open at both ends
balloon
rubber band
small rectangular piece of mirror

flashlight
Slinkies
a model of the ear (one for the whole class)
a labeled diagram of the ear

**Safety Precautions:** Be sure that all rough edges are filed off soup cans before providing them to student groups. Make sure there are no sharp edges on the mirrors; file if necessary. Encourage the students to use caution near edges of mirror and soup can.

**Discrepant Event:** Stretch a piece of the balloon over one end of the soup can. Secure it tightly with the rubber band. Glue a small piece of mirror on the balloon membrane, slightly off center. Shine a flashlight onto the mirror so that its reflection shows up on the chalkboard. Ask the students to observe the mirror's reflection on the board. Ask one student to come up and speak into the open end of the can. What happens to the mirror's reflection on the chalkboard when someone speaks into the can?

## Exploration *Which process skills will be used?*

Observing, experimenting, predicting, hypothesizing, inferring

### What will the students do?

Divide the students into groups depending on class size. Have one soup can reflector for each group. Provide each group with a flashlight. Ask the students to predict and then record what happens to the soup can reflectors as they vary the loudness of the sound. What do you think is causing the mirror's reflection to move? Think of this as you begin to play with a Slinky. Stretch and shake the Slinky, and record what the Slinky looks like as you do this. A diagram may be useful at this point. Try to label where the Slinky looks mashed together and where it looks thin on your diagram.

* Soup Can Reflectors

## Explanation/Concept Invention *What is the main idea? How will the main idea be constructed?*

*Concept:* Sound travels in waves. Waves consist of areas of compression and rarefaction. Waves move through the air.

+ What do you think caused the mirror to move? Can you actually see the balloon moving as someone speaks into the open end of the can? Speaking into the can set the balloon membrane vibrating.
+ Can you feel the vibration of the balloon if you lightly touch it as someone speaks into the open end? What type of pattern does the moving mirror make on the board? How is this pattern similar to the movement of the Slinky?
+ What would be a good name to describe the path sound travels in? (Waves.) Ask for a volunteer to share his or her drawing of Slinky movement with the class. Reproduce this drawing for all to see.
+ As you moved the Slinky, were you able to detect areas where the Slinky was mashed together? Were you able to detect areas where it was more spread out?
+ Share with the students that these Slinky movements are similar to sound waves. Areas where sound waves are mashed together are called *compression;* areas that are spread out are called *rarefaction.* Ask the students to complete this statement that answers the inquiry question: Sound travels in the form of _____ (waves). A wave has a ____ (high) and ____ (low) area. At times the waves are mashed together or _____ (compressed); at other times the waves are spread out.

## Expansion of the Idea *Which process skills will be used?*

Observing, manipulating materials, inferring, predicting, communicating

- *Slinky Waves*

- *Sound Waves and the Ear*

## How will the idea be expanded?

Ask the students to take turns laying their heads on their desks while another student stretches the Slinky out on top of the desk and releases it rapidly, or have another student hold a ruler over the edge of the desk and strike it quickly. Ask the student with his or her head on the desk what this felt like. What did your ear detect?

Provide the students with diagrams of the inner ear. Ask them to label what they believe is the path that sound takes as it reaches our ears. Use the ear model to trace this path for the students. Allow them to check their labeled predictions with the model you are tracing. Remind them that sound waves vary in strength. As the sound waves hit the eardrum, they cause it to vibrate in rhythm with them, causing sound messages to the brain. The human ear can interpret sound waves with frequencies ranging between 16 and nearly 20,000 vibrations per second. Those vibrations above 20,000 are termed *ultrasonic*.

### Science in Personal and Social Perspectives

- ✦ Why is it important that you never put anything in your ear smaller than your elbow? What kind of ear-cleaning products do you think are the safest to use?
- ✦ Have you ever tried to talk to your friends while you are under water swimming? Is it easy to understand someone talking under water? Why or why not?
- ✦ Interview people in different lines of work who use earplugs, such as factory workers, road construction crews, or building contractors. What types of earplugs do they use? How well do they think their earplugs work?
- ✦ Is it a good idea to wear headphones while riding your bicycle? Why or why not?

### Science and Technology

- ✦ How effective are earplugs in preventing potentially damaging sounds from reaching your eardrum?

- ✦ Write to the manufacturers of the various earplugs. What materials do they use to make their earplugs? Is any one material better than another? What is the most widely used brand of earplugs? (A teacher can assign this question as homework or as another expansion activity for the class to investigate.)

### Science as Inquiry

- ✦ At a track meet, why do you think you see the spark and smoke from the starter's gun before you hear the sound made by the gun? Can you explain this phenomenon in terms of sound waves?
- ✦ If someone in the room was speaking to you and you could detect only faint, muffled sounds, what might be the probable cause for your loss of hearing? How is sound supposed to travel from your ear canal to your brain?

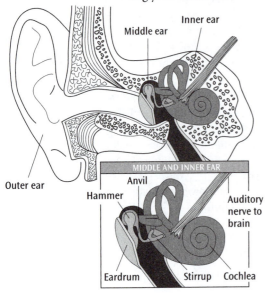

Inner ear

Middle ear

Outer ear

MIDDLE AND INNER EAR

Anvil

Hammer

Auditory nerve to brain

Eardrum    Stirrup    Cochlea

*History and Nature of Science*

+ What do you think would happen to you if you had a job working at an airport loading cargo onto planes and you did not wear protective headphones?
+ Would a piano tuner need to be aware of compression and rarefaction of sound waves? How could he or she apply this knowledge in his or her work?
+ Interview a local audiologist. What does his or her job entail? What kind of knowledge is needed to perform the job? Ask if he or she could share with you any cases where a person's job affected his or her hearing. Share the interview with the class.

## Evaluation  *How will the students show what they have learned?*

Upon completing the activities, the students will be able to:

+ identify areas of rarefaction and compression on a diagram of sound waves;
+ trace the path of the sound waves from their source through the ear when given a worksheet with a diagram of the ear. The students should be able to label the ear canal, eardrum, bones of the middle ear, and nerve to the brain.

# Sound Production

GRADE LEVEL: 5–8
DISCIPLINE: Physical Science

**Inquiry Question:**  Do energy changes make sound?

**Concept to Be Invented:**  Main idea—Sounds are produced by vibrations.

**Concepts Important to Expansion:**  A vibrating object has an energy source. Moving energy is referred to as *kinetic*. Vibrations that cause sound can be produced by hitting, plucking, stroking, or blowing an object.

## Materials Needed

*For Each Student Group*

| | |
|---|---|
| pencil | 1 balloon |
| paper | small piece of mirror |
| percussion instruments | 1 flashlight |
| one soup can with both ends cut out | chalkboard |

**Safety Precautions:**  Remind the students to exercise caution when making sounds with the instruments. They should be reminded not to hold them up to a friend's or their own ear when the sound is loud or piercing. During the expansion activity they must use care when handling the mirrors, and watch for sharp edges on the cans as well.

## Exploration  *Which process skills will be used?*

Observing, recording data, predicting, hypothesizing, experimenting

## What will the students do?

*Activity 1.* Ask the students to close their eyes, sit perfectly still, and not speak. Tell them to listen carefully to all the noises they can hear, even the slightest sounds that they normally ignore. After a few minutes ask them to open their eyes and write descriptions of every noise they heard and, if possible, identify what they believe is the source of those sounds. Students should describe noises in terms ordinarily used for sounds, such as high, low, loud, soft, hissing, rumbling, piercing, musical.

*Activity 2.* Tell the students that they are going to play a listening game. Ask the students to close their eyes while the teacher makes a sound and then try to guess what the sound was. The first one to guess what the sound was will make the next sound. Make sure everyone gets a turn.

*Activity 3.* Present various percussion instruments to the class, such as drums of various sizes, cymbals, pots, pot lids, and xylophones (toy ones will work as well). Ask the students to guess how you can get each one to produce a sound. Ask the students to predict what causes each one to make a sound. Allow the students to experiment with the various instruments, asking them to take note of how sound is produced on each instrument. Ask the students to describe what it feels like. After students have done this, have them strike the instrument again and then hold it tightly. Ask them if the sound stopped. Why did it stop?

## Explanation/Concept Invention   *What is the main idea? How will the main idea be constructed?*

*Concept:* Sounds are produced by vibrations.

*Activity 1.* Ask the students to go back to the first list they made. Make two columns on the board, one labeled *descriptive words* and the other *sound sources*. Ask the students to help fill in the chart from the lists they created. The class will be referring back to this list after they discuss the other two activities.

*Activity 2.* Ask each student: What type of sound did you make for everyone to guess? How was the sound made? What energy source did you use to make it? Add these sounds to the list on the board already; include a third column, *how made,* to the chart.

*Activity 3.* When you hit your instrument, what did you set up? How did you get the sound to stop on your percussion instrument? Go over the list on the board from each of the activities. As the students share that they had to strike the object in some way (e.g. hitting, plucking, stroking, and blowing) to set it in motion, share with them that this energy of motion is called kinetic energy. As they went from no motion of the object to motion, they changed energy from one form to another. Energy causes movement. All of these actions use energy to create vibrations. Vibrations are the source of sound. Ask them how they would now respond to the inquiry question: Do energy changes make sound?

## Expansion of the Idea  *Which process skills will be used?*

Experimenting, predicting, inferring

### How will the idea be expanded?

Divide the class into groups. Have each group stretch a piece cut from a balloon over one end of a soup can, using a rubber band to hold it tightly in place. Glue a small piece of mirror slightly off center. Darken the classroom, and hold the can at an angle to the black-

board. Using a flashlight, shine the beam so that it strikes the mirror and reflects on the board. Ask the group to predict what will happen to the mirror's reflection on the board as someone speaks into the open end of the can. Ask someone in the group to talk into the open end of the can. Ask the other members of the group to take note of what happens to the mirror's reflection as the person speaks into the can. Do your observations match your predictions? What do you think causes the changes in the reflection? What source of energy causes the balloon to vibrate?

• *Sound Movement*

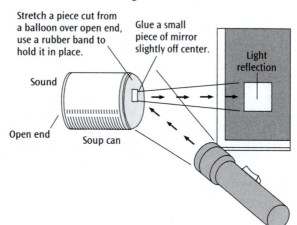

Stretch a piece cut from a balloon over open end, use a rubber band to hold it in place.

Glue a small piece of mirror slightly off center.

Light reflection

Sound

Open end     Soup can

### What is the home assignment?

This assignment may be done alone or with other family members.

1. Go home and sit down in your bedroom or the room of your choice, close your eyes, and be very quiet for 3 minutes. Listen carefully. Do you hear anything? Write down the sounds you hear and describe them.
2. If you have heard new sounds, what are they, and why do you think you haven't heard them before?
3. How did the quiet make you feel? (To show how the quiet made you feel, you may write a descriptive paragraph, write a poem, or draw a picture.)

• *Sound Game: "What Is Sound?"*

### How well can you match sounds?

Students will construct a game for younger students. After the students have made the game, they will take it to a primary class and supervise the younger students playing it.

### Materials Needed

At least twelve 6-ounce unmarked metal cans, small objects (materials used in cans to make noises could include dried rice, beans, peas, marbles, BBs, gravel, sand, bits of Styrofoam, puffed rice, or any other small objects found around the house), tape.

### Preparation

Place small objects in a pair of cans and then seal the cans with tape. Be sure children cannot see in the cans and that the cans are prepared in pairs with approximately the same amount of material in each set of cans.

*Procedure*

1. Shake the cans and listen to the noise they make.
2. Can you hear the different sounds they make?
3. Do any of the cans make the same sound?
4. If you find cans that sound alike, put them next to each other.
5. Have a friend listen to the cans and see if he or she agrees.
6. You may want to make more cans with different sounds to see how well your friends can tell the difference.

### Science in Personal and Social Perspectives

+ What would your life be like without sound?
+ What are some sounds that you hear around you and how are they made?
+ How have people made use of their knowledge that a vibrating body will produce a sound? What types of signals have we created because of this? (Fire alarms, smoke detectors, burglar alarms, fog horns.)
+ When you wake up in the middle of the night and hear creaking bed springs or creaking stairs, knowing what you now know about sound, how can you explain away any fears that you might have?

### Science and Technology

+ How do vibrating strings allow us to create a violin, a guitar, or a bass fiddle? Why is it that some of the sounds created by these instruments sound soothing to some, while others may think of them as simply obnoxious noise?
+ How do we record and transmit the sounds we make or the sounds that are made around us? Choose something that records sound or something that sound is recorded on. Draw a diagram explaining how it works.

### Science as Inquiry

+ Explain how it is possible to create a percussion instrument. Make one and describe how it works. Use terms like *vibration* and *energy* in your explanation.
+ Why do you think you enjoy certain types of music? Survey people of different ages as to their choices in music. Create a pie chart or bar graph to describe your results. Would you have predicted these results?

### History and Nature of Science

+ Why do you think it is important that a car mechanic is able to distinguish one sound from another? How does his or her job depend on recognizing engine sounds?
+ Do you think Beethoven was able to continue his musical career after he became deaf? Do you think it is possible for deaf people to "feel" sounds?
+ What other occupations can you think of in which reliance on sound is essential?

## Evaluation *How will the students show what they have learned?*

Upon completing the activities, the students will be able to:

+ describe sources of sound, explaining how a vibration is set up and the energy source for that vibration;
+ report on their home assignment "What Is Sound?" and share with the class their poems, paragraphs, or drawings about the sounds they observed;
+ work successfully with the younger students when they play the "What Is Sound?" game they made, helping the younger students invent the concept of vibration.

# Characteristics of Matter

GRADE LEVEL: 3–4

DISCIPLINE: Physical Science

**Inquiry Question:** What is matter?

**Concept to Be Invented:** Main idea—Anything that occupies space and has mass is called *matter*. Matter can be found in a solid, liquid, or gaseous state.

**Concepts Important to Expansion:** Physical change, atoms and molecules, matter can be neither created nor destroyed

### Materials Needed

*For Exploration (Per Student Group)*
2 Ziploc plastic bags (label one A and the other B); 1 teaspoon sodium bicarbonate (place in bag A and seal closed); 1 teaspoon calcium chloride, sold as ice melter during winter months (place in bag B and seal closed); magnifying glass; small medicine cups with 10 ml of water in each.

*For Expansion*
3 clear cups or plastic beakers; marbles, sand, water, graduated cylinder, and weighing scale

**Safety Precautions:** Remind students that safety goggles must be worn at all times. Since this is a guided discovery lesson, they are to listen to the teacher at all times before they begin to manipulate the materials—this is for their safety! Tell students not to taste anything during these activities.

## Exploration *Which process skills will be used?*

Manipulating materials, collecting and recording data, communicating, observing, hypothesizing, predicting, inferring

• *Plastic Bag Chemistry*

## What will the students do?

Since you are using unknown chemicals it is best to lead the students through a guided discovery. First ask the students to think about common household products they are familiar with that might look like a white powder. Write that list on the board and even bring in the objects they suggest. Have them there so that *all* students have something to draw upon when they are asked to make predictions later in this opening activity. Do the same with clear liquids.

Provide the students with a Ziploc clear plastic bag labeled A. Ask them to make and record their observations on the unknown in bag A and to make a prediction as to what they think the unknown powders may be. Once the students have had sufficient time to make those observations, ask them to set bag A aside. Now guide the students through the same process with unknown B. (Stress the importance of keeping bags sealed and not tasting the unknown substances. Encourage the students to make observations about the shape of the unknown white powders). Now ask the students to first make a prediction as to what they think will happen if they combine unknown A with unknown B. Ask the students to open bag A, taking care not to touch or eat the substance, and pour it into bag B, then seal the bag. Ask the students to record their observations once the two unknown powders are combined together. Did they behave as predicted?

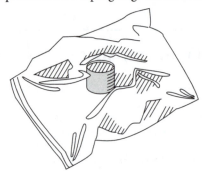

Set aside the bag of the combined unknowns A and B and provide the students with a small clear cup of an unknown liquid C. Again, ask the students to make and record as many observations about unknown C as possible and to make a prediction as to what unknown C could be. Remind them about safety when making observations of unknowns (eliminate the sense of taste as it is an unknown and gently waft the fumes of the unknown toward their nose, do not place the cup directly under the nose to smell).

Once they have completed recording their observations about unknown C, ask the students to make a prediction about what they think will happen if they combine unknown C with unknowns A and B. After they record their predictions then allow them to combine unknown C with the bag containing unknown A and B. Remind them to immediately seal the bag once C is combined with unknowns A and B.

Encourage them to observe the bag, making careful observations (not only looking at the bag but also holding it to feel for any changes in temperature) perhaps even drawing what they observed.

## Explanation/Concept Invention  *What is the main idea? How will the main idea be constructed?*

*Concept:* Anything that occupies space and has mass is called *matter.*

By working with the unknown white powders, students can make observations in which they realize that the unknown substances are in a *solid* state of matter. By observing the unknown *liquid* and the mystery solution, also in a *liquid* state, they can see they are using another state of matter. Upon mixing the *solid* with a *liquid*, they can see the bag expanding, thus observing the third state of matter, a *gas*. Careful use of questions will also get the students to realize that *solids* always retain their shape, no matter the container. *Liquids* take up the shape of the container, and a *gas* will take up as much space as you give it.

Ask the students the following questions to help get to the ideas stated above:

+ You drew pictures of the unknown white powders in bag A and in bag B. When you mixed them together, did they change their shape? (Work on the children's understanding of the concept of a solid, which does not change in shape. Physical change can be observed if they crush the solids; what was created is a *heterogeneous mixture*—a combination of two or more substances each distinct from the other.) If so, how? Why?
+ Share your predictions as to what unknown A, B, and C were. What did you base your predictions upon? (Based predictions on common white powders they were familiar with). If time permits, an entire expansion activity can be done where the students are given what one of the unknowns (A or B) is, and they use a variety of known powders to see if they get a similar reaction. Otherwise, at this point you should share with the students the identity of the unknowns.
+ What shape was the liquid in when it was inside the cup? What about when you poured it out? Why? (Work on the concept of liquids taking the shape of their container and only within the limit of the volume that the sample occupies.)
+ What happened when you mixed the solids with the liquids? What did you observe? (Listing all of their observations will allow you to expand on specific secondary concepts you want the students to understand, such as physical versus chemical change.)
+ Why did your bag get bigger? What took up that space in the bag? If you used a bigger plastic bag, would it be blown all the way up, too? Why? (Work on the concept of a gas taking the shape of its container.)
+ Ask the students to now respond to the inquiry question: What is matter?

If you use this activity for older students, you could also introduce the students to chemical nomenclature. Provide students with the chemical formulas for the unknowns involved in the activity (older students may help derive these formulas and help balance the equation).

$$CaCl_2 + NaHCO_3 + H_2O \rightarrow NaCl(aq) + HCl(aq) + CaCO_3 + H_2O$$
$$CaCO_3 + H_2O \rightarrow H_2CO_3 + CaO$$
$$H_2CO_3 \rightarrow H^+ + HCO^-_3 \ CO_2 \rightarrow (g) + H_2O$$

## Expansion of the Idea  *Which process skills will be used?*

Measuring, predicting, hypothesizing, observing, recording data

### *How will the idea be expanded?*

Again, this activity can be performed as a guided discovery or a class demonstration. Provide each student group with 3 clear cups or plastic beakers; marbles, sand, and some

• *Marble Matter*

water. Ask the students to weigh a cup, then fill the cup with marbles. Record their weight and number of marbles. Ask them questions such as the following: How many marbles did you put in the cup? Do you think you can put in any more marbles? Did the marbles take the shape of the cup? (Work here to make sure they understand that the marbles did not change their shape.) What was the weight of the cup? What state of matter are the marbles?

Ask the students to weigh another cup. Fill the cup with sand and then weigh it. Have them place a mark on the cup indicating the top of the sand. Use the same line of questioning for the marbles.

Now ask the students if they think both cups are full. Ask the students if they think they can pour any of the sand into the cup filled with marbles. Solicit responses. React to responses: I thought you told me the cup with the marbles in it was full; how can you possibly put anything else into this cup?

Have the students pour some sand into the cup of marbles. Mark the new level of sand on the sand cup. What happens? Were you able to add sand into an already-filled cup of marbles? Why? What is the weight of your new mixture? What is the weight of the sand remaining in the cup? Subtract this remaining weight of sand from the original weight of sand. How much sand did you lose? Subtract the original weight of the marbles from the new weight of the marble and sand mixture. Is this amount gained equal to the amount lost from the sand cup? (Reinforce the concept of matter—anything that occupies space and has mass; concept of states of matter—two different solids. Secondary concept—physical change, matter was not created or destroyed, it still has the same weight; nothing was lost, just placed in different containers.)

Weigh a third cup and fill it with water. Weigh this. Ask the students if they think it is possible to put water into an already-filled cup of sand and marbles. Why? Why not? What state of matter is the water? What do you know about liquids? (For older students, instead of weighing the water in a cup, introduce them to a graduated cylinder; have them measure out so many milliliters of water and record the volume of water in milliliters that they pour into the marble-sand cup.)

Was your prediction true? What happened when you tried to add water to the marble-sand cup? Why could the container that was already filled with marbles still hold more sand and water?

Do you think we could have started with the water, then the sand and marbles? Why? What does this tell you about the sizes of molecules of different materials or substances? (The concept of solids versus liquids leads into a discussion of the size of particles. Smaller-size particles can slip between the larger ones. Make an analogy to molecules. Introduction of this new term may lead into a new unit on atoms and molecules.)

### Science in Personal and Social Perspectives

+ Which would you rather take a bath in: water mixed with sand or water mixed with bath bubble beads? Why?

+ What would happen if you burned a dollar bill? Could you tape it back together and still have a dollar?

### Science and Technology

+ How has knowledge of chemical changes allowed the food industry to create cake mixes that can be made in a microwave rather than a regular oven?
+ Getting matter to change its shape has allowed us to create many large buildings, like the Sears Tower in Chicago. How is this so?

### Science as Inquiry

+ The students engage in manipulative skills during the activities.
+ For understanding the concept of physical versus chemical change, ask the students to explain why they can heat snow and get water, or why they can mix flour, water, baking soda, and sugar together, heat the mixture, and taste not these separate ingredients but a cake.
+ Why can't you put a round peg in a square hole?

### History and Nature of Science

+ Using a list of all of the concepts discovered in the activities, ask the students to survey their parents and other adults to see if they make use of any of these concepts in their work. Where do they see them utilized? Are these people in typical scientific careers? Can anyone use these science concepts?
+ Early scientists called *alchemists* thought they could turn simple elements into gold. Did everyone believe them at that time? Why or why not? Do you believe them? Why or why not?

## Evaluation *How will the students show what they have learned?*

Upon completing the activities, the students will be able to:

+ demonstrate a physical change when given a piece of paper;
+ provide examples of solid matter, liquid matter, and gas;
+ demonstrate how to capture a gas.

---

# Physical Properties of Matter

GRADE LEVEL: K–4
DISCIPLINE: Physical Science

**Inquiry Question:** How can objects be described?

**Concept to Be Invented:** Objects have many observable properties, such as size, weight, color, shape, behavior.

**National Science Education Standards:** K–4 Physical Science—Properties of objects and materials

◆ Objects have many observable properties, including size, weight, shape, color, temperature, and the ability to react with other substances. These properties can be measured using tools, such as rulers, balances, and thermometers.

◆ Objects are made of one or more materials, such as paper, wood, and metal. Objects can be described by the properties of the materials from which they are made, and these properties can be used to separate or sort a group of objects or materials.

**Science Attitudes to Nurture:** Curiosity, cooperating with others, tolerating other opinions, explanations, or points of view

### Materials Needed

Enough hard boiled, white eggs for half the class. Place the cooked eggs and an equal number of raw (uncooked) eggs, randomly, in a bowl. Allow each student to pick an egg out of the bowl.

l can of broth or canned liquid, 1 can of dog food, paper towels, clear container or bowl, 3 or 4 different brands of chocolate chip cookies, 1 ruler, 5 to 10 toothpicks, paper for recording data

**Safety Precautions:** Encourage students to use senses, except taste. Remind students to wash their hands after the Exploration activity, especially before they begin the Expansion activity.

## *Exploration* *Which process skills will be used?*

Observing, manipulating materials, collecting and recording data, communicating

• *Egg-Citing Observations*
Enter the classroom carrying the bowl of eggs. Act as if you are greatly troubled. Explain to the students that you boiled some eggs last night for dinner and placed them in the refrigerator. When you went to the refrigerator this morning, you found that someone had taken the cooked eggs and combined them with the raw eggs in the bowl. Now you have to determine which are cooked and which are raw without breaking any of them. Ask the students if they can help you solve your problem.

Ask each student to choose an egg from the bowl and to make as many observations about their egg as possible without breaking the egg open. Remind them not to break the egg. Allow sufficient time for students to collect their data and record their observations. For very young students, ask them to draw their observations. Once they have made their observations, move to the concept invention phase of this lesson.

## *Explanation/Concept Invention* *What is the main idea? How will the main idea be constructed?*

As students make their observations, encourage students who appear to be stumped to think of ways to make observations. Ask questions such as: When I make an observation, am I using only my eyes? What other things can I use to make an observation? Encourage the students to think about ways they can manipulate the egg

without dropping or breaking it. Remind the students to record the information they are discovering. Guide students to word the concept: Objects have many observable properties, such as size, weight, color, shape, behavior.

Solicit the students' observations. Make a list on the board. Once you have an observation from each student, go back to the original question: Which of these observations will help me solve my problem? Ask a student to restate the problem: Which eggs are raw and which are cooked?

Through the process of elimination, the students will find that some physical properties are more distinguishing than others. For instance, observing that the egg is white is not going to solve the problem, since all of the eggs the students have are white. However, observations such as: "It sounds as if something is moving inside when I shake my egg," or "My egg will spin or stand on end," are observations that will help solve the problem. Ask the students: Is one distinguishing characteristic enough to decide if any egg is cooked or raw? If some students think so, then ask them to make their prediction about whether their egg is cooked or raw based on that one distinguishing characteristic. Let one student crack an egg only to find that the prediction was incorrect. (Make sure that the student chosen to bring out the idea that one characteristic is not enough has in fact made a wrong decision.)

As you progress through the list of student observations, keep referring back to the original problem. As you narrow down their observations to those that help solve the problem, you may find that the students eventually come to an observation that stumps them: Some eggs spin easily and others sort of wobble but don't spin well. The students aren't sure if the raw or cooked eggs spin easily. At this point the teacher should bring

out the cans of broth and dog food. (Two cans of each are helpful.) Open the can of broth and pour it into a clear container. Ask the students what state of matter the broth is in. Have a student volunteer to spin the unopened can of broth and ask if it is easy or hard to get the can to spin.

Now open a can of dog food and empty it into a clear container. Ask the students what state of matter the dog food is in. Have a student volunteer to spin the unopened can of dog food and ask the student if it is easy or hard to get the can to spin.

## Expansion  *Which process skills will be used?*

Designing an experiment, observing, measuring, predicting, hypothesizing, recording data

This expansion activity is more appropriate for students in grades 3–6. For K–2 students, you may want to lead a guided discovery activity using the following ideas:

Remind the students about the concept they have learned about observable physical properties from the Exploration activity. Physical properties of matter help distinguish one kind of matter from another. Ask the students to design an experiment using

• *Chocolate Chip Exploration*

just physical properties to determine what the best brand of chocolate chip cookie is. Allow sufficient class time for groups of students to brainstorm ways in which they could use only physical properties to determine the best brand of chocolate cookie. Ask the students to submit a copy of their planned experiment and a materials list so that they can perform their experiment in the next class meeting. Suggested materials are included in the materials list at the beginning of the lesson. Be sure to read over the designed experiments to be sure that they are using only physical properties and also that appropriate safety standards are maintained.

On the second day, allow the students to act on appropriately planned lessons. On the third day, ask the different student groups to share the methods they used for determining the best cookie and the results of their experiment. Once all of the groups have had a chance to share their results, and especially if the results were different, ask the students if it is necessary to set some criteria for determining which cookie is best. The students should conclude that the term *best* is arbitrary—the members of the group must decide criteria for judging an object the *best*.

As a final discussion question, ask the students why you asked them to design their experiment around physical properties. Why could they not taste the cookie to determine the best?

### Science in Personal and Social Perspectives

+ If you had to describe your best friend to another student, how would you do that? Would a description, such as: "He or she is really nice and cute," be enough? Why or why not?
+ If you were talking with a group of people about the best movie you ever saw, do you think everyone in the group would agree with you? Why or why not?

### Science and Technology

+ How does the mineral industry determine which mineral is which?
+ Why has the auto industry gone from metal bumpers to plastic bumpers? What do properties of matter have to do with that decision?

### Science as Inquiry

+ Students engage in manipulative skills during the activities.
+ How can you accurately describe an object?
+ How can you tell the difference between a raw and cooked egg without cracking the egg open?

### History and Nature of Science

+ Pretend you want a new sidewalk in front of your house. You need to hire a cement contractor to do the work. One contractor you interviewed said it didn't matter what kind of material he or she used to pour your sidewalk. Does this person know much about distinguishing physical properties of matter? Would you be willing to hire that contractor? Why or why not?

+ Who do you think should be aware of the many different physical properties of matter for their work? What kinds of skills are needed for that profession? Have the necessary skills changed in the past twenty years?

## Evaluation  *How will the students show what they have learned?*

Upon completing the activities, the students will be able to:

+ determine, when given an egg, whether it is cooked or raw;
+ design an experiment to determine the best brand of paper towels;
+ list the physical properties of three or four different things (the teacher can choose any number of items: a rock, flower, penny, button, or anything else).

---

# Air

GRADE LEVEL:   **K–1**

DISCIPLINE: **Physical Science**

**Inquiry Question:**  How do we know that air is real?

**Concept to Be Invented:**  Air takes up space.

**National Science Education Standards:**  K–4 Physical Science—Properties of objects and materials. Objects have many observable properties, including size, weight, shape, color, temperature, and the ability to react with other substances.

**Science Attitudes to Nurture:**  Open-mindedness, curiosity, perseverance, positive approach to failure, cooperation with others

**Materials Needed:**  Balloons, clear plastic bags, plastic party horns, Styrofoam cups, soap bubble solution, drinking straws (bendable), clear plastic cups, large plastic tub or aquarium, scrap materials

**Safety Precautions:**  Wear goggles to avoid chemical eye splash. Avoid sucking soap solution into mouth.

## Exploration  *Which process skills will be used?*

Observing, identifying, comparing

Set the stage for exploration by demonstrating how to blow a balloon and to make "music" with the escaping air. Engage the children by asking: "What do you think is inside the balloon?" "What do you think makes this music?" Answers may differ, but most will refer to breath or air in the balloon. Pose the question: "Do you think air is real?" "Why?" Use the students' variety of answers to convey the need to investigate in order to find out if air is real. Avoid discussing the concept at this point.

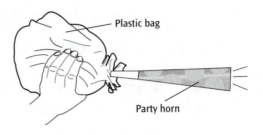

Plastic bag

Party horn

• *Party Horn*

Investigate by filling large plastic bags with air, closing the open end of the bag over the small "blow into" end of a party horn. Hold the bag closed against the horn and gently squeeze the bag to blow the horn (kind of like a bagpipe). Pose open-ended questions to the children about what they think makes the horn sound, what filled the bag, where the air came from, etc.

Investigate by giving each child a Styrofoam cup and have him or her punch a hole the size of the diameter of a straw 1 inch from the bottom, invert the cup and dip into soap bubble solution, and then insert a straw into the hole. Encourage the children to blow through the straw. Larger bubbles will result when the cup is inverted.

Caution the children to avoid sucking up the soap solution and demonstrate how to change their breathing to make the bubbles larger and smaller. Question: "What do you think is inside your bubble? How do you think the air got inside the bubble? How do you think you could remove the air from your bubble?"

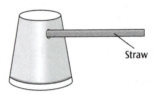

Straw

## **E**xplanation/Concept Invention   *What is the main idea? How will the main idea be constructed?*

Demonstrate how to fill a plastic cup with water and invert it in a water tank or a clean aquarium (you can use a large plastic tub or classroom's water table, if available). Ask the children prediction questions, such as: What do you think may happen to the water in the cup if you blow air into it? Demonstrate how to use a bent straw to blow air into the filled cup while it is in the water and inverted.

Ask the children to explain what they observe. Invite some of the children to try the same demonstration. Discuss what happened in each of the investigations and how air behaved the same as in this demonstration. Use a sentence starter and invite the children to offer ideas to complete it: "Air takes up _____." The desired answer is *space*, and the sentence represents the *concept* common to each investigation in this lesson. Ask children "How do we know air is real?" Relate the question to the concept statement and use the concept statement throughout the rest of the lesson.

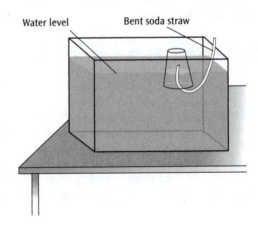

Water level

Bent soda straw

*Which process skills will be used?*

Classifying, communicating, and predicting

Permit all children to practice the demonstration (described in the Explanation phase). Encourage all children to describe the property: Air takes up space.

Set up an additional investigation that will be used for *Evaluation*. Partially fill several clear plastic shoeboxes or small clean plastic aquaria. Have several small potted plants on hand with dry soil. Immerse one plant into the water and observe the air bubbles as they emerge from the dry soil. (You can substitute a small cup of dry sand for the same effect.) Discuss: "What do you think causes the bubbles? Where do you think the bubbles come from?" Answers should reveal that the children understand the lesson's concept, are able to use it in their spoken communication, and can use it in a new setting. Continue to question and encourage children to communicate their findings as they investigate the following dry objects.

• *Air Bubbles*

| small pieces of wood | pieces of brick or fish tank gravel | crayons |
| small rocks | leaves | paper |
| pine cones | side walk chalk | clay |
| Popsicle sticks | classroom chalk | cloth |
| sponge pieces | aluminum foil (flat, folded, crumpled) | paper |

Use cooperative groups to predict and investigate what happens when the objects are immersed in water. Use a pictograph to classify objects as having air or no air. Pose the question again: "How do we know air is real?"

**Evaluation** *How will the students show what they have learned?*

Upon completing the activities, the students will be able to:

✦ observe changes to the balloons and water in the cups, and predict what they think will happen when changes are proposed, and communicate their observations;
✦ describe and illustrate examples of objects or conditions where "air takes up space";
✦ classify objects as having air or no air;
✦ give a response to the question "How do we know if air is real?" and a reason for their answer.

# Changing Matter

GRADE LEVEL: 5–8
DISCIPLINE: Physical Science

**Inquiry Question:** Do chemical changes result in useless matter?

**Concepts to Be Invented:** Main idea—An alteration of the composition or the properties of matter is called a *chemical change*. An alteration of the shape of matter without a change in its chemical composition is called a *physical change*.

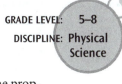

**Concepts Important to Expansion:** Small, single units of matter are called *monomers*. A substance that will speed up a chemical reaction without being affected itself is called a *catalyst*. A bond linking the chains of atoms in a polymer is a *cross-linker*. A compound formed by adding many small molecules together in the presence of a catalyst or by the condensation of many smaller molecules through the elimination of water or alcohol is a *polymer*.

### Materials Needed

*Per Student*

| | |
|---|---|
| 1 piece of scrap paper | 1 stirring rod or Popsicle stick |
| 1 clear cup | 1 lunch-size Ziploc bag |
| matches | |

*For Entire Class*

| | |
|---|---|
| 1 aluminum pie pan | liquid starch |
| 3 large containers of glue (enough to give each student 30 ml) | borate solution (50 g borax with 100 ml of water) |
| beaker or graduated cylinder for measurements | food coloring |
| | paper towels for cleanup |

*Items Used to Introduce the Problem*

| | |
|---|---|
| Teflon frying pan · | football helmet |
| compact disc | pair of nylons |
| plastic baby bottle | |

 **Safety Precautions and/or Procedures:** During the exploration phase, when the paper is burned, the teacher should make sure there is adequate ventilation in the classroom. The teacher should also be sure the matches are kept away from the students and use care when an open flame is present: sleeves must be pushed up, hair pulled back, and eyes protected. During the expansion phase, the students should be discouraged from putting their hands in their mouths. Be sure they wash their hands as soon as they are finished with the activity.

## Exploration  *Which process skills will be used?*

Observing, predicting, inferring

### What will the students do?

• *Physical and Chemical Paper Change*

*Introduction:* The teacher will allow the children to examine the following items: compact discs, baby bottles, Teflon pan, nylons, and a football helmet. As the students view the items, tell the students that you would like them to think about each item, and that by the time they finish the activities, they should be able to tell you what all the items have in common.

*Student Activity:* Give each student a piece of paper. Ask each of them to make it look different in some way. Then ask each to share what they did to make it look different.

## Explanation/Concept Invention  *What is the main idea? How will the main idea be constructed?*

*Concept:* An alteration of the composition or the properties of matter is called a *chemical change.* An alteration of the shape of matter without changing its chemical composition is called a *physical change.*

Ask such questions as: What did you do to make the paper look different? If they tore it up, ask, "If I taped it back together, would I still have a piece of paper? By changing its shape, did I do anything to change the molecules that came together to make that piece of paper?" Be sure to allow the students time to share their comments with one another. Explain that a change in shape with no loss of molecules is called a *physical change.*

If students suggest burning the paper, ask if they think they will still be able to use the paper once you change it by burning it. Then burn it over the aluminum pie pan. Is the paper still in a usable form? Why not? Explain that the paper underwent a *chemical change.* When it burned, carbon atoms were lost. Do all chemical changes result in useless matter? Think about how you might respond to this question as we go through the next guided activity.

## Expansion of the Idea  *Which process skills will be used?*

Observing, measuring, recording data, predicting, inferring

### How will the idea be expanded?

Ask the students to use the graduated cylinders to measure out 30 ml of glue. Pour it into the clear cup. Choose a color from the food coloring and mix it with your glue (use Popsicle sticks for stirring). Do you still have glue in front of you? What kind of change did the glue undergo?

- Polymer-Rubber Balls

What do you think will happen if you mix the colored glue with the liquid you have in front of you? (The teacher should place in front of half of the class the liquid starch, in front of the other half a borate solution). Please make some predictions, and share them with one another on each side of the room. What do you think will happen when you mix the glue with the unknown liquid in front of you? Make your predictions and record them.

Ask the students to measure out 30 ml of either the starch or the borate solution. Encourage the students to make predictions about how much of the solution they will need to bring about a change in the glue. Since they do not know for certain how much starch or borate solution they will need, encourage the students to add one of these slowly, stirring all the time, until they see a change. Record how much starch or borate solution was necessary to bring about a change in the glue. Record any new observations you may have made about the colored glue.

Did you create anything new, or can you still tell the glue from the starch or borate solution? Can you pick up this new piece of matter? (Encourage the students to do so—the more they manipulate it in their hands, the more the water will come out, and eventually they will have created their own rubber ball.) What do you think you can do with

it? What kind of change do you think you created by combining the glue with the starch or the borate solution? Why do you say this?

Go back to the original question: Do all chemical changes result in the creation of useless matter? How many of you think you created a new form of matter that is useful? What did you do differently from your classmates? What do you think you can do with your newly created piece of matter? How useful is it? As a teacher, you may encourage the students from the different sides of the room to compare their newly created rubber balls. Do they bounce the same? Roll the same? Feel the same? Here, two different catalysts were used to create this special kind of chemical change called a *polymerization reaction*. After they finish, the students may place their balls in a Ziploc bag, where they will stay fresh for a few weeks.

Do you think that other inventions could have been discovered just by people mixing things together in the lab and making careful observations about how much and of what materials they mixed together?

Teflon, used to coat pans, is one of these accidental chemical combinations that was discovered in a lab when scientists weren't looking for it. Chemists realized that it was possible to get small pieces of matter to link up chemically when a catalyst was used to force the reaction to occur. Sometimes these smaller pieces of matter, called *monomers*, add together in one long chain to create *polymers*. Saran wrap, Lucite, Plexiglas, and Teflon are polymers formed by this additive process. Polymers can also be formed by bringing monomers together, removing water or alcohol through a condensation reaction, and forcing the monomers to link together. This is what happened to form nylon, and this is what happened here to create a new form of matter—rubber balls! In addition to these synthetic polymers, silk, cellulose, and rubber are naturally occurring polymers.

Go back to some of the first items shown to the students: the football helmet, the baby bottle, the CD, the nylons, and the Teflon pan. Encourage the students to think about the activities they just participated in as they try to answer the very first question you asked: What do all of these things have in common?

They were all created by a chemical change in which small pieces of matter, called monomers, were linked together to form polymers. These polymer reactions created new kinds of matter that have proven to be very useful.

### Science in Personal and Social Perspectives

+ You're tired of the color of your bedroom, and you want to change the color of your walls. Will your room undergo a physical or chemical change?
+ Can you name any products created because of a polymerization reaction that have directly affected your life?
+ There is much controversy over the use of Teflon bullets. Police unions bitterly oppose their use. Why do you think this product, formed from a polymerization reaction, is of serious concern to our society?
+ Knowledge of chemical changes has led to the invention of many products that have greatly changed society. Can you think of any products that were created as the result of a chemical change?

### Science and Technology

✦ A technological advancement for many parents is the disposable diaper. Describe the materials used to make a disposable diaper. How has this technological advancement created more problems for society? Suggest possible solutions.

### Science as Inquiry

✦ Can you demonstrate the difference between a physical and a chemical change?
✦ Explain how a polymer can be created. How is this a unique type of chemical change?
✦ Can you name some monomers or polymers that are found in nature? How about some synthetic ones?

### History and Nature of Science

✦ Do you think a cement finisher or a beautician needs to understand how a chemical change can occur? Why or why not?
✦ Are physical or chemical changes common in the type of work your parents do? Identify one of the changes, and explain where it occurs.
✦ Interview a female over age sixty. Ask her to describe what nylon stockings were like when she was twenty. How and why did they change?

## Evaluation   *How will the students show what they have learned?*

Upon completion of the activities, the students will be able to:

✦ appreciate the need to think about a problem first, and then use clear, concise language to communicate the action taken on the problem;
✦ demonstrate the differences between physical and chemical changes;
✦ make predictions based on previous experiences;
✦ utilize the scientific method to solve a newly designed problem;
✦ explain how certain chemical reactions, such as polymer formation, can result in the creation of useful materials;
✦ explain what a football helmet, a compact disc, a Teflon pan, a baby bottle, and a pair of nylons have in common.

---

# Identification of an Unknown

GRADE LEVEL: 5–8
DISCIPLINE: Physical Science

**Inquiry Question:** Can I rely solely on physical properties to identify an unknown?

**Concept to Be Invented:** Main idea—Physical properties alone are not always sufficient characteristics to identify an unknown.

**Concepts Important to Expansion:** *Indicators* are used to bring about a physical or chemical change in an unknown. Common indicators are iodine, vinegar, and heat.

## Materials Needed

*For Exploration (for Class of 24)*

The following items make up the secret powders: 4 pounds of granulated sugar, 2 boxes of table salt, 4 pounds of baking soda, 4 pounds of cornstarch, 4 pounds of plaster of Paris.

The following items are necessary for all parts of the lesson: 20 plastic spoons, 1 box of toothpicks, 10 eyedroppers, 20 small cups or containers.

Some optional materials are newspapers, paper towels, broom and dustpan, black construction paper, hand lenses or microscopes.

*For Expansion (for Class of 24)*

To perform indicator tests the following items are necessary: 1 quart of vinegar, 1 roll of aluminum foil, 1 ounce of tincture of iodine, crackers, potatoes, 1 bucket of water or a water source in room, birthday candles (one per student group), small lumps of clay (one per student group), wooden clothespins (one per student group).

 **Safety Precautions:** Remind students of the following: never taste any of the unknown substances unless given teacher permission. Goggles must be worn at all times! Wash hands between testing different unknowns and immediately after the lab is completed. Remove all combustible material from the area of the flame during the heat tests during expansion. Roll up sleeves and tie back hair when using an open flame.

## Exploration  *Which process skills will be used?*

Observing, manipulating materials, inferring, collecting and recording data, communicating

### What will the students do?

• *Physical Properties of an Unknown*

Start off the lesson by asking the students the following: Have you ever thought about some of the common substances we use in our homes? For instance, how many of you can name some common white powder substances we may use in our homes? (List these on the board. If the ones used as secret powders are not suggested, make suggestions that will help the students think about those possibilities.) What are they used for? How do we know that what it says on the container is really what is inside? The following activity will provide you with skills to help identify unknown substances.

Provide each student group five small cups numbered 1–5 and containing five different secret powders. The students will also receive five toothpicks to use as stirring sticks, some black construction paper to dump their powders on, and a hand lens. Ask the students to try to determine what the unknowns are, based on their observations of physical characteristics. The following questions should serve as a guide to encourage the students to focus on physical properties: How are the powders alike? How are they different? Do they feel the same? Does any powder have an odor? Are they the same shade of white? Can you list three properties of each powder? Can you list more than three? Using the hand lens, can you discover anything new about the powders? Are all the powders really powders? Can you describe the particles that make up each powder? Do you think a powder can be identified by the shape of its particles? Describe which properties of the powders seem to be the same and which seem to be different. Which properties are helpful in describing a particular powder?

## *Explanation/Concept Invention* *What is the main idea? How will the main idea be constructed?*

*Concept:* Physical properties alone are not always sufficient characteristics to identify an unknown.

Ask the students to share answers to questions asked during the exploration phase. Refer back to the original list of common white powders from home. Ask the students to match up the unknowns to knowns based on physical characteristics they observed. Salt and sugar are made of cube-shaped particles, but salt is much more uniform and less broken. Cornstarch, baking soda, and plaster of Paris are similar in appearance, and it is hard to distinguish one from another simply on the basis of physical characteristics.

## *Expansion of the Idea* *Which process skills will be used?*

Designing an experiment, observing, measuring, predicting, hypothesizing, recording data, evaluating, controlling variables, interpreting data, reducing experimental error

### *How will the idea be expanded?*

*Discussion before the activity:* Ask students if they know why canaries were used in coal mines years ago, or what good it is to know the pH of pool water, or why a gas gauge in a car is useful. Once you obtain answers to these questions, ask what these three questions have in common. Work at getting to the idea that all of these are indicators of some sort: Canaries indicate the quality of the air, pH indicates the acidity or alkalinity of water, and a gas gauge indicates the amount of gas in the car.

    Indicators can be used to conduct tests on the secret powders to assist in a more accurate determination of the unknown. These indicators may bring about a physical or chemical change in the secret powder. (Be sure the students already know the difference between a physical change—one in which a change of shape can occur, but the chemical composition of the original material is not altered, such as freezing of water or shredding paper—and a chemical change—a change in the composition of the original material in which molecules are lost and cannot be put back into the material to return it to its original composition, such as burning sugar or mixing vinegar and baking soda.)

    During a discussion of the indicators, ask the students the following, to see if they can determine how the indicators can be used in determining the identity of the secret powders: What do you think might happen when water (or iodine, vinegar, or heat

*• Chemical Properties of an Unknown*

added) is mixed with the secret powder? How might you go about doing this without contaminating your secret powder sample? Why is it important to avoid contamination?

*Action:* Observe the reactions of the five secret powders when acted on by the water, iodine, vinegar, and heat. Reaffirm the notion of contamination at this point. Have the students use separate eye droppers for the water, iodine, and vinegar. Be sure they use different toothpicks and clean containers to mix the unknown with the indicator. The students should record their results.

*Water:* What happens to each powder when you put a few drops of water on it? Did each powder mix with the water? Did any of the powders disappear? Did you put the same amount of powder in each cup? Is this important? What will happen if you add 20 drops of water? 50? 80? Does additional water affect the powders? Did any powders disappear? Where did they go? Did the powder leave the cup?

As students work with the water, they will discover that sugar, baking soda, and salt are soluble in water. By comparing the number of drops needed to dissolve these powders, some students may conclude that sugar is more soluble in water than baking soda and that salt is the least soluble of the three. Both cornstarch and plaster of Paris are insoluble in water. Plaster of Paris will harden if permitted to stand for a short period of time. After hardening, plaster of Paris cannot be changed back into its original state. The concepts of solubility and evaporation, as well as the differences among solution, suspension, and mixture, can be highlighted through this portion of the activity if necessary.

*Iodine:* Place small amounts of secret powders in five separate cups. Add a few drops of iodine. Do all the powders react to iodine in the same way? How can iodine be used to distinguish one powder from another? Take a cracker and a piece of potato; how do these react with the iodine? Was this reaction similar to any of the secret powders' reactions? What do the cracker and potato have in common?

The cup containing cornstarch will show a striking blue-black color when iodine is added. A deep blue or blue-black color on contact with iodine is the standard test for the presence of starch. The starchier the food, the more obvious and deep the blue color will be.

*Vinegar:* Place small amounts of secret powders in five separate cups. Add a few drops of vinegar. What happens when you put a few drops of vinegar on each powder? Did any powder react more than others? Do you think that powders that dissolved in water will also dissolve in vinegar? Which powder do you think will take the least amount of vinegar to dissolve? The most? How can you find out? How can vinegar be used to distinguish baking soda from the other powders? If you place vinegar on an unknown substance and it bubbles, can you be sure that the substance is baking soda? Could it be another substance?

Baking powder fizzes actively when vinegar is added, while other powders fizz only slightly or not at all. Other powders can be tested with vinegar. A solution of powdered milk is curdled by vinegar.

*Heat:* Support a small candle in a lump of clay. This will supply sufficient heat to test the effects of heat on the powders. Fashion the aluminum foil into a small dish to be used to heat the secret powders. Use the clothespin as a handle for your aluminum dish when holding the dish over the flame. Be sure to make a separate dish for each powder.

Remove combustible litter from the area where the candle will be used. Roll up loose sleeves and tie back long hair while working with the burning candle. It is extremely important to use dry powder when performing this activity, to prevent spattering. Never use powders that have been mixed with any liquid. Place a small amount of powder in the dish and heat it.

Did any of the powders change when heated? Was an odor given off during heating? Do all the powders look the same after cooling? Compare them with samples of powders that were not heated. Were any new substances formed by heating?

When heated, baking soda and plaster of Paris seem to remain unchanged, while salt snaps and crackles. Starch turns brown and smells like burned toast. Sugar melts, bubbles, smokes, smells like caramel, turns brown, turns black, and finally hardens. The heat test, then, is a good way to detect sugar, since sugar is the only one of the secret powders to melt and turn shiny black when heated. The same reaction occurs to sugar even when it is mixed with any of the other powders.

After using the indicators, ask the students to share their results to help determine the identity of the unknown powders. Which powder turned black when iodine was added? Can you name the powder or powders that are soluble in water? Which liquid added to which powder caused bubbles? How can a hand lens help you to identify a powder? Is a hand lens helpful in identifying all substances?

### Science in Personal and Social Perspectives

✦ Why is it important for you to wash your hands before you eat any food?
✦ Has this activity changed your mind on decisions you make about whether you like a certain food? What about decisions on whether you want a certain person as your friend; do you base that choice on looks alone?

### Science and Technology

✦ Do you think an automobile manufacturer could be competitive if it based a car's performance ability on results from one test? Why or why not? Encourage interested students to research the performance tests that cars undergo.
✦ Which properties of coal or oil make them a useful form of energy for our power plants: physical or chemical?

### Science as Inquiry

✦ Students engage in manipulative skills during the activities.
✦ You are given 1 of the 5 powders. When tested with vinegar, it bubbles. Can you identify the powder? Can you be sure of its identity?
✦ You are given 1 of the 5 powders. It dissolves in water. Can you identify the powder? Are additional tests needed? Can you eliminate any powders?

### History and Nature of Science

✦ Can you think of any jobs in which avoiding contamination of materials is important?
✦ What care should be taken when mixing unknown substances with known substances? What good is knowing possible reactions? In what careers might this knowledge be necessary?

*Cornstarch:* The cornstarch can be used to demonstrate how dust explosions occur in coal mines or grain elevators. Cornstarch can also be used to explain how bread becomes toast.

*Baking soda:* The reaction of baking soda and vinegar results in the release of carbon dioxide gas. This gas can be used as a fire extinguisher. Most dry-powder extinguishers utilize baking soda; it can also be used to smother fires.

*Plaster of Paris:* This is nothing more than hydrated calcium sulfate. When mixed into a paste with water, it sets quickly and expands. It is because of this property that it is used as a fine casting material.

*Salt:* Salt can be used to lower the freezing point of water; examples are road salts and salt used in ice cream makers.

*Sugar:* Its numerous uses in foods are obvious, but also our knowledge of the chemical composition of sugar and the food calories it provides have led people to discover sweeteners that work like sugar but with fewer calories.

## Evaluation  *How will the students show what they have learned?*

Upon completing the activities, the students will be able to:

✦ when given 5 unknown powders, demonstrate the steps necessary to identify them by using physical properties;
✦ demonstrate how water, iodine, vinegar, and heat can be used to identify an unknown powder;
✦ explain the advantages of an indicator test over reliance on merely physical properties to identify an unknown.

## Bubbles

GRADE LEVEL: **5–8**

DISCIPLINE: **Physical Science**

**Inquiry Question:** How can we determine which type of detergent produces the largest bubbles?

**Concept to Be Invented:** *Variables* are things that can affect the outcome of an experiment. All variables that can affect the outcome must be identified and controlled so that the research question is truly answered without unintended interference.

**National Science Education Standards:** 5–8 Science as Inquiry—Students should develop abilities necessary to do scientific inquiry by designing and conducting a scientific investigation, using appropriate tools and techniques to gather, analyze, and interpret data, and develop descriptions, explanations, predictions, and models using evidence.

**Scientific Attitudes to Nurture:** Curiosity, open-mindedness, cooperation, avoidance of broad generalizations, willingness to withhold judgment until all evidence of information is examined.

**Materials Needed:** 3 different brands of detergent, glycerin, drinking straws

**Safety Precautions:** Wear goggles to avoid chemical eye splash.

# Exploration  *Which process skills will be used?*

Predicting, measuring, inferring

Offer a scenario that asks the class to determine which type of detergent produces the largest bubbles for a planned contest. Will it be the more expensive brand? Or, will an inexpensive brand do just as well? Pose the inquiry question. Ask the student groups to design their own experiment following general instructions. Introduce students to the materials and the requirements of an activity sheet that is prepared to record the measures of the diameters of at least four trials of at least three different brands of detergent. Measure the diameters of the soap rings left on the table surface after the bubbles are blown as large as possible and pop. Avoid telling the students the identities of the detergents until after the experiment. Bubbles can be made using 25 ml of detergent, 500 ml of water and 7 drops of glycerin. Take care not to structure the investigation, but encourage students to decide for themselves how to prepare the table surface, use the straws, determine duties of group members, etc. Construct a class data table using each group's record of the average diameters for each bubble solution.

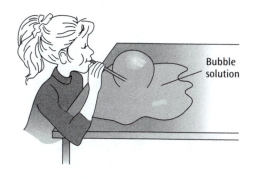

Bubble solution

• Detergent Bubbles

# Explanation/Concept Invention  *What is the main idea? How will the main idea be constructed?*

Compile the class's data into a table and investigate, taking care to examine the vertical columns for the range of measures and the horizontal rows for agreement or disagreement about the rank of bubble solutions by size. Identify the detergents used and the cost. Discuss questions such as: "Is there a difference in the size of bubbles? Does cost affect the difference in bubble size? What kinds of factors may have influenced the results of the experiments? Do you believe this is a reliable test? Why? Use the students' answers to lead to the lesson's concept: *Variables are things that can affect the outcome of an experiment.* Deepen students' understandings about the importance of variables and the meaning of the concept of *variables* through the *Expansion* phase.

# Expansion  *Which process skills will be used?*

Identifying variables, controlling variables, experimenting, investigating

### Science in Personal and Social Perspectives

✦ If left uncontrolled, what are some examples of variables that may cause us to get sick or become injured?

✦ Who needs to know about variables and use them in their daily lives? What are some examples of careers that use variables?

• Variables

### Science and Technology

✦ What are some examples of natural variables and examples that are mostly attributed to humans?

✦ What are some examples of technology that identify or control variables?

### Science as Inquiry

1. Discuss with classmates the different variables that may have affected the outcome of our investigation. Agree how to limit the influence of at least three variables, redesign the experiment, repeat, and report results. How do the size of the bubbles now compare with those of classmates?

2. Select one of the following research questions: (a) What detergent produces the most cost-affordable bubbles? (b) What formula additives produce the longest lasting bubble? Write a description about how to design an experiment to answer the research question. Take care to identify all variables and provide a description about how to control them in order to provide the most accurate answer to the research question.

3. For the upcoming school science fair, compose a research question that will compare experimentally two or more things. Identify all variables that may affect the outcome of the experiment and describe a research design that could produce an accurate answer to the question.

### History and Nature of Science

Name three scientists who have made important discoveries. At least one scientist must be a female or person of color. Research their discoveries. What are some examples of variables that they encountered? Report on how they identified and controlled variables. How might modern technology have made their discoveries easier or more accurate?

## Evaluation   *How will the students show what they have learned?*

Upon completing the activities, the student will be able to:

✦ describe what a variable is and why it is important;

✦ identify at least three affecting variables and how to control them or respond to them;

✦ plan a scientific investigation, conduct it, report the results, and describe in the report what steps assured accurate and repeatable results;

✦ exchange a scientific report with a classmate, examine the classmate's report, review it for proper identification and control of variables, and report a summary of the review.

# Using the Scientific Method to Solve Problems

**GRADE LEVEL:**  5–8

**DISCIPLINE:  Physical Science**

**Inquiry Question:**  Why is it important to follow a set procedure to solve a problem?

**Concepts to Be Invented:** Main idea—Problems should be thought out before action is taken to solve them. The *scientific method* is a useful tool in problem solving.

**Concepts Important to Expansion:** Matter can be combined in many ways. It can become a mixture, a solution, a suspension, or a colloid.

**Materials Needed**

| | |
|---|---|
| 1 liter 7-Up soft drink | 2 pounds cornstarch |
| 1 liter water | Efferdent tablets or Alka-Seltzer |
| 400 ml alcohol (90 percent or |    tablets |
|    higher concentration) | plastic bins or buckets |
| 1 gallon vinegar | paper towels for cleanup |
| 1 pound flour | balloons |

The teacher may also want to obtain any other clear liquids or unknown white powders the students decide to use in the experiments they design.

**Safety Precautions:** Goggles should be worn by teacher and students during all activities.

**Teacher Preparation**

*For clear liquid:* Pour about 400 ml of alcohol as close to 100 percent pure as possible into a container. Typical rubbing alcohol is 70 percent; the water content will cause the Efferdent to dissolve slowly. Therefore, 90 percent rubbing alcohol, also available over the counter, will be more effective.

*For white powder:* Add 1 cup of cornstarch to a large container or plastic bin (old dish-washing containers work well). Slowly add water until a gooey consistency is reached. This material will pour or drip slowly but will not splatter when struck with a quick blow. This is a non-Newtonian fluid. Rather than a solution or mixture, it is called a *colloid:* The starch is suspended in the water.

## *Exploration*   *Which process skills will be used?*

Problem solving, communicating, inferring, designing an experiment, recording data, measuring, observing, defining operationally, synthesizing and analyzing information

### *What will the students do?*

Ask the students to imagine traveling through space. All of a sudden the spaceship crash-lands. Tell them, "You have no idea where you landed. You do find several objects on the planet. Your hope is that manipulating these objects will give you some clues about the place where you have landed." Show them a container with a clear liquid in it. This is one of the things found at the landing site. Other items found were several packages of Efferdent tablets, used on earth to clean dentures. Ask them what they think will happen if you drop two tablets into the clear liquid. Encourage a variety of

• *Exploring with Efferdent Tablets*

predictions. Now drop the tablets into the liquid. Did you predict accurately? What do you think this liquid could be? In a few moments you will be given a chance to experiment to determine what it is and if there is a way to get the Efferdent to dissolve in it.

Explain to the students that in addition to the clear liquid and Efferdent tablets, they found some white powder and mixed it with water from their spaceship. Show them the mixture you created. Tell them, "You were trying to figure out what the powder was, especially because it didn't get all gooey like the paste you use at school. Some of you will need to design an experiment to determine what this white powder is."

Now assign the students on one side of the room to solve for one of the unknowns (what the clear liquid is—7-Up or vinegar, for example) and the students on the other side to solve for the other unknown (what the white powder is—flour or baking soda, for example). Encourage use of the scientific method to solve for the unknowns. Use the following guide questions to help plan student experiments: What do you think the problem is? How will you go about solving the problem? What materials do you think you will need? What will you do with those materials to help solve your problem? Do you think it will be important to keep accurate records of the information you collect while doing the experiment you designed?

## Explanation/Concept Invention  *What is the main idea? How will the main idea be constructed?*

*Concept:* Problems should be thought out before action is taken to solve them. The *scientific method* is a useful tool in problem solving.

Ask the students to share with you the methods they used to go about solving their problem. Key questions to get them to share are: Do you think it is important to plan before you act? Why? What steps did you use in designing your experiment?

This methodical way of problem solving is called the *scientific method*. The steps to be followed are:

1. State the problem.
2. Generate predictions or hypotheses to help solve the problem.
3. Design an experiment to help solve the problem.
4. Create a list of materials needed to solve the problem.
5. Gather the materials and act on the experimental design.
6. Collect and record the data.
7. Draw conclusions and share them with peers.

Ask the students if they did not follow the procedure about_____, could they easily communicate what they did to solve for their unknown to the students on the other side of the room so that they will get the same results? Let's try it!

## Expansion of the Idea  *Which process skills will be used?*

Problem solving, communicating, inferring, designing an experiment, recording data, measuring, observing, defining operationally, synthesizing and analyzing information

### *How will the idea be expanded?*

Trade what you wrote down to solve for your unknown with the students on the other side of the room. Could they replicate your experiment? If not what changes do you think you need to make to the method you followed? Make those changes based on the *scientific method*. Does it become easier for the students on the other side of the room to replicate your experiment with those changes in place? Now ask them where they think they landed. The students should reason that since they found objects on earth that behaved in ways they weren't familiar with, perhaps they could still be on earth.

• Exploring with Cornstarch

Once the students from each side of the room have discovered what the unknowns were, the students may want to play with the ooze formed with the cornstarch and water. Demonstrate to the students the balloon method for carrying their ooze in space. Obtain a plastic 1- or 2-liter soda bottle. Remove the cap and cut off the top of the bottle about 2 to 3 inches from the neck. Invert this, place a balloon over the bottle opening, pour the ooze into the funnel, and milk it into the attached balloon. Knot the balloon. Stretch the balloon into various shapes. What happens? Why can you do this?

### Science in Personal and Social Perspectives

+ Do you think you can use the scientific method to help you solve personal problems you have?
+ How would you go about explaining an important event that happened in your life to a friend? Will the story have the same impact if you leave out important details?
+ Do you think it is as important to be able to communicate accurately your feelings about some issue as it is important to be able to give directions for performing a particular task?

### Science and Technology

+ How important do you think it is to have motor oil that is the right weight in your car's engine? Can these differences in the oil's weight be affected if dirt particles were dissolved in the oil? Will dirt particles dissolve in the oil, or will they create a colloid?
+ Can solutions be created when the materials involved are at temperatures close to freezing? Do you think this knowledge will be important as we try to create space stations hundreds of miles from earth?

### Science as Inquiry

+ What are the differences among solutions, mixtures, suspensions, and colloids?
+ What steps are involved in the scientific method?

### History and Nature of Science

+ If you were an auto mechanic, would knowledge of solutions be beneficial? What kinds of solutions does an auto mechanic work with?
+ What other careers rely on knowledge of the differences among solutions, suspensions, colloids, and mixtures? Name three and state why.

**Evaluation** *How will the students show what they have learned?*

Upon completing the activities, the students will be able to:

+ take a given problem and design an experiment to solve it, using the steps in the scientific method;
+ demonstrate examples of mixtures, solutions, suspensions, and colloids;
+ upon looking at a diagram of a mixture, solution, suspension, or colloid, identify each combination of matter.

# Heat Energy

GRADE LEVEL: 1–4

DISCIPLINE: **Physical Science**

**Inquiry Question:** How can matter change from a solid to a liquid, or a liquid to a solid?

**Concept to Be Invented:** Main idea—Adding heat energy can change solids to liquids, or liquids to gases.

**Concepts Important to Expansion:** Removing heat energy can change liquids to solids, or gases to liquids.

### Materials Needed

hot plate
10 birthday candles
saucepan (double boiler)

aluminum foil
tablespoon

**Safety Precautions:** Ask the students not to move too close to the hot plate and not to touch the hot melted wax. Be sure to use a hot plate that has adjustable settings. Melt wax slowly. To avoid fires, melt in a double boiler.

**Exploration** *Which process skills will be used?*

Classifying, observing, inferring, generalizing, communicating

### What will the students do?

• *Liquid Birthday*

Allow the students to handle the birthday candles. Ask them to determine whether they are a liquid or a solid. Collect their responses. Once there is consensus as to their solid state, ask for suggestions on how the solid candle could be turned into a liquid. During this discussion, if no student suggests it, suggest using the hot plate to melt the candles. Place the candles in the double boiler over the hot plate, set at a low setting, and melt them. Ask the students to make observations as heat energy is added to the candles.

## *Explanation/Concept Invention*  *What is the main idea? How will the main idea be constructed?*

*Concept:* Adding heat energy can change solids to liquids, or liquids to gases.

To help the students create this concept, ask the following questions:

+ If you place your hand close to the pan (do not touch it!), does it sense that the pan is hot?
+ What happens to the candles as the heat energy moves from the hot plate to the pan? Can you explain why this is happening?
+ What is a common way in which birthday candles are melted?
+ What other types of things in your home release heat energy?
+ As the hot plate releases heat energy to the saucepan, it is transferred to the candles, causing them to melt. What can you do to change the candles back into solids?
+ Is heat energy added when an ice cube melts? How could you use heat energy to get water to turn to steam?
+ Ask the students to complete the following summary statements: By adding _____ _____ (heat energy) to a solid, I can change it to a liquid. By adding _____ _____ (heat energy) to a liquid, I can change it to a gas.

## *Expansion of the Idea*  *Which process skills will be used?*

Inferring, questioning, observing, communicating

### *How will the idea be expanded?*

Ask the students to make predictions about what will happen to the candles once the double boiler is taken off the hot plate. Give each child a piece of aluminum foil and a drop of the liquid wax. Ask the students to make observations of their wax. Divide the class in half. Ask half to determine ways in which they can turn the liquid wax back to a solid in the shortest time possible, the other half to determine ways to keep their drops in the liquid state. In which case do you need to add heat energy? Where is heat energy removed?

• Liquids
to Solids

### *Science in Personal and Social Perspectives*

+ Imagine you are riding in a car on a long trip through Florida in July. During the long ride you spend time coloring and drawing pictures. You leave your crayons on the car seat when you stop to eat lunch. What do you think you will find when you return to the car after lunch? Why?
+ Where in your home would be a good place to store candles? Why?

### *Science and Technology*

+ Why do you think it is important to understand why heat energy can melt a solid? Describe how this concept is applied in manufacturing glass objects, such as vases and mirrors.

✦ The oil used in a car engine is in a liquid state, yet when cool it is very thick. What do you think will happen to it as the car engine continues to run? Will this affect the design of an engine?

### Science as Inquiry

✦ What does it take to change a solid object into a liquid state?
✦ Can objects change their state of matter without gaining or losing heat energy?

### History and Nature of Science

✦ Aside from automobile engineers, are there other careers in which people must understand that the addition or subtraction of heat energy will change an object's state of matter?
✦ How do you think a hairdresser utilizes the concept identified in these activities? If you were having your hair done by a hairdresser, would you feel more comfortable if this person understood something about heat energy?

## *E*valuation  *How will the students show what they have learned?*

Upon completing the activities, the students will be able to:

✦ demonstrate how heat energy can be added to a rubber band without using fire or a hot plate;
✦ demonstrate how heat energy can be removed from an ice cube, draw a picture of it, and write three sentences describing how this is done.

## Magnets

GRADE LEVEL:  **K–2**

DISCIPLINE: **Physical Science**

**Inquiry Question:**  What is a magnet and what does it do?

**Concept to Be Invented:**  Magnets attract (pull) and repel (push) each other and certain kinds of metals.

**National Science Education Standards:**  K–4 Physical Science—Light, heat, electricity, and magnetism concepts. Magnets attract and repel each other and certain kinds of metals.

**Science Attitudes to Nurture:**  Open-mindedness, curiosity, perseverance, positive approach to failure, cooperating with others

**Materials Needed:**  Bar magnets—masking tape on the ends for Exploration, and a variety of additional magnet shapes (such as a horseshoe, disk, button, rod, and so on); an assortment of materials from the classroom including steel and iron objects, non-metal objects, and metallic objects, such as coins, aluminum cans, tinfoil, brass

**Safety Precautions:** Refrain from using iron filings. If iron filings are used, insist that students wear goggles to avoid filings getting lodged in their eyes. Adaptation for a student with visual impairment: Glue or tape a small object, such as a button, on one end of the bar magnets. The tactile relief will assist in identifying "same" ends of a magnet.

## Exploration   *Which process skills will be used?*

Observing, classifying, communicating, inferring

Suspend 2 bar magnets from a thread from a small table and demonstrate how one magnet can make another spin or swing or change position. Ask: Why do magnets seem to push or pull at each other? Do you suppose they always do this? Encourage children to investigate the behavior of 2 bar magnets by pushing and pulling them toward each other on a flat, nonmetal table. Cover N and S on the magnets with masking tape. Ask the children to use a crayon or marker to place an X on the ends that pull together and an O on the opposite ends. They will eventually notice that the X's attract each other and the same with the O's. Avoid dropping the bar magnets; they will tend to lose their strength, but the magnetic forces can be strengthened if you have a magnetizer available from a science supply catalog.

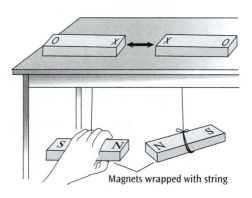

Magnets wrapped with string

## Explanation/Concept Invention   *What is the main idea? How will the main idea be constructed?*

Compose and use questions that cause the children to describe their experiences, such as: Which ends of the magnets seemed to pull together? Which ends seemed to push away? What kind of pattern did you notice? Remove the masking tape from the ends of the magnets and notice the N and S stamped on the bars. Ask the children to fill in the sentences that represent the concept, such as: "Magnets _____ away from each other when the ends are not the same." "Magnets _____ together when the ends are the same." Develop vocabulary, if appropriate, for students by using "attract" and "repel" or "pull" and "push."

## Expansion   *Which skills will be used?*

Classifying, communicating, inferring

Continue to use the language of "pull" or "attract" and "push" or "repel" as children investigate the behavior of different types of magnets. Ask them: Can you find a way to use the disk magnets and make them roll away from or toward another disk magnet?

Encourage the children to use a variety of magnets to examine the behavior of common metallic and nonmetallic objects from the classroom. Challenge them to group the objects and explain their reasons and to communicate their findings by making a chart to illustrate the types of objects that a magnet attracts. Discuss with the children where magnets exist in their homes and what these magnets do.

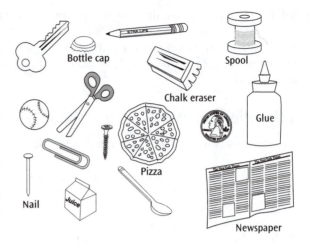

Bottle cap

Chalk eraser

Spool

Glue

Pizza

Nail

Juice

Newspaper

### **E**valuation  *How will the students show what they have learned?*

Upon completing the activity, the student will be able to:

+ identify like and unlike poles and label appropriately;
+ use the concept of push and pull or attract and repel appropriately to describe the behavior of magnets;
+ predict and test objects that may be attracted to a magnet;
+ classify objects as attracted or not attracted to a magnet.

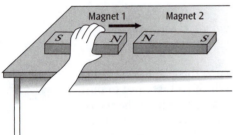

Magnet 1    Magnet 2

This picture shows a hand pushing Magnet 1 toward Magnet 2. The magnets are on a flat table. What do you think will happen to Magnet 2? _____

_____

_____

Why do you think this will happen? _____

_____

_____

## Simple Circuits

GRADE LEVEL:  3–4

DISCIPLINE:  **Physical Science**

**Inquiry Question:**  What does it take to make a light bulb light?

**Concept to Be Invented:**  A circuit is a pathway that electricity follows from the power source through the bulb and back to the power source.

**National Education Science Standards:** K–4 Physical Science—Electricity in circuits can produce light, heat, sound, and magnetic effects. Electrical circuits require a complete loop through which the electrical current can pass.

**Science Attitudes to Nurture:** Curiosity, open-mindedness, perseverance, positive approach to failure, cooperating

**Materials Needed:** Dry cells, wires, flashlight bulbs, bulb holders, switches, wire strippers, screw drivers, scissors, aluminum foil, paper clips, paper fasteners, masking tape, small pieces of cardboard

 **Safety Precautions:** Have students use not more than 5 dry cells in the same circuit to limit shock potential and to preserve light bulbs.

## Exploration  *What process skills will be used?*

Observing, predicting, classifying

Teacher's instructions to students: Using only the 3 pieces of equipment given to you, light the bulb. Once you are successful, find 3 other ways to light the bulb. You can use only the 3 pieces of equipment you have been given. Carefully draw a picture of each method you use to try to light the

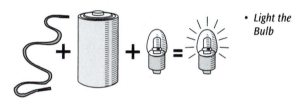

• Light the Bulb

bulb. Label your drawings *will light* and *will not light.* Be certain to show exactly where your wire is touching and how your bulb is positioned with the battery.

## Explanation/Concept Invention  *What is the main idea? How will the main idea be constructed?*

Concept: A circuit is a pathway that electricity follows from the power source through the bulb and back to the power source.

Have students draw their pictures on the chalkboard. Use your finger to trace the pathway that electricity from the battery flows through when the bulb light and when it does not light. This path is called a circuit. Using the students' own ideas and words, construct an explanation that a circuit is a pathway that electricity follows from the power source to the bulb and back to the power source. Show the students that contact with the bulb must be made in two specific places. The path must be complete from the battery, through the bulb, and back to the battery for the bulb to light. A key question to ask: In how many places must metal touch the bulb for it to light? The answer is: Two; the side and bottom conductors of the bulb must be included in the circuit.

# **E**xpansion  *Which process skills will be used?*

Making predictions, classifying, controlling variables

• *Parallel versus Series*

Challenge the students to light more than one bulb, combine batteries for more power, and add equipment, such as a bulb holder, a switch, and more wires. Ask what happens to other bulbs when one is unscrewed. Make a circuit so all bulbs go out when one is unscrewed: a series circuit. Make a circuit so the other bulbs remain lighted when one bulb is unscrewed: a parallel circuit or a separate series circuit; look carefully. Construct a paper clip switch and demonstrate its function.

### Science in Personal and Social Perspectives

✦ Name some devices you use that require an electrical circuit.
✦ What type of circuit is needed?
✦ What would your life be like without electricity controlled by circuits?
✦ How is electricity "made"? What resources are necessary? How has demand for electricity changed with population growth?

### Science and Technology

A set of car headlights is one example of a specific circuit used for safety purposes. When one light burns out or is broken, the others remain lighted.

1. What are other examples in which the type of circuit used is important for safety or convenience?
2. A flashlight uses a simple series circuit and is an example of technology. How has the simple flashlight improved or affected your life? Your community? The world?
3. Use the idea of a circuit to make a flashlight out of these materials: cardboard tube, wire, two D-cell batteries, flashlight bulb, paper clip, two paper fasteners, bottle cap, tape.

### Science as Inquiry

Plan, conduct, and explain investigations that illustrate short circuits, open and closed 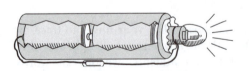 circuits, series and parallel circuits. Identify new concepts in new lessons, such as resistance, cell versus battery, and electromagnetism. Use the concept of open and closed circuit to solve circuit puzzles.

### History and Nature of Science

✦ Thomas Edison experimented thousands of times before he successfully found a material suitable as a filament that could be used to complete the circuit in a light bulb. How would our world be different today if Edison had never succeeded?
✦ Who needs to know about circuits? Name careers, and have students identify those careers that they previously did not know about that rely on some knowledge of electrical circuits. Some possibilities include electrician, appliance repair person,

architect, city planner, electric power producer, computer engineer, car/truck repair person.

+ How have the expectations changed over time for people in these careers?

## Evaluation  *How will the students show what they have learned?*

Upon completing the activities, the students will be able to:

+ correctly identify all of the circuits as complete or incomplete by marking them *will light* or *will not light;*
+ construct a working switch from cardboard, 2 paper fasteners, a paper clip and 2 wires;
+ construct, demonstrate, and describe the operation of a series circuit and a parallel circuit. Each circuit must include at least 2 bulbs and be controlled by the paper clip switch;
+ accurately draw a diagram and correctly label the parts of the circuit they use to make their flashlights;
+ construct a flashlight that functions properly. (Students must show the teacher that the switch turns the light on and off);
+ cooperate with group partners, volunteers to assist those who request help, and a demonstrate a positive approach when having difficulty with manipulative tasks;
+ describe three ways to use circuits and identify at two different inventions that control the flow of electricity through those circuits;
+ describe at least three safety precautions to avoid accidents with electricity;
+ use inquiry skills to solve correctly four circuit puzzles.

# Structure Strength

GRADE LEVEL: 5–8
DISCIPLINE: Physical Science

**Inquiry Question:** Is it the materials or the way in which they are arranged that give a structure its strength?

**Concept to Be Invented:** Main idea—The strength of a structure depends on the arrangement of the materials used in construction.

**Concepts Important to Expansion:** A variety of materials can be used to create a structure. A triangular arrangement of materials provides a more stable structure than a square.

## Materials Needed

| | | |
|---|---|---|
| straws | toothpicks | toilet paper tubes |
| clay | Popsicle sticks | paper towel tubes |
| glue | string | rolled sheets of newspaper |
| pins | | |

**Safety Precautions:** Remind students to use care in handling the pins to attach straws together, not to stand on chairs when building tall structures, to ask the teacher for help, and not to throw any of the building materials.

## Exploration *Which process skills will be used?*

Observing, predicting, manipulating materials, hypothesizing, inferring

### What will the students do?

• *Simple Construction*

Divide the class into five working groups. Provide one group with straws, another with toothpicks, another with Popsicle sticks, the fourth with toilet paper or paper towel tubes, and the fifth with sheets of newspaper rolled slightly longer than the paper towel tubes but just about the same diameter. Allow each group access to clay, pins, glue, or string to attach the building materials together.

Ask the students to make observations about the materials provided. Ask them to make predictions about how the materials could be used. Encourage the students to think beyond the usual uses for the materials. Allow them to manipulate the materials and to put them together in as many ways as possible. Ask the students to draw pictures of the different creations. Ask them to identify which of their creations remained standing the longest.

## Explanation/Concept Invention *What is the main idea? How will the main idea be constructed?*

*Concept:* The strength of a structure depends on the arrangement of the materials used in construction. A variety of materials can be used to create a structure.

Key questions to ask to help identify these concepts are:

+ What kinds of things did you create with these materials?
+ Did anyone create a structure that remained standing?
+ What did that structure look like?
+ What kinds of materials did you use?
+ How long did your structure remain standing?
+ Why do you think one structure stood longer than another?
+ Do you think you could use the same materials yet make your structure stronger? How do you think you could do that?

## Expansion of the Idea *Which process skills will be used?*

Observing, predicting, manipulating materials, hypothesizing, inferring

### How will the idea be expanded?

• *Triangle Construction*

Let's look at what each team has created. Your challenge at this point is to answer the inquiry question: Is it the materials or the way in which they are arranged that give a structure its strength? Give the students time to revisit their original creations and make any changes necessary to derive an answer. Ask them to share their answers. Share with them structures that are sturdier when they are arranged in a triangular shape, versus those left as squares. Lead the students to complete this statement: The strength of a structure depends on the _____ (arrangement) of the materials used in construction.

### Science in Personal and Social Perspectives

- ✦ Take a field trip with an adult family member to the attic or basement of your house or that of a friend. What kinds of support systems are found in the house? What materials were used? In what arrangements are those support systems placed?
- ✦ Think of some common objects found around your house that you typically use once and throw away. Do you think you could use them to create a structure? How long do you think a structure would last if it was built out of the material you have in mind?

### Science and Technology

- ✦ Can you name three famous buildings that are known for the uniqueness of their structure?
- ✦ Why do you think that certain areas in the United States have strict laws about the types of structures that can be built there?

### Science as Inquiry

- ✦ Can you make a house out of a deck of cards? How is it possible? Why is it possible?
- ✦ Do you think you can support a 2-pound weight in a structure made out of old newspapers? How will you manipulate the newspapers to make this possible? Try it.

### History and Nature of Science

- ✦ Choose one of the following occupations and explain how important knowledge of structural arrangement and strength is to that occupation: mechanical engineer, civil engineer, architect, contractor.
- ✦ Do you think a paper carrier or someone working in a fast-food restaurant would use the ideas you discovered through these activities in his or her work? How?

## *Evaluation* *How will the students show what they have learned?*

Upon completing the activities, the students will be able to:

- ✦ work in cooperative groups of four and use drinking straws and clay to build a bridge that spans across the classroom. The strength of the structure built will be tested using metal washers.

✦ view two toothpick structures and determine which of the two has the greater strength and be able to explain why (create them according to the accompanying picture).

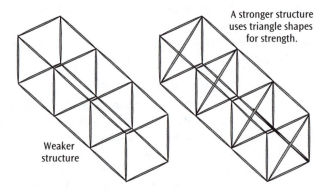

A stronger structure uses triangle shapes for strength.

Weaker structure

✦ draw a picture of a structure that could survive in an area where strong winds occur often. Write a narrative explaining what the structure is and why it was so designed.

# Make a Sinker Float: Clay Boats

GRADE LEVEL: 5–8

DISCIPLINE: Physical Science

**Inquiry Question:** Why can heavy objects float?

**Concept to Be Invented:** If the upward force of the liquid is greater than the downward force of an object, the object will float because it is buoyed (lifted up or supported) by the water. This concept is called buoyancy, and it explains why some heavy objects, such as steel ships, will float in water.

**National Science Education Standards:** 5–8 Physical Science—Motion and forces. If more than one force acts on an object, then the forces can reinforce or cancel one another, depending on their direction and magnitude. Unbalanced forces will cause changes in the speed and/or direction of an object's motion.

**Science Attitudes to Nurture:** Open-mindedness, cooperating with others, avoiding broad generalizations, willingness to withhold judgment

**Materials Needed:** Small tubs or buckets to hold water, small objects that will sink or float in water, modeling clay (Plasticine), small uniform objects to use as cargo (weights, such as ceramic tiles or marbles) in the clay boats, a container modified like the illustration (Expansion), a small container to catch the water that spills from the modified container, and a scale or balance to measure the weight of the spilled water

**Safety Precautions:** Have students notify you in case of spills. Use a room with a nonslip floor surface, if possible.

# Exploration  *Which process skills will be used?*

Observing, estimating, predicting

Have the students examine the variety of objects given to them and predict whether each object will sink or float in the water. Have the students write their predictions on organized data sheets that you provide. Use as one of the objects a lump of clay about the size of a tennis ball. Provide time for the students to test their predictions and then gather the students together to explore what their predictions reveal.

• *Buoyancy*

# Explanation/Concept Invention  *What is the main idea? How will the main idea be constructed?*

If objects of different sizes and weights are used in the Exploration phase, students will discover that heaviness is not the factor that determines whether an object will sink or float. For example, a large piece of 2 × 4-inch wood will be heavier than a glass marble or a metal washer, but it will float while the marble and washer will sink. Explain that Archimedes, a Greek philosopher, is credited with discovering that an object immersed in a liquid (water) will appear to lose some of its weight. Ask students to speculate why this seems

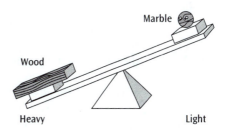

to be. A suitable explanation may be: If the upward force of the liquid is greater than the downward force of the object, it will float because the object is buoyed (lifted up or supported) by the water. This factor is called buoyancy and is the conceptual focus of the lesson. Steel has been given a special shape (the ship) that gives it a greater volume, which helps to spread its weight across a larger amount (volume) of the water, making it possible for the buoyant upward forces of the water to be greater than the downward force of the ship's weight. How might buoyancy be affected by the amount of cargo a ship carries? Why is it important to keep a ship from taking on water? What were you able to do with the clay to help it to float? What did you do to the clay's mass respective to the volume of the container's water?

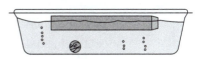

# Expansion  *Which process skills will be used?*

Inferring, hypothesizing, investigating

Weigh the lump of dry clay and the smaller container to be used to catch the water spill; record the measures. Take the lump of clay and use the device as illustrated. Carefully lower the clay into the container of water and measure its weight while it is submerged. Catch the water that spills out of the container and weigh the container again; subtract the dry container weight to determine the weight of the water displaced by the sinking clay. The weight of the submerged clay should be less than the dry weight because of the

• *Clay Boats*

upward (buoyant) force of the water. Challenge the students to find a way to change the shape of the clay so that it will float in water. Challenge them to see who can make the clay boat that will carry the largest amount of cargo before it sinks. Have students draw pictures of their boats' shapes and/or measure the size of the boats' bottoms. Capable students could cal-

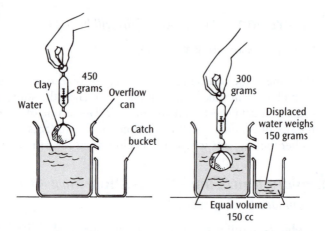

culate the surface area of the boats' bottoms and graph the amount of cargo carried (before sinking) as a function of area. Ask them to observe carefully what happens to make their clay boats sink and to describe later what they observe.

### Science in Personal and Social Perspectives

Ask the students why the Coast Guard requires flotation devices on boats and why these devices make it possible for a person who otherwise might sink to float. Why does the Coast Guard set passenger limits on pleasure craft?

### Science and Technology

Ask the students to search for other inventions that apply the buoyancy principle. Ask how these uses have had an impact on people. Examples might include floats connected to switches or valves that control pumps or appliances, seat cushions on airliners that are removable and can be used as flotation devices, channel buoys for navigation or to mark danger zones.

### Science as Inquiry

+ Ask the students to identify other examples of buoyancy in liquids and to describe differences. As examples, ask the students to redo their sink-or-float tests in denatured or isopropyl alcohol, or a mixture of alcohol and water, or water with different amounts of salt added. (This can lead to another concept and another lesson: specific gravity.)

+ Ask the students to explain why a submarine can sink and float, and how it is possible for a submarine or a SCUBA diver to remain at a particular depth.

+ Construct a Cartesian diver using a 2-liter soft drink container filled with water. Place a glass medicine dropper in the container and put the cap on tightly. Squeeze the sides of the container, release and watch what happens to the dropper. Why does the dropper sink and rise? What is necessary to keep the submarine dropper at a constant depth in the container?

+ Ask the students to explain why it is easier to swim and float in salt water than in fresh water.

*History and Nature of Science*

As an Expansion assignment, have the students search for pictures and examples of careers that require some knowledge of the buoyancy concept. Examples may include ship builders, navy and marine personnel, fishermen, marine salvage crews, plumbers, SCUBA divers. How have the inventions used by these changed over time?

Read Pamela Allen's *Mr. Archimedes' Bath* (1991) to the class and discuss what the author needed to know about science to write this children's book.

## *Evaluation*  *How will the students show what they have learned?*

Upon completing these activities, the students will be able to:

✦ (with the ball of clay and/or Cartesian diver) demonstrate and explain the concept of buoyancy;

✦ draw a picture of what happens when their clay ball is placed in water and when its shape is changed. They will be able to write a paragraph in their own words that explains why and how the clay floats;

✦ demonstrate proper use of the balance when weighing the clay, dry and submerged;

✦ measure and calculate the area of the clay boats and graph the maximum cargo carried as a function of the surface area of the boats;

✦ research the buoyancy inventions used by a single career over a period of time (perhaps fifty years) and explain how different understandings of buoyancy and technical advancement influenced persons in these careers.

# Mirrors and Reflection

GRADE LEVEL: 5–8

DISCIPLINE: Physical Science

**Inquiry Question:**  What is a mirror?

**Concepts to Be Invented:**  Main idea—An object must be shiny, smooth, and reflect light to be called a *mirror*. Light bouncing off a shiny surface is called *reflection*.

**Concepts Important to Expansion:**  Mirrors with a bowl-shaped surface are called *concave;* those that are rounded outward are called *convex*.

## Materials Needed

*For Each Student Group*

| | |
|---|---|
| at least one 2-inch square mirror | black paper |
| 1 metal spoon | scrap paper |
| aluminum foil | pencils |
| clear plastic | Mylar paper |

**Safety Precautions:**  Be sure that rough edges on mirrors are filed or taped. Demonstrate to the students the proper handling of mirrors and Mylar paper: hold them by the edges to avoid fingerprints. Stress the importance of sharing.

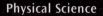

## Exploration  *Which process skills will be used?*

Observing, predicting, making assumptions, brainstorming, recording data

### What will the students do?

• *Mirrors and Reflectors*

Allow the students to observe various materials and predict if they will be able to see themselves. Ask the students to brainstorm ideas of when and where they have seen mirrorlike materials such as the ones they are working with. Manipulate the materials to see if they can see images of objects in them. Ask the students to describe their observations. Encourage the students to think about the position of that object in the mirrorlike materials versus what it looks like when they look at it directly. Ask the students to predict what their name will look like after they write it on the paper, and look at it in each of the materials. Instruct the students to write their name and view it in the mirror and each of the other materials. Can you see it in all of the objects? Does it look the same as it is written? Why or why not? Can you write it so that you can read it correctly when you look in the mirror?

## Explanation/Concept Invention  *What is the main idea? How will the main idea be constructed?*

*Concept:* An object must be shiny, smooth, and reflect light to be called a *mirror*. Light bouncing off a shiny surface is called *reflection*.

Assist the students in creating these concepts by doing the following: Refer back to the list brainstormed during the exploration phase. If terms like *smooth, reflect, light,* and *shiny* are not listed, add them to the list. Ask the students to help explain the meaning of those terms. Can an object be considered a mirror without light? Does the surface of the object need to be shiny? Can surfaces that are rough or bumpy give images as clear as shiny, smooth surfaces? A mirror is _____ (any shiny, smooth object that can reflect light).

## Expansion of the Idea  *Which process skills will be used?*

Observing, predicting, manipulating materials, classifying, inferring

### How will the idea be expanded?

• *What is a Mirror?*

Using the same materials from the exploration activity, ask the students to classify them into groups of things that are shiny, things that are smooth, and things that reflect light. Were you able to classify all of the materials? Could some of the materials fall into more than one group? Which materials were shiny and smooth and reflected light? Can you call these objects mirrors?

Can the spoon be considered a mirror? Describe the images seen inside the spoon. Where have you seen mirrors like these before? Have you ever been to a grocery store and seen these kinds of mirrors? What purpose do these mirrors serve? Mirrors with a bowl-shaped surface are called *concave*; those that are rounded outward are called *convex*.

### Science in Personal and Social Perspectives

+ Mirrors are used quite a bit in our everyday lives. When and where have you seen mirrors? What is their purpose?
+ How often do you use a mirror? Describe the mirrors that you use.

### Science and Technology

+ How do different people use mirrors? What can be learned by looking in a mirror?
+ How do scientists use mirrors? Have you ever used a microscope that uses mirrors? Did you ever see a telescope that makes use of mirrors?
+ Can you list at least three machines that make use of mirrors? Draw a working diagram of one of them.

### Science as Inquiry

+ Why is a light source needed in order for an object to be considered a mirror?
+ Which type of mirror would you use if you wanted objects to appear larger than they actually are: concave or convex?
+ Why do words appear to be written backward when viewed in a mirror?

### History and Nature of Science

+ What careers are linked to the use of mirrors? Do your parents use mirrors in their work?
+ Would some careers be more difficult without mirrors? Think of your school bus driver.
+ The German chemist Justus von Liebig was instrumental in creating the mirror that we currently use. Trace the history of the mirror, describing the role von Liebig played.

## *E*valuation  *How will the students show what they have learned?*

Upon completing the activities, the students will be able to:

+ write their names upside down and backwards on a piece of paper to illustrate their knowledge of what a mirror can do;
+ describe the three properties of a mirror or mirrorlike object and use them in sentences;
+ classify materials into *shiny, smooth,* and *reflects light* categories.

---

# The Slinky Potential

GRADE LEVEL: 7–8
DISCIPLINE: Physical Science

**Inquiry Question:**  Why *do* slinkies slink?

**Concept to Be Invented:**  Main Idea—Energy is a property of many substances and is associated with mechanical motion. Stored energy is called potential energy. Energy of motion is called kinetic energy.

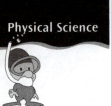

**Concepts Important to Expansion:** Energy can be transformed from one form to another. Momentum is described as the mass of an object times the velocity of the object. Momentum is always conserved.

## Materials Needed

*For Exploration*

1 Slinky or equivalent-type toy per student group

access to a flight of stairs wide enough for the Slinky to fit, but

not so wide that the top of the Slinky ends up falling over itself onto the same step

*For Expansion*

a gold ball and a Ping-Pong ball for class demonstration and/or, if time permits, one each per group

access to a hard floor surface for dropping the balls, preferably

near a wall where ball heights can be marked

tape to mark ball height on wall

**Safety Precautions:** Caution students about acceptable behavior while working with the Slinky on the stairs. Ask the students to watch one another as they descend the stairs with the Slinky to avoid falling.

As a precaution students should wear goggles when dropping the golf and Ping-Pong balls, as they cannot control the height and angle of the rebound when the balls are dropped simultaneously.

## Exploration  *Which process skills will be used?*

Manipulating materials, communicating, observing, inferring

### What will students do?

• *Energy Conversions with a Slinky*

Have the students, working in teams, go to designated areas within the school building where they have access to a flight of stairs. Remind them of safety measures while working on the steps. Ask them to predict what will happen to the Slinky when it is placed on the top step of a flight of stairs and they push the top half of the Slinky toward the edge of the step. Ask them to predict how many stairs it will descend before it stops. Do you think it will make it to the bottom of the stairs? Give them an opportunity to have at least three trials with the descending Slinky.

## Explanation/Concept Invention  *What is the main idea? How will the main idea be constructed?*

*Concept:* Energy is a property of many substances and is associated with mechanical motion. Stored energy is called *potential energy*. Energy of motion is called *kinetic energy*.

Ask the students to describe the motion of the Slinky as it descended the steps. Ask them to explain the conditions necessary for a successful journey from the top to the bottom of the steps. What variables must they adjust so the Slinky can move down the entire flight of stairs?

The students should begin to talk of the Slinky uncoiling and coiling as it moved down the steps. Ask them what they think "pulled" the Slinky down. They should be talking about the force of gravity pulling on the end of the Slinky as it moved down the steps.

Explain to them that the Slinky had energy stored in it as it was sitting on the top of the step. This is known as *potential energy*. By pushing the top of the Slinky to get it started down the stairs you imparted some of your own energy to the Slinky. Once gravity takes over, that stored or potential energy is converted to kinetic energy as the coils pull the trailing end of the Slinky down. This energy has now given the trailing end of the Slinky momentum. It is that momentum that causes the end to move up and past the high point of the arc as the Slinky falls over on itself. Gravity then takes over and continues to pull the Slinky down. Again this process is repeated as the Slinky moves down the stairs, transforming gravitational energy and the potential energy of the spring into kinetic energy until it reaches the bottom of the stairs. With this explanation, ask your students at what point in the Slinky's descent does it have its greatest kinetic energy? (When it falls from one step to the next.) At what point is the potential energy the greatest? (When it is poised ready to fall from one step to the next.)

Can you make the Slinky walk back up the steps? Why or why not? (You can't do this because you'd have to create potential energy from nothing. This would be against the law of conservation of energy, which states that energy cannot be created nor destroyed.) In this lesson the students should conclude that energy can be transformed from one form to another. This will be reinforced in the expansion activity.

Now that we have had this discussion about how the Slinky behaves who can answer our inquiry question: Why *do* Slinkies slink? (Students should demonstrate through their responses that they understand the differences between potential and kinetic energy).

## Expansion of the Idea   *Which process skills will be used?*

Observing, predicting, identifying, and controlling variables

### How will the idea be expanded?

Hold a Ping-Pong ball and a golf ball up in front of the class. Ask the students to predict how high they think the Ping-Pong ball will bounce if you drop it from chest height onto a hard floor below. Ask them to predict how high they think the golf ball will bounce if you drop it from chest height onto a hard floor below. Collect all predictions—then drop each ball one at a time. Ask some students to mark a spot on the wall behind you with tape at the height of the ascent with the first bounce for each ball. How accurate were their predictions? They should have discovered that when dropped separately from the same height the balls will bounce to approximately the same height.

Now ask the students to predict what will happen when you drop both balls at the same time with the Ping-Pong ball positioned on top of the golf ball. Record these predictions. *Note:* Be sure to practice this before you do it in front of your students so that when the balls are released simultaneously, the Ping-Pong ball will shoot straight up, 10 to 15 feet.

• Energy Transfer— Having a Ball!

Now drop the balls so that the Ping-Pong ball is positioned over the golf ball. Ask the students again to mark the height of the bounce for each ball. Did the balls respond as predicted? What do you think happened? At what point did the balls have potential energy? When was that converted to kinetic?

Ask the students where the energy came from to cause the Ping-Pong ball to bounce so high? (It came from the golf ball.) What happened to the golf ball if it transferred some of its energy into the Ping-Pong ball? (It bounced lower than it did before.) Repeat this activity or allow the student teams to repeat this activity so they come to understand that particular scientific phenomena become laws when they hold up with repeated testing. In this case they will be justifying the law of conservation of momentum.

In this activity, energy is transferred from the golf ball to the Ping-Pong ball. This demonstrates how momentum is conserved. Momentum is described by the formula $M$ (momentum) = $m$ (mass) × $v$ (velocity). When dropped separately, each ball gained momentum based on the mass of the ball.

A sidebar conversation may need to occur about how friction plays into this experiment. The classroom is not an ideal setting because it can not demonstrate a perfectly elastic collision. There is some loss of kinetic energy with each bounce due to friction. If friction from the air were not present, the ball would bounce at the same height with each bounce.

When the Ping-Pong ball was dropped directly over the golf ball, momentum had to be conserved. In order for that to happen the mass of the golf ball times the velocity of the golf ball had to equal the mass of the Ping-Pong ball times the velocity of the Ping-Pong ball ($m_{gb} \times v_{gb} = m_{ppb} \times v_{ppb}$). Since the golf ball has greater mass than the Ping-Pong ball, to make the equation equal the velocity of the Ping-Pong ball had to increase proportionally. Thus what they observed was the transfer of energy from the golf ball to the Ping-Pong ball to maintain the law of conservation of momentum.

### Science in Personal and Social Perspectives

+ How can you apply the concept that energy can be transferred while playing a game of baseball?
+ Why is it important to wear a helmet when roller blading or skateboarding? Where is energy transferred from if you are moving along on your skateboard and you hit the pavement and you do not have a helmet on?

### Science and Technology

+ What role do air bags in automobiles play if a car stops suddenly? How has the knowledge that energy can be transformed from one form to another been applied in air bag technology?
+ Explore the different materials used to make bike safety helmets. Which material absorbs energy transformation more efficiently? What kind of a rating scale do helmet manufacturers use?

### Science as Inquiry

+ Collect balls of various sizes and masses. Predict which ball will allow the Ping-Pong ball to bounce higher when it is used instead of the golf ball in the expansion activity. Support your predictions and justify your outcomes by applying the concept of momentum to the mass and velocity of the balls using the formula $M = m \times v$.

### History and Nature of Science

+ Explore the possible professions that apply the concept of energy transformations to their work end product.
+ In recent record the number of accidents on amusement park rides has increased. Using the concepts you learned in these activities, create a job description for a person responsible for inspecting amusement park rides.

## *Evaluation*  How will the students show what they have learned?

Upon completing the activities, the students will be able to:

+ explain the difference between potential and kinetic energy and demonstrate this using a toy such as a Slinky or a top or a Frisbee;
+ accurately predict which ball will have greater velocity when dropped simultaneously and vertically in the following order: a basketball under a Ping-Pong ball, a basketball under a volleyball, and a small rubber ball under a Ping-Pong ball;
+ create a campaign for increased use of safety helmets while skateboarding, demonstrating the concept that energy can be transformed from one form to another.

## Toys in Space

GRADE LEVEL: 5–8

DISCIPLINE: Physical Science

**Inquiry Question:**  Can I play with my yo-yo in outer space?

**Concept to Be Invented:**  Main idea—Things that behave one way on earth will behave differently in space due to zero-gravity conditions.

**Concepts Important to Expansion:**  An astronaut will experience weightlessness while traveling through space. Toys can be used to explain a variety of scientific principles.

**Materials Needed:**  *Toys in Space* video (available from NASA, Lewis Research Center, Cleveland, OH) and toys used in the video: wheel-o, yo-yo, paddle ball, ball and jacks, self-propelling car, magnetic marbles, spinning top, Play-Skool Flip Mouse, gyroscope

**Safety Precautions:**  Teacher and students should wear goggles to be sure that no eye injuries occur.

## *Exploration*  Which process skills will be used?

Observing, predicting, manipulating materials, hypothesizing, inferring

• Toy
Behavior
in Zero
Gravity

### What will the students do?

Provide the students with the toys from the materials list. Ask them to play with the toys and make observations about how they function. After adequate time has been spent playing with the toys, ask the students to make predictions as to how they think the toys would function in zero gravity. Encourage the students to make as many predictions as possible.

## Explanation/Concept Invention  *What is the main idea? How will the main idea be constructed?*

*Concept:* Things that behave one way on Earth will behave differently in space due to zero-gravity conditions.

To assist the students in developing this concept, ask them the following questions: How do the toys work in the classroom? Can you demonstrate them for me? How does gravity behave on Earth? What does it do to objects on Earth? If there were no gravity on Earth, how do you think these toys would behave? Have you ever seen movies of astronauts as they travel in space? How do they look? If you were an astronaut, could you play with your yo-yo in outer space? Think about how you can respond to this as we move to the next activity.

## Expansion of the Idea  *Which process skills will be used?*

Observing, predicting, manipulating materials, hypothesizing, inferring

### How will the idea be expanded?

• Toys and
Newton

Show the NASA videotape *Toys in Space*. Discuss afterward the discrepancies between the students' predictions and what really happened. An astronaut will experience weightlessness while traveling through space. So, can you play with your yo-yo in space? Of course, you can—but does your yo-yo respond the same as it does on Earth?

Toys can be used to explain a variety of scientific principles. If the students really show an interest in the behavior of the toys under zero-gravity conditions, you may want to introduce the students to some of Newton's laws, which govern the behavior of these toys on Earth. If you want the students to really understand them, then take care to plan additional activities that engage the students in science processes to enhance their understanding of these laws. The laws are as follows:

1. *Law of inertia:* Every body continues in its state of rest or of uniform motion in a straight line, except insofar as it is compelled by forces to change that state.
2. Force equals mass times acceleration.
3. The force exerted by an object A on another object B is equal in magnitude and opposite in direction to the force exerted by object B on object A.

### Science in Personal and Social Perspectives

+ How do you decide what kinds of toys to play with? Did you ever think that you could use them to help explain science concepts?
+ Why do you think you or your friends choose particular toys to play with? Is it important that you play with the same things as your friends? Why or why not?
+ Can you choose one of your toys and explain how or why it works? Ask your friends to help you decide which science concept is applied to explain why your toy works.

### Science and Technology

+ Toys are actually like models of particular systems. Why do you think it would be easier to make a toy model of some invention first? What advantage would that give to certain industries?

### Science as Inquiry

+ Is it possible for toys on Earth to behave the same way when under zero-gravity conditions? Is it possible for toys in space to behave the same way when on Earth?
+ Describe two different scientific concepts that can be explained using a bicycle.

### History and Nature of Science

+ Do you think a wheel-o could have been invented if the creator did not understand something about magnetism?
+ If you were to become a toy designer, would knowledge of science concepts be useful in your career?

## Evaluation   How will the students show what they have learned?

Upon completing the activities, the students will be able to:

+ describe one scientific concept that can be explained with the use of a roller skate;
+ create a toy using materials of their choice that can be fun and explain a scientific concept;
+ design a toy that can still function in the absence of gravity and write a few sentences to describe it.

---

## Simple Machines: The Lever

GRADE LEVEL: 5–8

DISCIPLINE: Physical Science

**Inquiry Question:** How can one person do the work of ten?

**Concept to Be Invented:** Main idea—A lever is a rigid bar that pivots around a point that is used to move an object at a second point by a force applied at a third point. The pivot point is the *fulcrum*, the object moved is the *load*, and the place where the force is applied is the *effort*.

**Concepts Important to Expansion:** There are three kinds of levers. A *first-class lever* is a fulcrum between effort and load; the effort moves in the opposite direction of the load, as in a seesaw or a balance. A *second-class lever* is a load between the fulcrum and the effort; effort is applied in the same direction as the load should be moved, as in a wheelbarrow or a bottle opener. A *third-class lever* is an effort between the fulcrum and the load, which magnifies the distance moved by the load but reduces its force, as in a hammer, a catapult, or a fishing rod. Additional terms that may be introduced in this lesson are *resistance, friction, work,* and *machine.*

**Materials Needed**

*Per Student Group, for the Discrepant Event*

| | | |
|---|---|---|
| sandpaper | marbles or beads | hand lotion |
| water | cooking oil | paper towels or wipes |

*For Exploration*

goggles, one long piece of board (18" × ¼" works well), one fulcrum (proportional in size to the long board—for the 18-inch board, triangular pieces cut out of a 2 × 4 work well), any proportionally sized objects to be used as load, such as blocks of wood, small books, metal chunks, or cylinders

*For Expansion*

| | | | |
|---|---|---|---|
| goggles | 2 plastic spoons | 1 rubber band | peanuts |

 **Safety Precautions:** Remind students that safety goggles must be worn at all times. Discourage students from sending the load material flying across the room. Warn them of the potential danger to themselves and other students.

**Discrepant Event:** *Which process skills will be used?*

Observing, hypothesizing, inferring, drawing conclusions

*What will the teacher and students do?*

Do not show the students what you are giving them. Ask them to put out their hands and place a small amount of one of the following in their hands: sandpaper, nothing, water, hand lotion, cooking oil, two or three marbles or beads. Tell them to be sure not to let anyone else see what they have. Once everyone has received one of the items, then ask the class to rub their hands together (all at the same time) with the objects still in their hands. After the students have had time to do this and to comment on what just happened, then ask questions such as: What did your hands feel like? Who had the hardest time rubbing his or her hands together? The easiest? Why? Did your hands change temperature? What do you think caused your hands to get hot/cold/no change? Why was it easy for some and not for others? What do you think is prohibiting you from sliding or rolling the objects in your hands? (Resistance.) What is this resistance to movement called? (Friction.) What did you need to do to overcome friction? (Exert some energy—effort.) By using effort to move your hands over a distance, you have done work. What do we call an object that will do the work for us? (A machine.)

## Exploration  *Which process skills will be used?*

Manipulating materials, collecting and recording data, communicating, observing, hypothesizing, predicting, inferring

### What will the students do?

*Instructions:* Use a long board and a triangular-shaped block in as many combinations as you think possible to move the weighted object (blocks, books, metal pieces). Draw the methods you tried. Discuss possible solutions with your peers. Try to record the results of those as well.

• Lever
Creations

## Explanation/Concept Invention  *What is the main idea? How will the main idea be constructed?*

*Concept:* A lever is a rigid bar that pivots around a point, which is used to move an object at a second point by a force applied at a third point.

Have the students draw the results of their manipulations on the board. With help from the class, identify on their drawings the pivot point, the object being moved, and the place where they had to apply a force to get the object to move. Solicit class ideas as to names for these points. Identify the pivot point as the *fulcrum,* the object moved as the *load,* and the place where force was applied as the *effort.*

Key questions to ask: Did these inventions make it easier for you to do work? What do we call objects that make our work easier? What has the machine we invented allowed us to do? What do you think we call it? Why? Once the concept *lever* has been invented, ask the students if they can see any differences in the placement of the three points on any of their diagrams. If necessary, supply diagrams that show different placements of the points. Key questions: Is there any advantage to changing the position of the three points? What happens to the direction of the effort and load in each of the diagrams? Can you see some practical uses for the different positions of the points? As you go through the different arrangements of the points, identify the three classes of levers: A *first-class lever* is a fulcrum between effort and load; the effort moves in the opposite direction of the load, as in a seesaw or a balance. A *second-class lever* is a load between the fulcrum and the effort; effort is applied in the same direction as the load should be moved, as in a wheelbarrow or a bottle opener. A *third-class lever* is an effort between the fulcrum and the load, which magnifies the distance moved by the load but reduces its force, as in a hammer, a catapult, or a fishing rod. Now that we've discussed your inventions tell me: How can one person do the work of ten?

## Expansion of the Idea  *Which process skills will be used?*

Hypothesizing, inferring, manipulating materials, observing, communicating, collecting and recording data, making assumptions, predicting, formulating models

• Spoons
and Nuts

• Lever
Scavenger
Hunt

### How will the idea be expanded?

*Instructions:* Given 2 plastic spoons, a rubber band, and some peanuts, design and demonstrate a first-, second-, and third-class lever. Share your inventions with the class.

### Home extension: Which process skills will be used?

Inferring, manipulating materials, making assumptions, formulating models, observing, analyzing, classifying

### What will the students do?

Have the students ask an adult to go with them on a lever scavenger hunt. Make a list of all of the places where levers are being used in some form or another. How many of these are combination levers? How many are compound levers of the first, second, or third class? Bring these lists back to school to share with the class.

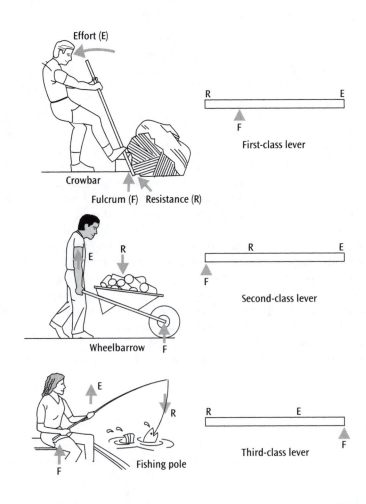

First-class lever

Second-class lever

Third-class lever

### Science in Personal and Social Perspectives

+ Where in your home did you find a lever being used? Did any of these places surprise you? Were any of these uses a case where two of the lever types were used in combination? (Nail clippers, manual typewriter, piano.) Did you find any compound levers? (Scissors, pliers, nutcracker, tweezers.)
+ When you need to cut a piece of paper, why is it easier to use scissors instead of a knife? What advantage does using a pair of scissors have over using a knife for cutting?
+ Which simple machine makes it possible for people to play a piano?

### Science and Technology

+ Why would it be difficult for you to wear your ice skates in the house but not your roller skates? How have industries used this information to overcome friction?
+ How do you think the invention of the parking meter has affected your city? How about cities like Chicago or New York?

### Science as Inquiry

+ Students will be able to explain the function of the fulcrum, load, and effort; various combinations of these points can create a first-, second-, or third-class lever. They will be able to explain how machines help us to do work and to overcome friction.
+ This activity lays the foundation for new concepts to be identified in new lessons, such as the relationship between effort and work, mechanical advantage, other types of simple machines, and so on.

### History and Nature of Science

+ Archimedes of Syracuse was perhaps the greatest of the Greek mathematicians and scientists. He lived from 287 to 212 B.C. He is credited with inventing the catapult, which the Greeks used during the Second Punic War against the Roman army. It is said that Archimedes was slain during this war while he was studying mathematical figures, which he habitually drew in the dust. What do you think he meant when he said, "Give me a fulcrum on which to rest, and I will move the Earth"?
+ Who needs to know about levers? Which careers rely on the use and/or knowledge of levers? (Manufacturers of playground equipment, laborers, dock workers, piano makers, typewriter manufacturers, parking meter repair persons.)

## *Evaluation*  *How will the students show what they have learned?*

Upon completing the activities, the students will be able to:

+ classify the following items as a first-, second-, or third-class lever: hammer, nutcracker, seesaw, wheelbarrow, balance, bottle opener, fishing rod;
+ identify the fulcrum, the effort, and the load on each item, when given a hammer, wheelbarrow, and nail extractor;
+ predict the direction of the load when effort is applied with each of the following: fishing rod, balance, bottle opener.

# Earth and Space Science Lessons

| LESSON NAME | NSE CONTENT STANDARDS FOR EARTH & SPACE SCIENCE | GRADE LEVEL | ACTIVITIES |
|---|---|---|---|
| **Astronomy** | | | |
| The Solar System and the Universe | Objects in the Sky | K–3 | Rhythm Activity • Postcard Writing |
| The Expanding Universe | Earth in the Solar System | 5–8 | Expanding Balloon/Universe • Build a Solar System Salad |
| Constellations | Earth in the Solar System | 5–8 | Connect the Stars • Evening Field Trip • Create a Constellation |
| **Geology** | | | |
| Earth Layers | Properties of Earth Materials | K–4 | Clay Earth Layers • Clay Continents |
| Fossils | Properties of Earth Materials | 2–4 | Fossil Observations • Plaster Molds and Casts |
| Investigating Soil | Structure of the Earth System | 5–8 | Soil Separation and Rock Crushing • Soil Components |
| Rock Types | Structure of the Earth System | 5–8 | Rock Categorization • Rock Collection Field Trip |
| Cooling Crystals | Structure of the Earth System | 5–8 | Making Crystals • Crystal Differences in Rocks |
| Weathering | Structure of the Earth System | 5–8 | Freezing Bottle • Weathering Field Trip • Rock Identification • Chemical Weathering • Mechanical Weathering |
| Crustal Plate Movement | Earth's History | 5–8 | Moving Plates • Mapping Volcanoes and Earthquakes • Oatmeal and Cracker Plate Tectonics |
| Aging Human/ Aging Earth | Earth's History | 7–8 | Living Human—Living Earth • The Rock Record |
| **Meteorology** | | | |
| Rain Formation | Objects in the Sky | K–4 | Rain in a Jar • Water Drop Attraction |
| Dew Formation | Objects in the Sky | K–4 | Soda Bottle Condensation • Thermometer Reading and Dew Point |
| Radiant Energy | Objects in the Sky | 2–4 | Temperature and Colored Surfaces • Temperature: Sun versus Shade • Magnifiers: Capture the Sun • Sun Tea |
| Water Cycle | Structure of the Earth System | 5–8 | |
| Weather Forecasting | Structure of the Earth System | 5–8 | Weather Log Creation • Weather Map Symbols • Weather Data Collection |
| Air Mass Movement | Structure of the Earth System | 5–8 | Coriolis Effect: Globe • Coriolis Effect: Top • Air Movement: Dry Ice • Oil and Water Fronts • Create a Rain Gauge • Air Masses and Parachutes |
| Air Pressure | Structure of the Earth System | 5–8 | Balloon Balance • Paper Blowing • Newspaper Strength |
| Solar Heating | Earth in the Solar System | 5–8 | Temperature versus Surface Color • Optimum Thermometer Placement |
| Air Movement and Surface Temperature | Structure of the Earth System | 5–8 | Convection Current and Surface Temperature in an Observation Box • Paper Bag Balance |
| Uneven Heating of the Earth | Structure of the Earth System | 5–8 | Tower of Water • Aneroid Barometer • Uneven Heating and Air Pressure • Air Pressure versus Water Temperature • Air Temperature versus Movement of Air • Heat Transfer on a Wire • Heat Movement Through Air • Heat Transfer Through Metal • Movement of Smoke over Hot and Cold Surfaces: Clouds • Movement of Smoke over Hot and Cold Surfaces: Wind Patterns |

# The Solar System and the Universe

GRADE LEVEL: K–3
DISCIPLINE: Earth and Space Science

**Inquiry Question:** Would you vacation on Mars?

**Concept to Be Invented:** Main idea—The Earth is part of the solar system.

**Concepts Important to Expansion:** Planets differ from one another.

### Materials Needed

*For Exploration*
books on planets, such as Jeff Davidson, *Voyage to the Planets* (Worthington, OH: Willowisp Press, 1990) and Joanna Cole, *The Magic School Bus Lost in Space* (New York: Scholastic, 1988)

*For Expansion*
postcard outline, poster paper, paints, and markers, resource books on the planets

**Safety Precautions:** The students should be reminded to sit and listen without poking or hitting one another. During the expansion activity, they should clean up any paint spills immediately, and they should not put markers or paint brushes in their mouths.

## Exploration *Which process skills will be used?*

Observing, questioning

### What will the students do?

+ You should read books such as *Voyage to the Planets* or *The Magic School Bus Lost in Space* to the students. Ask them to recall questions as you are sharing the book with them.

+ Teach the students the following chant, clapping the beat. Allow them to fill in the planet of their choice once they get the rhythm down:

• Rhythm Activity

> A—B—CDE, How many planets can there be?
> F—G—HIJ, There are nine we know of today.
> K—L—MNO, To which one would you like to go?
> P—Q—RST, I'd like to visit Mercury.
> U—V—WXY, I've been watching it in the sky.
> Z—Z—ZZZ, Know anyone who'll come with me?

## Explanation/Concept Invention *What is the main idea? How will the main idea be constructed?*

*Concept:* The Earth is part of the solar system.

Ask the students to recall the names of the planets from the stories and chanting activity. Share with them that it has been found through observations of the nighttime sky and satellite observations that Earth is just one of nine planets that move around the sun. Each of the planets has unique characteristics because of their distance from the sun. Ask them if they would like to vacation on Mars or any of the other planets? In the next activity we will discuss your make-believe trip.

## **E**xpansion of the Idea  *Which process skills will be used?*

Inferring, observing, questioning

### *How will the idea be expanded?*

• *Postcard Writing*

Once the students know the chant and sing it with all nine planet names, ask them to choose one of the nine as a place they'd like to go on vacation. Break the students into nine planet vacation groups. Provide the student teams with grade-level appropriate resource books on the planets. Ask them to plan a drawing of their planet as close to reality as possible, and then work as a cooperative group to create one drawing of that planet. Draw a sun on your mural paper. Ask the different groups to come up to the mural and place their planet in its appropriate order from the sun.

Give each student a copy of the postcard outline. Ask them to write postcards to family members, describing their trips to the planets they drew. Teach them how to address a postcard. Ask them to design an appropriate stamp for the planet they visited. When all of these are completed, tape the postcards near the planet of origin.

### Questions that help invent additional concepts

+ Is the Earth all alone in space? (No, there are eight other planets.)
+ What else is found in Earth's neighborhood? (Planets, moons, dust, meteors.)
+ How do we know there are other planets in our neighborhood? Has anyone ever seen them? (We can see them in the sky; they look like stars. We have satellites that have gone close to them and sent back pictures to Earth.)
+ What is unique about your planet? (Answers will vary.)
+ How close to the sun is your planet? (Answers will vary.)
+ Are all the planets the same size? (No. Go into detail about their planets.)
+ Do you think you could live on your vacation planet as easily as you can on Earth? Why or why not?

Students will apply knowledge they learned about their planets to answer these questions.

### Science in Personal and Social Perspectives

+ Do you think if Earth were as close to the sun as Mercury, you could still live on it? Why or why not?
+ If someone told you he or she could take you on a plane ride to the planet Mars, would you believe it? Why or why not?

### Science and Technology

+ Do you think a person can invent a way so that it will be possible to live on any of the other planets? How do you think we can do this?

### Science as Inquiry

+ Students will be able to name the nine planets, list their order from the sun, and discuss one characteristic of each after completing and participating in the above activities.

### History and Nature of Science

+ Do you think that a person responsible for monitoring the air quality of the planet Earth can learn anything from understanding what the atmosphere is like on the planet Jupiter?
+ How important is it that space scientists know the positions of the planets before launching satellites or rockets into space? What kinds of skills do space scientists need in order to do their jobs?

## Evaluation   *How will the students show what they have learned?*

Upon completing the activities, the students will be able to:

+ answer the questions included in the expansion phase of this lesson, as well as the new outcomes questions;

◆ draw lines from the picture of a planet to a group of words that briefly describe the planet. The picture question below is an example of the kind of question that could be made for this assessment:

Water and oxygen present

◆ create a planet mobile (this can be done as a home extension) out of the following materials: wire coat hanger, paint, tape and/or glue, papier-maché or balls of different sizes, string, and cardboard, paper, or newspaper.

# The Expanding Universe

**GRADE LEVEL:** 5–8

**DISCIPLINE:** Earth and Space Science

**Inquiry Question:** How far is far when discussing distances between planets?

**Concepts to Be Invented:** Main idea—Our universe appears to be expanding. Distances between parts of the universe are vast.

**Concepts Important to Expansion:** Planets orbit about the sun. The planets are very small and very far away from the sun.

## Materials Needed

*For Exploration*
round balloons (one for each student), wide-tip felt markers (black and red)

*For Expansion*

| | | |
|---|---|---|
| 1 fresh pea | the school track | 1 small walnut |
| 1 large walnut | 1 dried pea | 1 smaller bean |
| 1 8-inch head of cabbage | 1 bean | 1 grapefruit |
| 1 big orange | 1 9-inch head of cabbage | a bicycle |

**Safety Precautions:** Advise students to use extreme caution while blowing up the balloon. Do not allow children to chew on the balloon.

## Exploration *Which process skills will be used?*

Observing, predicting, hypothesizing, inferring

*What will the students do?*

Instruct each student to

• *Expanding Balloon/Universe*

1. inflate a round balloon partially, pinching the neck closed with thumb and fore-finger;
2. make specks with a wide-tip felt marker all over the surface of the balloon, noting their positions and letting them dry;
3. blow more air into the balloon and look at it, again noting the position of the specks.

## Explanation/Concept Invention  *What is the main idea? How will the main idea be constructed?*

*Concept:* Our universe appears to be expanding. Distances between parts of the universe are vast.

Help the students invent the concept by asking them such questions as:

✦ What has happened to the distance between the specks? (It has increased, expanded.)
✦ What do you think will happen to the specks if you continue to add air to the balloon? (They will continue to move away from one another.)
✦ Imagine that the balloon is space and one of the specks is the neighborhood Earth is found in. Put a red mark on one of the specks to represent Earth's neighborhood. Blow up the balloon some more while watching the red speck. What do you think you could say about space if you were on this red speck? (Earth is very far from other parts of the universe.)

## Expansion of the Idea  *Which process skills will be used?*

Observing, communicating, formulating models, recording data

*How will the idea be expanded?*

• *Build a Solar System Salad*

Have students observe the fixings for a solar system salad (see materials needed). They should decide which of the items correspond to the nine planets and Earth's moon. The

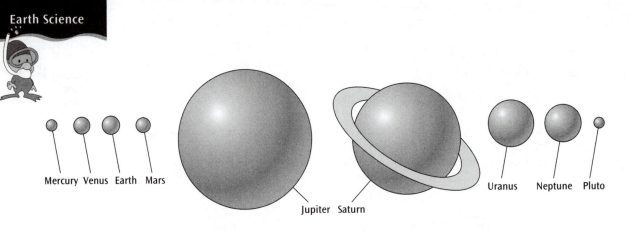

Mercury Venus Earth Mars

Jupiter Saturn

Uranus Neptune Pluto

students should check with one another to come to some consensus. Then they will discuss decisions with the teacher.

After a discussion on relative sizes, take the salad items out to the school track. While bicycling around the track, drop off the planets to show their relative distance from each other. Allow all the students to participate. Some may be lap counters; others should do the riding. To make it really effective, each student should ride the bicycle. As the children grow tired, the vast distances between the planets will be apparent to them. Each lap represents 211,265 miles in space.

*Mercury:* ⅖ lap          *Saturn:* 9½ laps

*Venus:* ¾ lap          *Uranus:* 19½ laps

*Earth:* 1 lap          *Neptune:* 30 laps

*Mars:* 1½ laps          *Pluto:* 39⅖ laps

*Jupiter:* 5½ laps

### What questions can help invent additional concepts?

+ Which of the salad fixings did you have a hard time assigning a planet to?
+ Did you find it necessary to look in some reference books to help you decide which item represents which planet?

*Mercury:* Fresh pea          *Jupiter:* 9-inch cabbage

*Venus:* Walnut          *Saturn:* 8-inch cabbage

*Earth:* Larger walnut          *Uranus:* Grapefruit

*Moon:* Dried pea          *Neptune:* Big orange

*Mars:* Bean          *Pluto:* Small bean

+ How did your legs feel after you dropped off the solar system salad fixings?
+ Imagine you are out in space dropping those items off at the different planets. What would be the total distance you would have traveled? (*Hint:* What is the distance from the sun to Pluto?)
+ If the center of the football field represents the sun, what can you say about the planets with respect to the sun? What do the planets do?

### Science in Personal and Social Perspectives

✦ Do you think it will ever be possible for you to travel to the other planets? Would you like to do this? Why or why not? What do you think you would need to pack for your trip?

✦ Would you purchase a ticket today to spend some time in a space station? Do you think you will live long enough to use the ticket?

### Science and Technology

✦ Do you think space stations will solve the problems of pollution and overpopulation on Earth?

✦ Do you think the vastness of space will allow us to ship our garbage out into space and never be affected by it on Earth? How do you think this will be possible?

### Science as Inquiry

✦ The students will be able to explain the concept of the expanding universe and discuss the implications that has for life as we presently know it on earth.

✦ Why is it possible to view planets in the nighttime sky? Do all of the planets always maintain the same orbital paths?

### History and Nature of Science

✦ If it was your job to create a satellite that would move through outer space, sending back to earth information about other planets, what kinds of knowledge do you think you would need to have? What would be the qualifications for your job? Pretend you need to employ someone to fill such a job. Write a job description and give it a title. Does the race or sex of the person applying matter?

## Evaluation  *How will the students show what they have learned?*

Upon completing the activities, the students will be able to:

✦ complete the activities above.

✦ write a few sentences after they participate in the bicycle activity about how they felt when they finished and what they think about the distances between the planets. Ask the students to share their feelings with one another. How tired they became and how much they want to share with others what they did will provide an effective measure of success.

✦ when provided with ten different kinds of vegetables for a solar salad, use these new items to arrange the members of the solar system. Also ask them to decide how far they would have to be from one another if 1 inch equals 1 million miles.

# Constellations

**Inquiry Question:** What star patterns do you see in the sky?

**Concept to Be Invented:** Main idea—Constellations are groups of stars.

**Concepts Important to Expansion:** Big Dipper, Little Dipper, Polaris or North Star, Cassiopeia, Perseus, and the Pleiades found in Taurus

### Materials Needed

*For Exploration*

construction paper

1 pen or pencil per student

overhead projector

4 or 5 flashlights

**Safety Precautions:** Remind students to be careful not to poke themselves or others with the pen or pencil.

## Exploration  *Which process skills will be used?*

Observing, predicting, hypothesizing, inferring

### What will the students do?

• *Connect the Stars*

The students will view a dot-to-dot pattern presented to them and predict what the pattern will look like once the dots are connected. This pattern is made on the chalkboard by using an overhead projector and black construction paper with holes punched in it for dots as the transparency. Place several different patterns on the overhead. Have the students take turns connecting the dots on the chalkboard.

## Explanation/Concept Invention  *What is the main idea? How will the main idea be constructed?*

*Concept:* Constellations are groups of stars found in the sky. Ask the students questions such as the following to help invent this concept: What do you think these patterns represent? Do you recall seeing these same patterns anywhere? Review each of the patterns again and ask once again if anyone recalls seeing these patterns anywhere.

Patterns represent star constellations. Star constellations are made up of a group of stars and are given a name traditionally based on the pattern they make in the sky. These constellations were named by people in the past and usually have a story or legend attached to them.

Once again, project the patterns up on the board, again connecting the dots. This time go through the names of the constellations presented, and give a brief history of how they got their names. Some easy constellations to showcase are the Big Dipper, the Little Dipper, Cassiopeia, Perseus, and the Pleiades found in Taurus.

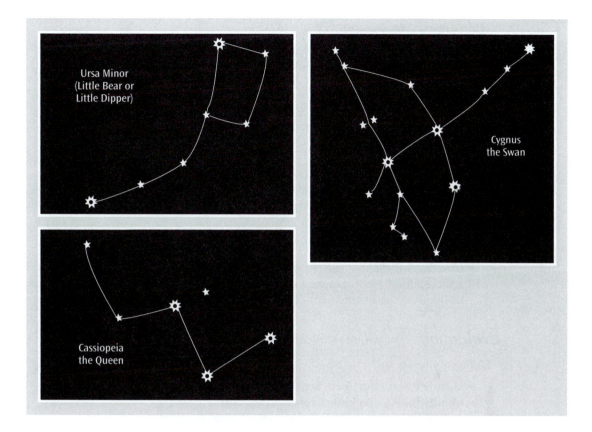

Identify the North Star—Polaris—for the students. Explain how all the other constellations in the Northern Hemisphere appear to revolve around this star. Thus, at different times of the year only certain star patterns are visible in the nighttime sky in the Northern Hemisphere. We call these star patterns _____ (constellations).

## Expansion of the idea  *Which process skills will be used?*

Observing, communicating, formulating models, recording data

### *How will the idea be expanded?*

◆ Take the students on an evening field trip to an area where electric lights are minimal. Be sure you pick a clear night. Ask everyone to bring a blanket and lie on the grass. Try to identify as many constellations as possible.

• *Evening Field Trip*

◆ Ask the students to create a constellation of their own and name it, much as the ancient Greeks and Indians did as they observed stars in the nighttime sky. Have them write reports about how their constellations got their names. Share the reports orally with the class.

• *Create a Constellation*

*Science in Personal and Social Perspectives*

+ How can star constellations help you if you get lost at night?
+ How can you develop watching stars into a hobby?

*Science and Technology*

+ What kind of equipment can you use to improve your view of the stars?
+ How has astronomy equipment been perfected since the time of Galileo's first telescope?

*Science as Inquiry*

+ How can we use our knowledge of constellations to find a particular star in the sky?
+ Why do all stars in the Northern Hemisphere appear to revolve around Polaris? Is this our closest star?

*History and Nature of Science*

+ How are constellations used by astronomers who study other phenomena in the sky?
+ Is there any difference between an astronomer and an astrologer? Do they both use their knowledge of constellations in some form? How?

## Evaluation  *How will the students show what they have learned?*

Upon completing the activities, the students will be able to:

+ identify Polaris, the North Star;
+ identify the Big and Little Dippers in the northern sky;
+ explain how at least two different constellations got their names;
+ identify the star closest to Earth.

## Earth Layers

GRADE LEVEL: **K–4**

DISCIPLINE: **Earth and Space Science**

**Inquiry Question:**  Why does the Earth have layers?

**Concept to Be Invented:**  Main idea—The planet
Earth is made up of three layers: the *core, mantle,* and *crust.* The differences in the layers are caused by the amount of heat and pressure upon them and the material found within each.

**Concepts Important to Expansion:**  Large land masses found on the crust of the Earth are called *continents.* Large bodies of water on the crust are called *oceans.*

**Materials Needed**

*For Exploration (One Per Student)*
2-inch diameter ball of red, yellow, and gray clay; plastic knife; white construction paper; 3 crayons of red, yellow, and gray

*For Exploration (for Entire Class)*
Green and blue clay, green crayon, globe of the Earth, tennis ball, soccer ball. Maps of ocean floors are useful but optional.

 **Safety Precautions:** Remind students to be careful not to poke themselves or others with the plastic knife. Be sure to wash hands after using the clay. Remind them not to eat the clay.

# Exploration *Which process skills will be used?*

Observing, manipulating materials, predicting

*What will the students do?*

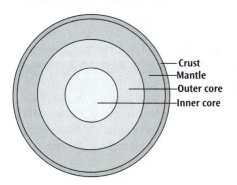

Guide the students through this portion of the lesson by first asking them to pick up the red clay and work it into a ball. Ask them to then flatten out the yellow clay and wrap it around the red ball of clay. Finally ask them to flatten out the gray clay and then wrap it around the yellow-covered ball of clay. Ask the students to use their plastic knives carefully to cut the clay ball in half. Ask them to draw on their construction paper what the sliced-open clay ball looks like.

• *Clay Earth Layers*

# Explanation/Concept Invention *What is the main idea? How will the main idea be constructed?*

*Concept:* The planet Earth is made up of three layers: the *core, mantle,* and *crust.* The differences in the layers are caused by the amount of heat and pressure upon them and the material found within each.

Tell the students you'd like them to think of the clay ball as a *model* or representation of Earth. Since the students are most familiar with things found on the surface of the Earth, ask them to give you suggestions of things they find there. If possible, draw pictures of their suggestions or write the names on the board. Ask if anyone has an idea for another name to call Earth's surface. You might make an analogy to a pie that has a different material on the inside than outside. What do you call the outer covering of the pie? *Crust*—this same name is given to the outer surface of the Earth. Ask the students to label the gray layer on their diagram the *crust.*

Now ask the students to look past the outer covering and focus on the yellow layer. The yellow clay represents the mantle. This layer of Earth is in a slightly liquid form. It is under enough pressure to heat the rock and melt it. Ask the students to label the yellow layer on their diagram the *mantle.* Share with them that this is where the magma comes from during volcanic activity. When there are cracks in the crust, the magma gets pushed up from the mantle through the weight of the earth's crust.

Continue with questions to get the children to think about what the very middle of something is usually referred to. Get the students to think about what they call the center of an apple. The red ball represents the *core*. Because the core is under such great pressure it is very hot, leaving the outer core in a solid state and the inner core in a semi-liquid state. Ask the students to label the red layer on their diagram the *core*.

Ask the students to reflect on what they now know about the characteristics of the Earth's layers to answer this question: Why does the earth have layers?

## *Expansion of the Idea*  *Which process skills will be used?*

Manipulating materials, observing, hypothesizing, inferring

### How will the idea be expanded?

- Clay
  Continents

Hold up the tennis ball. Ask the students how they think the tennis ball is like the Earth. Encourage them to use the terms *crust, mantle,* and *core*. Hold up a soccer ball. Ask the students how the soccer ball is like the Earth. Hold up the globe. Tell them that this represents what Earth would look like if they were up in the sky looking down. Ask the students to observe the globe carefully. After they look at the globe, ask the students if they think the soccer ball or the tennis ball is more like Earth's surface. Engage the students in a conversation about how the soccer ball is not one solid piece but many pieces sewn together. The crust of Earth does not look like one solid piece but like many pieces separated by water. The pieces appear to fit together. Ask the students for suggested names for the land masses and the bodies of water. If none are given, tell the students that the land masses are called *continents* and the bodies of water are called *oceans*. If maps of the ocean floor are available, share them with the students. Be sure to point out that the crust still exists below the ocean water.

Provide the students with some green and blue clay. Ask them to put their two halves of clay back together again, gently sealing the gray clay so that they have one ball of clay again. Ask the students to use the green clay to place some land masses or continents on their Earth. Ask them to add blue clay between the continents to represent the oceans. Then ask them to use their green and blue crayons to draw the continents and oceans on their drawings and to label them.

### Science in Personal and Social Perspectives

- ✦ It has been found that the movement of the semiliquid material in the mantle of the Earth causes the crust to move. When the crust moves, earthquakes occur. Have earthquakes ever occurred where you live? What should be done to protect people during earthquakes?
- ✦ What continent do you live on?

### Science and Technology

- ✦ How has knowledge about continent movement changed the way we construct buildings?
- ✦ Can earthquakes be detected? How?
- ✦ Do you think if technology could come up with a way to drain the oceans that would be better for life on Earth? Why or why not?

### Science as Inquiry

+ Which layer of the Earth is very hot yet still in a solid state?
+ The land masses on the surface of the Earth appear to fit together, yet many are far apart. Do you think they were once together? If so, why?
+ Is there crust under the oceans? How do we know this?

### History and Nature of Science

+ A seismologist would need to understand that the Earth is in layers. Why do you think this is true? What do you think a seismologist does?
+ Should oceanographers be concerned about the Earth's layers?
+ Many oil companies get their oil out of the North Sea. Do you think these companies used their knowledge of the Earth's layers to find their drilling sites? Why or why not?

## Evaluation  *How will the students show what they have learned?*

Upon completing the activities, the students will be able to:

+ draw a diagram of a cross section of the Earth and label the continents, oceans, crust, mantle, and core;
+ identify from a diagram the different layers of the Earth;
+ explain how the Earth can be compared to a soccer ball;
+ point out continents and oceans on a globe.

## Fossils

GRADE LEVEL:  2–4

DISCIPLINE:  Earth and Space Science

**Inquiry Question:**  What is a fossil?

**Concept to Be Invented:**  Main idea—A record of an ancient animal or plant found in sedimentary rocks is called a fossil.

**Concepts Important to Expansion:**  *Fossils* provide clues to ancient environments. Evidence that humans were present during primitive times is called an *artifact*. A hollow space left in sedimentary rock when a plant or animal body decays is called a *mold*. When sediments fill the hollow space and harden, the hardened sediments formed in the shape of the plant or animal are called *casts*.

### Materials Needed

*For Exploration*
A variety of fossil samples for class observations, construction paper, and crayons or markers.

*For Expansion*

seashells (1 or 2 per student)          plaster of Paris
leaves or plants                        water
1 aluminum pie tin per student          1 plastic spoon per student
petroleum jelly                         paper towels
2 paper cups per student                old newspapers

*Note:* Plastic samples of seashells, readily available through science equipment suppliers, may be preferred over actual seashells. Young children will find these easier to work with.

**Safety Precautions:** Students should be reminded not to eat the plaster. Take care to avoid water spills. Should they occur, wipe them up immediately.

## Exploration   *Which process skills will be used?*

Observing, brainstorming, predicting, hypothesizing, communicating

### *What will the students do?*

• *Fossil Observations*
Pass the fossil samples around to the students without telling them what they are looking at. Ask the students to make careful observations about these unknown objects and to share their observations with the class. Encourage the students to think about what these things could possibly be. Is it a plant or an animal? Is it an image of a plant or an animal, or a piece of the real thing? Do you think it is still on the earth? How do you think this could have been formed? Allow the students sufficient time to brainstorm with one another ideas on the fossils' possible origins. Ask the students to draw the unknown object and to color it the way they think it would look if the actual object (plant or animal) were right in front of them. If the students are capable of writing sentences, ask them to write three or four sentences below their pictures describing how they think the image in the rock was formed.

## Explanation/Concept Invention   *What is the main idea? How will the main idea be constructed?*

*Concept:* A record of an ancient animal or plant found in sedimentary rock is called a *fossil.*

Help the students invent the concept by asking them to share with the class the drawings they created. Some questions to ask the students to help invent the concept are:

◆ Why did you choose those colors for your drawing?
◆ Depending on the unknown you observed, was it easy or difficult for you to decide what this would look like if it were right in front of you? Why?
◆ How do you think this was formed?
◆ Will you please share with us your ideas?

Through this line of questioning the process of fossilization can be brought out. When an animal or plant dies, it is covered with mud, rocks, sand, and so on. Pressure is applied over many years, so the layers turn to stone, leaving an imprint of the plant or animal. The records of ancient animals and plants found in sedimentary rocks are called fossils. Additional source books or films on fossils may be shared with the class at this time. Also share examples of local fossils.

## Expansion of the Idea  *Which process skills will be used?*

Observing, manipulating materials, predicting

### How will the idea be expanded?

Ask the students to bring in seashells or leaves to use in making an image, or provide these or plastic models for them. Ask the students to use the old newspapers to cover their desktops. Give each student a pie tin. Provide enough petroleum jelly so that the students can spread a thin-to-medium film over the bottom and sides of the pie tin. Remind them to be sure that the entire inside of the tin is covered with jelly. Once they have chosen the item they want to make an image of, instruct the students to cover the shell or plant with a thin layer of petroleum jelly. Place the shell or plant in the bottom of the pie tin so that the flattest side rests on the bottom of the pan.

• *Plaster Molds and Casts*

**Step 1.** Pour plaster into a pie dish.

**Step 2.** Push shell into plaster. After drying an hour, carefully remove shell and allow plaster to dry overnight.

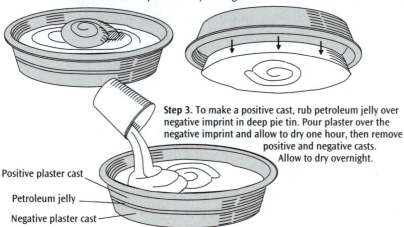

**Step 3.** To make a positive cast, rub petroleum jelly over negative imprint in deep pie tin. Pour plaster over the negative imprint and allow to dry one hour, then remove positive and negative casts. Allow to dry overnight.

Positive plaster cast
Petroleum jelly
Negative plaster cast

In one of the cups for each student, place enough dry plaster of Paris so that when mixed it will be enough to cover the bottom of the pie tin with about 15 mm (½ inch) of plaster. In the second cup place enough water so that each student will have created the proper consistency of plaster once he or she mixes (using the plastic spoon) the dry powder with the water. Once the students have mixed their plaster, instruct them to pour it carefully over the shell or plant into the pie tin. They should allow about 1 hour for the plaster to harden. Remember: As the plaster dries it will become quite warm and then cool. Wait until it has cooled before removing it from the tin.

Once the plaster has hardened, turn the pie tin upside down over the paper-covered desk and tap the tin lightly to remove the plaster cast. The plaster will still be quite wet at this time, so the students need to be reminded to use care as they remove their shells or plants from the plaster. Once the shells or plants are removed, set the plaster casts in a safe place to cure fully (dry out and harden). This should take at least a day. Once the casts are cured, the students will have what is known as a *negative imprint* or *mold* of a plant or animal. If desired, a *positive imprint* or *cast* can now be created by spreading additional petroleum jelly over the surface of the negative imprint and placing it back into a deeper petroleum-jelly-lined pie tin. On top of the first cast pour additional plaster. After it has hardened (about 1 hour) carefully turn the tin upside down and remove the old and new plaster casts. Since the surface of the old cast was thoroughly covered with petroleum jelly, the two casts should readily come apart with a knife blade. The new cast formed from the negative imprint is called a positive imprint. After this has had a chance to harden thoroughly (about one day), the students may want to paint or color with markers their newly formed fossils.

### Science in Personal and Social Perspectives

- ✦ Why do you want to know about fossils? Has our study of fossils given you any ideas about what life was like in the past?
- ✦ Do you think you could have lived during the time when dinosaurs roamed the land? Why or why not?

### Science and Technology

- ✦ How can fossils tell us what ancient environments were like?
- ✦ Evidence left by early people is called an artifact. Some examples are arrowheads, ancient beads, and animal skins used as clothing. Why do you think we don't call them fossils?

### Science as Inquiry

- ✦ Why can fossils be found only in sedimentary rocks?
- ✦ Can you find fossils where you live? Where do you think you would go to look for fossils?

### History and Nature of Science

- ✦ Paleontologists (fossil experts) study and learn from fossils. If you were a paleontologist, what kind of information would you share with others on the imprints you just made?

- How is an archeologist's job different from a paleontologist's? An excellent book for this topic is Gloria and Esther Goldreich, *What Can She Be? A Geologist* (New York: Lothrop, Lee and Shepard, 1976).
- Describe how the Leakeys (Louis, Mary, and son Richard) used fossil evidence to determine the changes in human body form throughout history.

## Evaluation *How will the students show what they have learned?*

Upon completing the activities, the students will be able to:

- demonstrate how a fossil can be formed by using sand, water, and a seashell;
- pick out the fossils when given several items to choose from, such as a seashell, a leaf, a sedimentary rock with a shell imprint or leaf imprint on it, a geode, or an igneous rock such as obsidian;
- tell or write in their own words what a fossil is and what information it can provide humans.

## Investigating Soil

GRADE LEVEL: 5–8
DISCIPLINE: Earth and Space Science

**Inquiry Question:** What is soil and how is it formed?

**Concept to Be Invented:** Soil is made from finely ground rock and organic material.

**National Science Education Standards:** Grades 5–8—Earth/Space Sciences. Soil consists of weathered rocks, decomposed organic material from dead plants, animals, and bacteria. Soils are often found in layers, with each having a different chemical composition and texture.

**Science Attitudes to Nurture:** Activities that investigate and analyze science questions.

**Materials Needed:** Soil samples from local area, hammers, 1 piece of white construction paper/per student, old newspaper paper/per student, 1 magnifying glass/per student, local sedimentary rock samples (these are easily broken), 1 pair of goggles per student, sand, 2 small transparent plastic jars or containers with lids, organic matter such as leaves or grass clippings, water, soil samples from local area.

**Safety Precautions:** Students must wear goggles while smashing rocks with hammers. Wrap the rocks in newspaper and then strike them with a hammer. This will prevent rock pieces from flying and causing injury.

If you choose to take the students outside to collect soil samples, be sure proper safety procedures are followed. Pair the students and make sure they know the boundaries for soil sample collection.

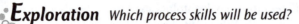

## *E*xploration  *Which process skills will be used?*

Observing, recording data, classifying

• *Soil Separation and Rock Crushing*

Engage the class by posing the inquiry question and involving the students in predicting answers. Explore by providing the class with soil samples collected from the local area, or if possible, take the students around the school grounds to collect soil samples. Ask the students to cover their desktops with old newspapers and then place the white construction paper on top of the newspaper. Arrange the students in cooperative groups of three to four to make observations of the soil samples. Use the magnifying glasses to make detailed observations of the individual particles. Encourage students to draw or write a description of their observations. Pose divergent questions to stimulate observations using the basic process skills.

After the students have made as many observations as possible, ask them to try to separate their soil samples into different parts. *Divergent question to ask: How many different ways do you think you can use to separate the soil samples?*

Give each cooperative group a hammer and several pieces of local sedimentary rocks like sandstone or limestone. Remind students to *put on and keep on* their goggles at all times during this section of the activity. On top of the newspaper-covered desks, ask the students to wrap the rock samples in newspaper and then pound the rocks with hammers. *How do the rock samples compare to the sediments you separated from the local soil sample? (Open-ended evaluative question to stimulate independent thought.)*

## *E*xplanation

Ask the students to share the results of their observations. As they share use the following line of questioning to help the students invent the concept:

◆ What kinds of things did you observe? *Convergent question—implies specific answers based on their observations.*

◆ How did the components of the soil compare in size? Shape? *Encourages detail observations to respond to the convergent close-ended question.*

◆ How many different ways did you separate your soil samples? Suggestions may include size or color; rocklike or plantlike. *An open-ended evaluative question.*

+ What did your rock look like before you crushed it with the hammer? Afterward? *Convergent question—implies specific answers based on their observations.*
+ How do the crushed rock and your soil sample compare? *An evaluative question asking for analysis and synthesis of results.*

Continue using questions, moving from divergent types from the Exploration phase to more convergent and evaluative questions to help the students create a working definition for soil: "Soil is made from finely ground rocks and organic material."

## Expansion *Which process skills will be used?*

Manipulating materials, observing, inferring, classifying, estimating, predicting

Provide each cooperative group with two transparent plastic jars with lids. Ask the students to label one jar *local soil* and the second *homemade soil*. Ask the students to fill the first jar halfway with one of the local soil samples. Ask the students to place, in the second jar, some of the crushed rock they just smashed, some sand, and some grass clippings or leaves, so that half of the jar is filled. Into both jars pour enough water to cover all of the solid materials. Place the lids on the jars and shake vigorously. Solicit predictions about what will happen in each jar after it sets for 1 hour, for 3 hours, and overnight. Ask the students to record their predictions and then place the jars where they will not be disturbed for the times indicated.

• *Soil Components*

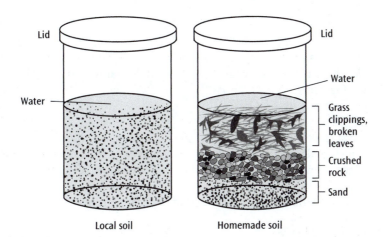

Local soil                    Homemade soil

Use the following questions to help the students conclude that the rocks and plants found in the local area will determine the kind of soil formed. Weathered sandstone will create a sandy soil, more finely ground particles will create a silty soil, and very fine particles will create a clay soil. Note the questions start as close-ended, convergent types of

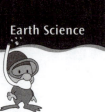

questions—this is to help the students to focus on the expansion activity. Next they move into more open-ended divergent and evaluative questions—all designed to help the students create an understanding of the relationship between local rock and the type of soil formed in the area:

✦ What did the two samples look like after 1 hour? After 3 hours? The next day?
✦ If you did not look at jar labels and just at samples, how could you tell the difference between the soil in the two jars? How are they similar? How are they different?
✦ Look at the settled materials. How much of the sample do you estimate is sand? Silt? Clay?
✦ Based on your estimates how would you classify the soil?
✦ What do you think will happen to the grass or leaves if you let the jar sit for one week, one month, or three months? Solicit predictions and then set the jar in a safe place so that students can observe it over a three-month period.
✦ What do you conclude about the local rock found in the area and the soil type after looking at your results and the results of the whole class?

### Science in Personal and Social Perspectives

What kind of soil is found around your home? What types of plants would grow well in the soil? Not grow well? How might soil types impact agricultural decisions?

Should people be concerned about farmers using excessive amounts of fertilizers in soils? Why? What can be done to prevent excessive use of fertilizers?

Do you think it is better to have a sandy or a silty soil in your garden? Why? Do you put fertilizers on your soil? If so, why?

### Science and Technology

✦ As you have discovered, not all soils are alike. Do you think it was important to keep this fact in mind as tractor tires were developed? Why?
✦ What do you think *no-till* means, and why would farmers be urged to use this method of farming?

### Science as Inquiry

✦ What are at least three components of soil?
✦ What influence does local bedrock have on the type of soil found in an area?
✦ How might the rate of weathering and erosion in an area affect the formation of soil?
✦ Where do you think the minerals found in soils come from?

### History and Nature of Science

✦ What are the responsibilities of a soil agronomist?
✦ How important is it for a land developer to understand soil formation?
✦ What is organic farming? How do these methods of farming differ from other methods?

## Evaluation

Upon completing the activities, the students will be able to:

+ take a soil sample and demonstrate the steps necessary to estimate the amount of sand, silt, and clay in the sample;
+ explain how the type of soil found in a local area is dependent on the local bedrock and ground cover; and
+ write a persuasive argument on why grass is necessary to cover soil, or on how soil is different from dirt.

## Rock Types

GRADE LEVEL: 5–8

DISCIPLINE: Earth and Space Science

**Inquiry Question:** Are all rocks made the same?

**Concept to Be Invented:** Main idea—Rocks may be classified into three groups: *igneous, sedimentary,* and *metamorphic,* depending on how they are formed.

**Concepts Important to Expansion:** *Igneous* means "fire formed." Cooled magma and lava create igneous rocks such as granite and obsidian. *Sedimentary* rocks are formed in water due to layers of sediments building up from weathered igneous, metamorphic, and other sedimentary rocks, or decaying organic matter; examples are limestone and sandstone. *Metamorphic* rocks are very hard rocks that may be formed from igneous or sedimentary rocks under extreme heat and pressure; marble and gneiss are examples.

### Materials Needed

*For Exploration (for Each Cooperative Group of Students)*
several samples of igneous rocks, sedimentary rocks, metamorphic rocks, 1 jar, 2 sheets of construction paper, sand, mud, and pebbles

*For Expansion (for Each Student)*
goggles, hammer and chisel, collection bag, 3 empty egg cartons, old newspapers, and a marker

**Safety Precautions:** Remind students to handle rock samples carefully. No throwing rocks! If you choose to take the students outside to collect rock samples, be sure proper safety procedures are followed. Pair up the students and make sure they know the boundaries for rock sample collection.

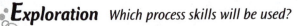

## Exploration *Which process skills will be used?*

Observing, classifying, inferring

### What will the students do?

- *Rock Categorization*

Divide the class into cooperative learning groups of three or four students. Provide each group with sand, numerous rock types, and pebbles. Ask the students to categorize the rocks. What's different about them? How are they alike? After the students have shared the results of their categorizing, ask them to set those samples aside in the categories they identified.

Give each cooperative group a jar and ask them to put rocks, sand, mud, and water into it. Put a lid on the jar and shake it for a few moments. Ask the students to draw a picture of what the jar looks like after the materials have settled.

## Explanation/Concept Invention *What is the main idea? How will the main idea be constructed?*

*Concept:* Rocks may be classified into three groups: igneous, sedimentary, and metamorphic, depending on how they were formed.

Ask the students to fold a sheet of construction paper into three parts. Now go back to the different piles of rocks the students first categorized. Ask them what kinds of differences they noted. Explain that rocks come in all shapes, colors, and sizes. However, they weren't all made the same way. Use the example of lava from a volcano. What happens to the lava when it dries? It becomes a hard rock called *igneous*, meaning "fire formed." Cooled magma and lava create igneous rocks like granite and obsidian. In the first part of the construction paper, draw or describe how igneous rock is formed. Provide the students with various samples of igneous rocks to observe.

Refer back to the shaken jar. What does it currently look like? Steer the students toward looking at the layers of materials. Did your group classify any of the rock samples based on whether you could see layers? What do you think rocks formed from the buildup of materials in layers are called? *Sedimentary* rocks are formed in water due to layers of sediments building up from weathered igneous, metamorphic, and other sedimentary rocks, or decaying organic matter. Limestone and sandstone are sedimentary. In the second part of the construction paper, draw or describe how sedimentary rocks are formed. Provide the students with various samples of sedimentary rocks to observe.

Ask the students if they think they classified any rocks that have not yet been described. Have the students share those rocks with the rest of the class. Make sure they do not fit under igneous or sedimentary categories. Explain to the students that the igneous or sedimentary rocks can be put under extreme heat and pressure inside the Earth, which changes the look of the rock. These are called *metamorphic* rocks; examples are marble and gneiss. Metamorphic rocks are very hard. In the third part of the construction paper, draw or describe how metamorphic rocks are formed. Provide the students with various samples of metamorphic rocks to observe.

Summarize how rocks are formed by completing these statements: Rocks formed "from fire" are called _____ (igneous); rocks when placed under heat and pressure change into _____ (metamorphic) rocks; and rocks formed from the buildup of materials in layers are called _____ (sedimentary).

## Expansion of the Idea   *Which process skills will be used?*

Observing, classifying, collecting, comparing, communicating

### How will the idea be expanded?

This expansion activity may be done as a home extension activity or as a class field trip. Identify a site where students will be permitted to collect rock samples. Either take them as a class or provide instructions to parents to take the students to the collection site. Be sure the students are given instruction on how to use the hammer and chisel to extract rock samples from the bedrock. Encourage the students to break their samples into pieces small enough to fit into the egg carton depressions. Remind the students to think about the different colors and textures that different kinds of rocks have. Classify the collection into igneous, sedimentary, and metamorphic, and designate one egg carton for each rock type. After a sufficient amount of time has passed (one or two months), ask the students to bring their collections to school to share with the class.

• *Rock Collection Field Trip*

### Science in Personal and Social Perspectives

✦ If you were going to build a home along the ocean, would you want the underlying rock to be igneous, sedimentary, or metamorphic? Why?
✦ Have you ever washed your hands with a pumice-based soap? Have you ever used a pumice stone to smooth away rough skin? Where do you think this comes from?

### Science and Technology

✦ Which type of rock is best used for building purposes?
✦ Would you trust a bridge made of sedimentary rocks? Do you think it would last as long as a bridge made with igneous rocks? What about a bridge made of metamorphic rock?
✦ Which type of rock would be a wise choice to build a dam with?

### Science as Inquiry

✦ Where in the world would I easily find an igneous rock? A sedimentary rock? A metamorphic rock?
✦ Can an igneous rock be formed from a sedimentary one? Can a sedimentary rock be formed from a metamorphic or igneous rock?
✦ What kind of rock is the local bedrock?

### History and Nature of Science

✦ Would a civil engineer responsible for placing a bridge across the Mississippi River between Illinois and Missouri need to understand the type of bedrock found in the area before plans for the bridge could be made? Why or why not?

✦ As a construction worker you decide to build your own home. You want to make it out of stone. Which kind of rock type would you use, and why? Is it important that a construction worker or even a home owner know the differences among igneous, sedimentary, and metamorphic rocks?

## *E*valuation  *How will the students show what they have learned?*

Upon completing the activities, the students will be able to:

✦ look at six different rocks and identify whether they are igneous, sedimentary, or metamorphic;
✦ identify different areas of the world where the three different rock types can be found;
✦ reflect, and then write a description of an igneous rock formed when lava cooled outside the Earth.

## Cooling Crystals

GRADE LEVEL: **5–8**
DISCIPLINE: **Earth and Space Science**

**Inquiry Question:**  Why do some rocks, made of the same materials, have different names?

**Concept to Be Invented:**  The rate at which a crystal cools affects the size of the crystal.

**National Science Education Standards:**  Grades 5–8—Structure of the Earth's system. Changes in the solid Earth can be described as the rock cycle. Old rocks are buried, then compacted, heated, and often recrystallized into new rock.

**Science Attitudes to Nurture:**  Curiosity, perseverance, open-mindedness when evidence for changes is given

### Materials Needed

*For Exploration (for Each Group)*

3 glass caster cups
3 small test tubes (10-ml)
test tube holder
paradichlorbenzine (PDB) flakes
  (found in supermarkets, hardware
  stores, pharmacies)

1 150-ml beaker
heat-proof glove
grease pencil
crushed ice
2 500-ml beakers
tongs

*For Exploration (for Entire Class)*
hot plates, paper towels

*For Expansion*
samples of the igneous rocks rhyolite, granite, and obsidian; 1 hand lens per student

 **Safety Precautions**

> ✦ Review with the students proper use of heating equipment—such as the hot plates used in this activity. Remind them the hot plates purposely have short cords so that they are plugged in close to the wall, NO extension cords should be used. Keep the table/desk that the hot plate is on close to the wall to minimize the risk of someone tripping over the cord.
> ✦ Extreme care should be used near the hot plate and in handling the hot water and the PDB.
> ✦ Goggles should be worn at all times, NO excuses.
> ✦ Be sure the room is well ventilated when melting the PDB.

## *Exploration*  *Which process skills will be used?*

Observing, predicting, manipulating materials, recording data, drawing conclusions

As safety is very important with this activity, it is important to conduct this as a *Guided Discovery Activity.* Lead the student teams in a step-by-step process.

• *Making Crystals*

**Step 1:** Ask the students to fill one of the 500-ml beakers with 300-ml of water. Place a caster cup in the beaker. Boil the water on the hot plate. Again, remind the students to place the hot plate flat on the table/desktop as close to the wall as possible to avoid anyone tripping over the cord. Fill the other 500-ml beaker with crushed ice. Place the second caster cup in the beaker. Leave the third caster cup at room temperature.

**Step 2:** Ask the students to observe some PDB flakes. Be sure to remind students that goggles are to be worn at *all* times and that these observations are made in a well-ventilated area of the room. If no fume hood is present, be sure windows are opened. Ask the students to record their observations.

**Step 3:** Once the water in the beaker begins to boil, ask one student from the group to put on the heat-proof glove and carefully remove the 500-ml beaker from the hot plate. Set it on a heat-proof surface, away from risk of getting knocked over while the students perform Step 4.

**Step 4:** Again, in a well-ventilated area, ask the students to fill each of the 3 small test tubes with PDB flakes, and to half-fill the 150-ml beaker with water. Place the 3 test tubes in the beaker containing the water. Place the beaker on the hot

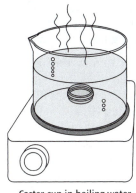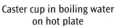

Caster cup in boiling water on hot plate   Caster cup in ice   Caster cup at room temperature

plate. Heat the beaker gently until the PDB melts. Be sure a team member is carefully watching for the PDB to melt and that goggles are still on *ALL* students.

**Step 5:** Instruct students to go back to the 500-ml beaker and using the tongs carefully remove the caster cup from the boiling water. Dry the cup and label it *A*. Once the PDB flakes have melted in each of the test tubes, instruct one student from each team to use the test tube holder to carefully remove one test tube from the beaker and pour the liquified PDB into this caster cup. Ask the students to time how long it takes for the PDB to completely become a solid, to record the time, and to record their observations of the PDB when placed in caster cup A.

**Step 6:** Ask the students to now remove the second caster cup from the beaker with ice. Dry the cup quickly and completely. Label it *B*. Ask another student from each team to use the test tube holder to carefully remove another test tube from the beaker and pour the liquified PDB into the caster cup labeled B. Ask the students to time how long it takes for the PDB to completely become a solid, to record the time, and to record their observations of the PDB when placed in caster cup B.

**Step 7:** Ask the students to take the third caster cup which was sitting at room temperature and label it C. Then ask yet another student from each team to use the test tube holder to carefully remove another test tube from the beaker and pour the liquefied PDB into the caster cup labeled C. Again, ask the students to time how long it takes for the PDB to completely become a solid, to record the time, and to record their observations of the PDB when placed in caster cup C.

Encourage the teams to use the hand lens to draw pictures of the now cooled PDB in each of the caster cups—A, B, and C.

## *E*xplanation/Concept Invention   *What is the main idea? How will the main idea be constructed?*

Ask the student teams to help create a set of class data on cooling rates for the liquified PDB in caster cups A, B, and C. Collect student drawings of the cooled PDB from the caster cups to share with the entire class. Use the following questions to help make the concept behind the guided activity concrete:

✦ Which caster cup took the longest for the PDB to solidify? Which took the least amount of time?
✦ Was there a difference in the PDB when it solidified in hot caster cup (A) compared to cold caster cup (B)?
✦ How does the rate of cooling affect the size of crystals?
✦ Look at the various drawings of the solidified PDB in casters A, B, and C. How are they different? What caused this difference? What conclusions can you draw?

The students should conclude that the rate at which a crystal cools affects the size of the crystal formed.

## *Expansion of the Idea*  *Which process skills will be used?*

Observing, recording data, generalizing, formulating models

This Expansion activity can be completed as an open discovery activity once the students are reminded of the safety issues and proper teacher supervision makes sure that students follow them. The student teams can be free to explore at their own pace. Remind students to wear goggles during the expansion phase, in case rock samples are dropped, to avoid getting rock chips into eyes.

> • *Crystal Differences in Rocks*

Ask the students to observe the crystals in the samples of granite, rhyolite, and obsidian with a magnifying glass. Have them draw the crystals in each sample on paper. Ask them to compare the crystals in the caster cups with the samples of granite, rhyolite, and obsidian and to respond to this question in their science journals: Which PDB crystals are most similar to the crystals in the rock samples? (Cup A, granite; cup B, obsidian; cup C, rhyolite.)

Granite, rhyolite, and obsidian are igneous rocks essentially made of the same material. Ask the students to use what they learned in the exploration phase to provide an explanation as to why they look different. Ask the students to record team responses to the following questions in their science journal so that responses can be shared once all the student teams have completed their observations: Where would igneous rocks have a chance to cool slowly? Where would igneous rock cool rapidly? If you saw a rock that contained large interlocking crystals, what would you say about the way it formed? Some suggested answers are: The more slowly a crystal cools, the larger the crystals are. Granite cooled slowly and crystals were able to form. Rhyolite cooled more rapidly than granite, but more slowly than obsidian. Igneous rocks cool slowly deep in the Earth. They cool rapidly on the surface. Large interlocking crystals form slowly inside the Earth.

As a class, now ask the students to respond to the Inquiry Question: Why *do* some rocks, made of the same materials, have different names?

### Science in Personal and Social Perspectives

- ✦ What kinds of crystals do you eat regularly? (salt and sugar)
- ✦ How does the size of a crystal determine its quality? Do you think your knowledge of how crystals form will assist you in determining the quality of precious rocks and gems?

### Science and Technology

- ✦ The strength and quality of rocks are important for construction. What is the best type of rock for long-lasting buildings?
- ✦ How has the scarcity of quality gems on the market affected your life, your community, or the world?

### Science as Inquiry

- ✦ What kinds of rocks are found in the area where you live? Can you classify them according to their crystal structure?
- ✦ Are crystals found in sedimentary rocks? Why or why not?

*History and Nature of Science*

✦ What kinds of careers would use information on crystal formation? Some possibilities include geologist, geophysicist, volcanologist, jeweler, sculptor, and geographer.

✦ Choose one of the career suggestions from the question above and research the skills necessary to enter that career. Provide an oral report to the class.

## *Evaluation* *How will the students show what they have learned?*

Upon completing the activities, the students will be able to:

✦ (with drawings of crystals of different shapes and sizes) identify where a crystal is cooled (on the Earth's surface or inside the Earth) and at what rate;

✦ examine samples of igneous rocks and explain why they have different-sized crystals;

✦ and explain how the prices of precious jewels are affected by crystal formation.

## Weathering

GRADE LEVEL: 5–8

DISCIPLINE: Earth and Space Science

**Inquiry Question:** If rocks are so hard, what causes them to break apart?

**Concept to Be Invented:** Main idea—*Weathering* is the name given to the various mechanical and chemical processes that break down rock.

**Concepts Important to Expansion:** erosion, soil formation, rock formation—igneous, sedimentary, metamorphic

### Materials Needed

*For Discrepant Event*
soda bottle and cap, water, freezer

*For Exploration*
field site to collect data, stereomicroscope, hammer

*For Expansion*
dilute hydrochloric acid (HCl); igneous, sedimentary, and metamorphic rock samples

 **Safety Precautions:** Review with the students ahead of time the rules that should be followed for everyone's safety during the field trip. Visit the field site before the students do to guard against any possible hazards at the site.

• *Freezing Bottle*

The day before you begin this lesson, take a glass soda bottle and ask a student to fill it with water all the way to the top. Cap the bottle so that no water can escape. Now ask the students what they think will happen to this bottle if you place it in the freezer for a day. Record their predictions on the board, where they will remain untouched until the next day. Twenty-four hours later remove the bottle from the freezer. If the bottle was totally filled before freezing, it should now be cracked, as the ice expanded upon freezing. Ask the students what they observe. Did it behave according to their predictions? Why did this happen? What happens to water when it freezes? Based on your observations, do you think water could do this to other items besides glass? Think about this as we engage in today's activity.

## Exploration   *Which process skills will be used?*

Observing, hypothesizing, predicting, measuring, using spatial relationships, recording data

### What will the students do?

Tell the students that they are going on a field trip around the school grounds to answer the following question: If rocks are so hard, what causes them to break apart? An old road or empty prairie or field will be an ideal site. Remind the students about appropriate care of a collection site. Remind them to take care as they travel through the site and to try not to destroy any animal homes or wildflowers or plant growth. Ask the students to look for rocks that appear to be broken apart. They are to record a description of the area in which they find them, taking care to note the soil conditions (wet, dry, sandy, clay), an estimate of the original size of the rock, a physical description of the rock (color, shininess, hardness, porosity), and a prediction based on their findings as to what they think caused the rock to break apart. A small sample of the rock should be collected for further study in the classroom. Upon returning to the classroom, the students will make a composite chart of their field observations. Headings for this chart could include *collection site, soil conditions, rock size, physical properties* (color, luster, hardness, pore size), *possible cause for breakage.*

* Weathering
Field Trip

## Explanation/Concept Invention   *What is the main idea? How will the main idea be constructed?*

*Concept: Weathering* is the name given to the various mechanical and chemical processes that break down rock.

Draw the students' attention to the composite chart in the front of the room. In order to guide the students in inventing the concept of *weathering*, ask such questions as: In looking at this chart, are there any we can group together? Do any of them sound as if the different groups of investigators were looking at the same rocks?

Ask the students to bring up the sample rocks whose descriptions sound similar. Do you think these are the same rocks?

Once double sightings have been eliminated, begin to focus on the chart again, this time asking, Is there any one area where broken rocks were found more often than any other? Or is there any one soil condition where broken rocks are found more often than any other?

If this is the case, then ask the students if they think this soil condition contributed to the presence of broken rocks. If it is a very wet area, then you can relate this back to the discrepant event—how the freezing and thawing of water will contribute to the cracking of the rocks. If this is a dry area, ask the students if they made note of any vegetation growing in the area. They may have found the broken rocks due to roots growing through the surface of the rock. It may be a very dry area where wind blows through rather rapidly, causing the rocks to break up.

Based on the results of our field study—if rocks are so hard, what causes them to break apart? Solicit ideas from the students. Share with them that the name of this process that causes the breaking up of rock due to running water, wind, rain, or roots is called *weathering*.

What happens to the rock pieces as they are carried by the rain, wind, or running water? What term can we use to describe the carrying away of this weathered material? (Erosion.) Ask the students if they observed the soil where they found the rock. Was it similar in composition to the rock itself? Engage the students in a discussion of how the weathering of rocks assists in soil formation.

## **Expansion of the Idea**  *Which process skills will be used?*

Observing, classifying, experimenting, predicting, inferring, interpreting data, recording data, communicating

### *How will the idea be expanded?*

- Rock Identification

If your students collected rock samples that fell into one type (all igneous, or all sedimentary, or all metamorphic), then in addition to their samples, provide them with rock samples from the missing rock groups. Ask the students to try to group the rock samples according to the characteristics from the composite chart from the first activity. Suggest to them that based on hardness, porosity, and composition, they should be able to group their rock samples into three different groups.

Once they have their samples in three groups, the students can perform the following experiments to determine possible sources of weathering.

- Chemical Weathering

*Acid Test.* Take one sample from each rock group. Predict what will happen to the rock when you drop three drops of dilute HCl on it. Do you think each rock will react the same way? Which one do you think will weather the most? In nature, what type of weathering could we consider this to be? (This is known as *chemical weathering.*)

*Rust/Oxidation.* Do you notice any color changes in your rock? Are there what appear to be rust spots on the rock? What do you think causes this?

- Mechanical Weathering

*Water.* Cover the three different rock samples with water and place them in a freezer for a day. Do the rocks crumble easily in your hands? If you strike them with a hammer lightly, do they fall apart? Are the insides still wet? Which rock type was most susceptible to the freezing water? Since the water simply froze and broke the rock apart, this is known as *mechanical weathering.*

*Roots.* In what area did you find this rock? Are there still traces of plant matter on the rock? Did you see any roots pushing up right through the surface of the rock?

Do the roots cause chemical or mechanical weathering? Overall, which rocks are most easily weathered and which are most difficult to weather? Can you guess how each of these rock groups was originally formed based on your weathering observations? Lead a discussion on rock formations: igneous, sedimentary, and metamorphic. Detailed discussions will be provided in a separate lesson for each rock type.

### Science in Personal and Social Perspectives

+ Why does one need to use special fishing lures if a river or lake is muddy or murky due to erosion?
+ What would you suspect was happening if the water in your favorite fishing stream looked clean, yet the number of fish began to dwindle? You have noticed that some of the rocks along the bank are beginning to crumble and wash downstream. What could you do to verify your suspicions? Whom would you talk to about this problem?

### Science and Technology

+ What role does strip-mining of coal or clear-cutting of timber play in allowing the forces of weather to affect erosion?
+ How has an increased understanding of the forces of weathering and erosion caused us to change our farming practices since the Dust Bowl days of the 1930s?

### Science as Inquiry

+ How does weathering differ from erosion? What factors contribute to soil formation? What processes have occurred to create the different rock types? Can you name the three different rock types?
+ In which rock formation would you most likely place a building like the Sears Tower? Why? Which rock type would you be least likely to use to build a house? Why?

### History and Nature of Science

+ Why would a civil engineer need to understand the processes of weathering and erosion?
+ Do you think a contractor or cement finisher would find knowledge of weathering, erosion, soil, and rock types useful in his or her work?
+ Research the great pyramids of Egypt. How were they built? What are they made of? When were they built? Would they still exist if they were first built in Chicago?

## *E*valuation *How will the students show what they have learned?*

Upon completing the activities, the students will be able to:

+ draw a diagram showing the relationships among rock types, soil types, weathering, and erosion;

+ when given a weathered rock sample and a description of where the sample was found, suggest the most probable source for its weathering;
+ list at least four agents of erosion;
+ discriminate between constructive and destructive geologic forces.

# Crustal Plate Movement

GRADE LEVEL: **5–8**

DISCIPLINE: **Earth and Space Science**

**Inquiry Question:** Is the earth's surface one solid piece?

**Concept to Be Invented:** Main idea—The theory of plate tectonics states that the crust of the Earth is not one solid piece but rather several separate plates that are in motion on top of molten material.

**Concepts Important to Expansion:** Continental drift, earthquakes, volcanoes

### Materials Needed

*For Exploration (for Each Group of 4 to 6 Students)*

4 wood blocks
1 liter of water
a heat lamp or 150–200-watt bulb
   and socket

plastic shoebox (heavy plastic type,
   which will not melt under lightbulb)
food coloring
stacks of books to raise box above lamp

*For Expansion*

maps of the world showing the crustal plate boundaries, a list of places famous for volcanic eruptions, a list of sites of recent earthquakes

**Safety Precautions:** The students should be reminded to use care with the heat source. Don't place the heat source too close to the plastic box or books. Use care around water and electricity. Wipe up any water spills immediately. Do not touch heat source with wet hands.

## **E**xploration *Which process skills will be used?*

Experimenting, observing, predicting, inferring

### What will the students do?

• *Moving Plates*

Each student group should place its plastic box on two stacks of books. The box should be high enough so that a heat source (lamp) will fit beneath. Pour water into the box. Place the 4 small wood blocks in the box. All the blocks should touch, forming a square. Place the heat source beneath the box directly under the center of the blocks. Turn the light on and place a drop of food coloring in the water where the 4 blocks meet. Observe the blocks for about 5 to 10 minutes. What happens to each of the 4 wood blocks? What happens to the food coloring?

## Explanation/Concept Invention   *What is the main idea? How will the main idea be constructed?*

*Concept:* The theory of plate tectonics states that the crust of the Earth is not one solid piece, but rather several separate plates that are in motion on top of molten material.

Ask the students to share their observations on the movement of the 4 wood blocks and the food coloring. Why do you think this happened? If you were to relate this activity to the Earth's crust, what do you think the blocks represent? (Early land masses that separated millions of years ago.) What would the water represent? (The molten layer of the Earth called the *mantle.*) What happened to the temperature of the water over time? (It warmed up.) What happened to the food coloring? (It slowly moved along the surface as the water continued to warm.) Through questioning along this line, help the students to conclude that the theory of plate tectonics states that the crust of the Earth is not one solid piece but rather several separate plates that are in motion on top of molten material.

## Expansion of the Idea   *Which process skills will be used?*

Observing, predicting, making conclusions

### How will the idea be expanded?

Pair up the students. Provide each pair with a world map indicating the boundaries for the crustal plates. The students should be free to mark on the maps you provide. Provide the students with a recent list of volcanic and earthquake activity. Ask them to plot on the map the places where the most recent earthquakes and volcanoes have occurred. You may give them a list of volcanic and earthquake activity for the past fifty years to plot. Ask the students to share some observations they have made about the relationship between earthquakes and volcanoes from this exercise. The students should conclude that most earthquake and volcanic activity occurs where two or more crustal plates come together.

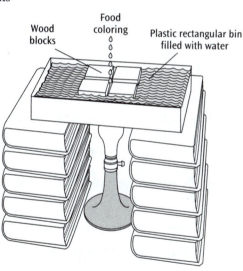

Wood blocks

Food coloring

Plastic rectangular bin filled with water

• *Mapping Volcanoes and Earthquakes*

### Science in Personal and Social Perspectives

✦ Would you choose to live along a crustal plate boundary? If you did, how might it affect your life?

✦ Do you think the government should help pay to repair homes for people who chose to build their homes on a known crustal boundary?

### Science and Technology

✦ Are you aware of any other theories about formation or movement of the Earth's crust? What part do you think technology has played in theory change and advanced knowledge about different phenomena?

✦ How do we use our knowledge about movement of the Earth's crust when we construct buildings in areas where crustal plates are known to move?

### Science as Inquiry

✦ Is there still movement of the Earth's crust? How do we know?

✦ A lot of volcanic activity occurs in the Hawaiian Islands. Are they on the edge of a crustal plate? If not, what is causing the volcanic activity? Research the formation of these volcanic islands.

✦ Explain how a solid crust can move. What does the mantle layer of the Earth have to do with this movement?

### History and Nature of Science

✦ Who is Charles Lyell? What career changes led him to many geological discoveries?

✦ Would a seismologist be concerned with crustal plate movement? Why?

✦ Why would a civil engineer be concerned with the location of crustal plate boundaries? What does a civil engineer do?

## **E**valuation  *How will the students show what they have learned?*

On completing the activities, the students will be able to:

• *Oatmeal and Cracker Plate Tectonics*

✦ demonstrate the theory of plate tectonics by using a bowl of oatmeal and some soda crackers;

✦ identify the area known as the Ring of Fire on a world map and explain what it is;

✦ briefly explain the theory of plate tectonics.

## Aging Human/Aging Earth

GRADE LEVEL: 7–8

DISCIPLINE: Earth and Space Science

**Inquiry Question:**  Are the processes that shaped the Earth in the past still occurring today?

**Concept to Be Invented:**  The Earth's processes we see today, including erosion, movement of crustal plates, and changes in atmospheric composition, are similar to those processes that occurred in the past.

**Concepts Important to Expansion:**  Earth history is also influenced by occasional catastrophes such as the impact of an asteroid or comet.

**Materials Needed**

*For Exploration*

pictures of the Earth, including views from space and close-up pictures of various biomes

pictures of the other planets and Earth's moon

journal or notebook to record data

access to older community members

audio or videotape recorder

*For Expansion*

geologic maps of your state and the region where your school is located. These are maps that show the ages of the various rock layers identifying the periods and epochs, and the depth of each layer from the surface.

geologic time scale

access to reference materials on the geology of the local region, or access to geologists who live/work in the region

**Safety Precautions:** During the exploration activity the students should work in pairs and never go into an interview without a formal introduction by a trusted adult.

## Exploration   Which process skills will be used?

Observing, inferring, predicting, communicating, comparing and contrasting, formulating hypotheses, using space-time relationships

### What will students do?

*Introduction.* The teacher should hang pictures of the Earth around the classroom—scenes from the major biomes such as pictures of forests, mountains, deserts, etc. An old calendar may be a good source for such scenes. Also hang pictures of the other planets and the moon around the classroom. Ask the students to look around the room at all of the pictures. After students have had time to view the pictures, ask them why they think scientists call the Earth a "living planet." Solicit their responses. To get them started, use guiding questions, such as what do you think is evidence of living things? Do you see any evidence of that in any of the pictures found around the classroom?

• *Living Humans— Living Earth*

Encourage them to think about changes in the surface of the Earth; recall for them events in recent years, such as the earthquake in Iran, volcanoes in Mexico, and the numerous hurricanes that strike from the Atlantic Ocean. All of these are evidence that the Earth's surface is constantly changing shape, wearing down one area and building up another. The forests and grasslands are evidence that on the planet Earth the sun's energy is being used to grow new life.

Ask them to ponder this question: How is your body like the planet Earth? Solicit student ideas. These may include things like our bodies have mountains and valleys—high and low spots; we are covered with a thin crust—our skin; and we make use of the sun's energy to get food to help us grow as well. Like the Earth, changes have happened to our bodies over time. We've grown since we were babies, we've acquired some cuts

and bruises, but even with that our bodies have repaired themselves. This is much like the planet Earth does after a catastrophe like a forest fire or flood.

Conclude with this statement: Just as there are changes in our living bodies over time, so too has the living Earth changed.

*Student Activity.* Assign the students to "interview teams." Explain to them that their task is to identify and interview a person in their community who can share information on changes in the physical environment of the community over time. Stress that the purpose of the interview is to capture stories on changes in the ecology of the region—not social changes. Remind the students of the introductory discussion's conclusion: Just as there are changes in our living bodies over time, so too has the living Earth changed. Ask them to use this conclusion to shape their interview questions. For instance, the students could ask the interviewee to recall something he or she liked to do outdoors when young, like swimming in a certain pond or walking across a frozen creek in the dead of winter. The students could then ask if a young person could still do that today. Is the pond still there? Has the creek been widened or does water still flow there?

Provide the students with audio or videotape recorders for the interviews. Teach them skills in setting up an interview, the proper etiquette in calling the person they want to interview, introducing themselves, showing respect and courtesy to the person speaking, etc. For safety's sake stress to the students the importance of performing the interview as a team. Never go into the person's home without at least another student or a parent present while they conduct the interview. If at all possible, invite the person to the school for the interview.

Ask the students to prepare a multimedia presentation on the ecological changes they discovered through their interviews. Ask them to speculate on causes for the identified changes and to pick at least one change and research the exact reason for that change. For example, if a person said, "As youngsters we used to swim across the Mississippi River," and your students know that this is not possible today because the spot the person talked about is now much wider than it was then, the students should do some research to find out why the river is much wider today. Encourage them to bring in pictures and/or video of the sites in the past and present.

## Explanation/Concept Invention  *What is the main idea? How will the main idea be constructed?*

*Concept:* The Earth's processes we see today, including erosion, movement of crustal plates, and changes in atmospheric composition, are similar to those processes that occurred in the past.

Hold a public forum for the students to present their findings. Invite the people who were interviewed, parents, and the community to hear the students' presentations. A public forum presentation will provide a real-world context for the students' work and demonstrate the importance of good communication skills, both spoken and written. As the students share their findings, ask them to classify the causes for the ecological changes as "human-made" or due to "nature." Discuss how both may occur, or how humans may speed up natural causes like erosion. Now that we've looked at geologic events of the past, and changes in our local geology today, how would you complete this sentence: Processes that shape the earth today, such as volcanoes, earthquakes, and erosion, are the _____ (same) processes that were shaping the Earth in the past.

## Expansion of the Idea  *Which process skills will be used?*

Observing, inferring, hypothesizing, interpreting data

### How will the idea be expanded?

Provide the students with a series of maps showing the rock record for your region and for your state. These are typically available through your state department of natural resources, geology division. The major geologic eras, periods, and epochs should be marked on the maps, as well as the relative thickness of the layers represented. Also provide the students with a geologic calendar, which provides the names and duration for all of the geologic eras, periods, and epochs. If the students have never worked with a geologic calendar, review the components, explaining the differences between eras, periods, and epochs.

• *The Rock Record*

Using the maps, ask the students to compare the rock record of the local region to the geologic calendar. Are all of the epochs present in your region? What epoch is missing in your region? How does your region compare with the rest of your state? Are there differences in the thickness of the rock layers? Are the same layers missing throughout the state as are missing in your local region? Ask the students to reflect on their findings from the interview activity. Knowing what and why geologic changes happened in recent times from the interviews with the local people, can you project how some of the rock layers may be absent from the rock record?

Ask the students to determine where in their local rock record did humans first appear on the planet? How far below the surface is that rock layer? When did the dinosaurs first appear on the planet? How far below the surface is that event in your local rock record? What about animals like a horse or a mastodon? When did they first appear on Earth? How far below the surface is that event in your local rock record? Why aren't all of these animals still found on Earth today? Would a process like erosion or even an earthquake wipe out the dinosaurs? What do you think happened in Earth's history to eliminate some animal species? Can we tell this from the rock record?

Use the reference materials on the geology of the local region to provide some answers to these questions. Invite a local geologist or even a paleontologist or a paleobotanist to come in and talk to the class about the local geologic record, explaining the geologic processes that have occurred in their state and region. Conclude this activity by having the students share answers to the questions posed, to restate the primary concept that processes that occurred in the past still occur today, and that the Earth's history is also influenced by occasional catastrophes such as the impact of an asteroid or comet.

### Science in Personal and Social Perspectives

✦ While we cannot always control the impact that nature has on our local ecology, we can control human impact. Identify one local ecological change caused by humans and propose solutions to minimize such impact in the future.

✦ The rock layers below the surface were formed by natural processes that occurred, in some cases, hundreds of thousands of years ago. Engage in a debate about the pros and cons of extracting rock below the surface just because we own the land above the surface.

### Science and Technology

✦ Humans have applied various technologies to extract rock from the Earth. Some mining operations take place at the surface, typically called surface or strip mining. Mining below the ground makes use of a "longwaller." Research these two types of technology, describing how they each work, determining which has the least impact on the local environment, and defending your response.

✦ To map the ocean floor, sonar is used. What is this device? Can it be used to provide a rock record of the layers of the ocean floor also? If not, how do we determine what the rock record is below the ocean floor?

### Science as Inquiry

✦ Review the local rock record. What kinds of rock can be found within the first two hundred feet below the surface? Propose a way to verify that the map of the local rock record is correct. Describe in detail what you would need to do to investigate the validity of the map.

### History and Nature of Science

✦ Would a paleobotanist be a good source of information on changes in our local ecology? Why? What does a paleobotanist do?

✦ Some scientists believe that by studying the gases that surround a planet like Jupiter today, we can have insight into the ancient atmosphere that surrounded Earth. Why would we want to know more about the Earth's early atmosphere? What can we learn about our own planet from studying the gases that surround other planets?

### Evaluation  *How will the students show what they have learned?*

Upon completing the activities, the students will be able to:

✦ discuss the age of the Earth's crust at different locations (i.e., ocean floor, different continents) by describing where it is older in other places, and using that information to explain how the Earth's crust has changed over the last billion years;

✦ explain why even though the Earth's history is very long and the time of human life on Earth is incredibly short, we have permanently altered our environment. A student will be able to discuss the implications of the environmental crisis as it exists in the context of Earth history;

- when provided with a rock record history of two different areas, explain the differences between the two records;
- explain the difference between a geologic era, period, and epoch.

# Rain Formation

GRADE LEVEL: K–4
DISCIPLINE: Earth and Space Science

**Inquiry Question:** Why does it rain?

**Concept to Be Invented:** Main idea—Raindrops form as water vapor condenses and falls from the sky.

**Concepts Important to Expansion:** Water cycle, condensation, evaporation, precipitation

### Materials Needed

*For Exploration (for Each Group of 4 to 6 Children)*
1-quart glass jar with lid, hot-to-boiling water, ice cubes

*For Expansion*
clear plastic lid (coffee can lid), pencil, water, plastic cup, eyedropper, paper towels

**Safety Precautions:** The students should be reminded to avoid bumping the tables once the exploration activity is set up. If the hot water spills out, it could hurt the children. If the glass jar breaks, it could cut someone.

## *Exploration* Which process skills will be used?

Observing, predicting, recording data

### What will the students do?

Set groups of 4 to 6 students around a table. In the middle of the table place a 1-quart jar with enough hot-to-nearly-boiling water to cover the bottom of the jar. The teacher should ask the students to make predictions about what will happen when they cover the jar with the lid turned upside down, holding 3 or 4 ice cubes. After the students have recorded their predictions and shared them with the class, instruct someone from each group to place the lid carefully over the jar and place the ice cubes on top of the inverted lid. Ask the students to watch the jar for 4 or 5 minutes. Ask them, What did you observe? Was it as you predicted? Record these observations.

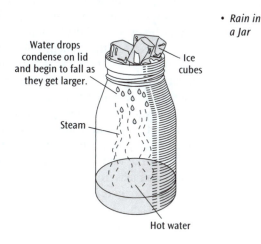

- Rain in a Jar

Water drops condense on lid and begin to fall as they get larger.

Ice cubes

Steam

Hot water

## **E**xplanation/Concept Invention *What is the main idea? How will the main idea be constructed?*

*Concept:* Raindrops form as water vapor condenses and falls from the sky.

The students should have observed that water drops collected on the inside of the lid. As time progressed, more water drops formed. As the drops became bigger, it got to the point that the lid could no longer hold the drops, and the drops began to fall back into the jar. Ask the students the following questions to help them conclude that raindrops form as water vapor condenses and falls from the sky. What observations did you record? Where do you think the drops of water on the lid came from? (From the *condensation* of water vapor inside the jar. The hot water in the jar *evaporated* and changed into a *gas*—water vapor. When the water vapor hit the cool lid, it *condensed* and changed back to a *liquid*.) What happened to the drops of water as they collected on the lid? (They got bigger as more water vapor *condensed* and collected on the jar lid.) At what point did the water drops start to fall from the jar lid? (As they collected on the lid, they grew bigger and soon pulled together with other drops. Their weight pulled them down.) What do you call water drops that fall from the sky? (Rain.) Ask the student teams to create a drawing of an area with land and a lake and sky with some clouds in it. Ask them to use this drawing to trace a drop of water from the lake to the sky and back again. How does this demonstrate why it rains?

## **E**xpansion of the Idea *Which process skills will be used?*

Observing, inferring, measuring

### *How will the idea be expanded?*

• *Water Drop Attraction*

Pair up the students. Provide each pair with a plastic coffee can lid or the like, an eyedropper, a cup of water, and some paper towels. Ask the student pairs to do the following: One student should hold the plastic lid bottom-side-up.

The other student should fill the eyedropper with water and squeeze as many separate drops of water on the lid as possible. The child holding the lid should then quickly turn the lid over. Hold the lid at least 8 to 10 inches over the tabletop, directly over some paper towels. Ask the student not holding the lid to use the point of a pencil to move the tiny drops together. What happens when you do this? Ask the students to switch roles, allowing one to hold the lid and flip it and the other to use the eyedropper and pencil. Did the same thing occur?

The water molecules appear to attract one another. As you pull them together, it seems as if they readily jump to one another. As they grow bigger, they eventually are overcome by gravity and fall from the lid. Water may fall like this from the sky, not just in the form of rain. The teacher may solicit ideas from the students on other forms in which water falls from the sky (snow, sleet, hail). Explain to the students that all of these are called *precipitation*.

### Science in Personal and Social Perspectives

+ Why do you think it rains more in certain places than in others?
+ Read the poem "Little Raindrops," by Aunt Effie (Jane Euphemia Browne), to the class. After it is read, ask the students if they think they are affected by emotional changes with changes in the weather.

### Science and Technology

+ Why do you think meteorologists study rain patterns? Do these patterns affect where people will build cities?
+ Why do scientists *seed* rain clouds in dry areas? Do you think farmers in these areas want to be able to make it rain when water is scarce? Why?

### Science as Inquiry

+ What do you call it when water turns into water vapor? (Evaporation.)
+ When water vapor collects on an object to form water droplets, what is it called? (Condensation.)
+ What do you call water that falls from the sky? (Precipitation.)
+ What do we call the process by which water evaporates, condenses, and falls from the sky? (The water cycle.)

### History and Nature of Science

+ How important do you think it is for a farmer to understand the water cycle?
+ If you were a botanist working in the desert, why would you be curious about how a cactus grows?
+ When you watch a local weather forecast, does the meteorologist help explain where the next rainfall will come from?

## Evaluation  *How will the students show what they have learned?*

Upon completing the activities, the students will be able to:

+ show how they can make rain when given a jar of hot water, a pie tin, and some ice cubes;
+ explain where evaporation, condensation, and precipitation are occurring in the jar demonstration they set up;
+ draw a picture of something they think they would not have in their life if it did not rain. Ask them to explain the reasoning behind choosing that object.

# Dew Formation

**Inquiry Question:** Why do my shoes get wet if I walk through the grass on a cool, dry, summer morning?

**Concept to Be Invented:** Main idea—Cold surfaces collect more water drops than warm surfaces do.

**Concepts Important to Expansion:** Dew, frost, temperature measurement with a thermometer, dew point

## Materials Needed

*For Exploration (for Each Group of 4 to 6 Children)*
minute timer or clock with minutes marked off, glass soda bottle, clear container large enough for the bottle to fit in, ice cubes, water, paper towels

*For Expansion*
drinking glass, thermometer, ice cubes, water, paper towels

**Safety Precautions:** The students should be reminded to use care when handling the bottles. Wipe up any water spills so that students do not slip on wet surfaces.

## Exploration  *Which process skills will be used?*

Observing, predicting, measuring, inferring, recording data

### What will the students do?

• *Soda Bottle Condensation*

Set groups of 4 to 6 children around a table. In the middle of the table place a container large enough to hold a soda bottle. In this container place 4 or 5 ice cubes and enough water so that once the bottle is placed in the container, it will be covered with cold water up to its neck. Give one child in the group a glass soda bottle. Remind the other students that they each will get a turn. If enough bottles are available, each child may be given one at this time. Ask the children to wrap their hands around the bottle for 2 minutes to try to get it very warm. When the 2 minutes are up, ask the students to exhale inside the bottle. What did you observe? Record those observations.

Then ask the students to make predictions about what will happen after they put the bottle into the container of ice water for 2 minutes, take it out, quickly wipe it off, and again exhale into the bottle. After they have recorded their predictions and shared them with the class, the students should take turns putting their bottles into the ice water container, taking them out, wiping off the excess water, and then exhaling inside them. What did you observe? Was it as you predicted? Record these observations.

## Explanation/Concept Invention  *What is the main idea? How will the main idea be constructed?*

*Concept:* Cold surfaces collect more water drops than warm surfaces.

Ask the students to reflect on their observations by asking the following:

+ What observations did you record when you exhaled on the warmed bottle?
+ What observations did you record when you exhaled on the cooled bottle?
+ Was there a difference between the two? Why do you think this happened?
+ When the students exhaled into their warmed bottles, they may have observed some condensation, but very little. Their warm breath and the warmed bottle did not differ greatly in temperature. Therefore, water vapor did not condense readily. When the students exhaled into the cooled bottles, the difference in temperature between their breath and the bottles was enough to make water drops collect on the cold bottles. The students will be able to conclude that cold surfaces collect more water drops than warm surfaces when you ask them the following questions about what they did.
+ Now ask them to respond to the inquiry question: Why do your shoes get wet when you walk through the grass on a cool, dry, summer morning? Remind them to think about the summer air temperature compared to the ground temperature. (The cool grass allowed water vapor to come out of the warm air and condense on the grass.) Do you know what we call the water you find on grass in the morning? (Dew.) When it's a very cold morning, this dew appears to be frozen. What name do we give it then? (Frost.)

## Expansion of the Idea  *Which process skills will be used?*

Observing, measuring, comparing, recording data

### How will the idea be expanded?

Pair up the students. Give each pair a thermometer. Practice reading the thermometer. Be sure each student knows how this is done. As the students work in pairs, ask them to fill a glass with ice and add enough water to cover the ice. Record the temperature their thermometer is reading. Place the thermometer in the glass. Watch the outside of the glass and record the temperature at which water begins to form on the outside of the glass. Explain to the students that for this particular day, with this particular amount of moisture in the air, the temperature they just recorded would be called the *dew point* for

• *Thermometer Reading and Dew Point*

the day. When the air reaches that temperature, then *dew* will begin to form on the grass outside.

### Science in Personal and Social Perspectives

✦ Other than the noise involved, why do you think it is not a good idea to mow grass very early on a summer morning?

✦ Explain how your feet could get wet when you run through the grass in the spring.

✦ Why does frost form on car windows in the winter?

### Science and Technology

✦ Do you think auto manufacturers are concerned with dew formation when they build new cars? Do you think the auto manufacturers think carefully about the kind of paint they put on new cars because they know dew may form on them? What would happen to a car if dew formed on it day after day and there was no protective paint on it? Would the same thing happen to your bicycle?

✦ How does a rear window defogger/deicer eliminate frost on the car window?

### Science as Inquiry

✦ What do you call it when water turns into water vapor? (Evaporation.)

✦ When water vapor collects on an object to form water droplets, what is it called? (Condensation.)

✦ When water collects on a cold surface, what may form? (Dew or frost.)

✦ What is a *dew point*?

### History and Nature of Science

✦ Why would a landscaper be concerned about dew/frost formation? Have you ever seen plants wrapped in cloth or covered in plastic bags? Why do you think landscapers or home owners do this?

✦ Do you think a person in the lawn-care business should pay attention to weather forecasts that give the dew point? Do you think it could be used to help the person decide when to start work in the morning?

## *E*valuation  *How will the students show what they have learned?*

Upon completing the activities, the students will be able to:

✦ use a bottle and a bowl of ice water to demonstrate how dew can form;

✦ demonstrate how to determine dew point using a glass, ice cubes, and a thermometer;

✦ explain why their shoes get wet when they run through grass on a sunny summer morning.

# Radiant Energy

**Inquiry Question:** What kind of energy do we get from the sun?

**Concept to Be Invented:** Main idea—The sun produces energy in the form of heat, referred to as *radiant energy.*

**Concepts Important to Expansion:** The sun's heat energy can be used to perform work.

## Materials Needed

*For Activity 1*
2 pie pans, sand, 2 coins, 2 black plastic bags

*For Activity 2*
large glass jar with lid, water, thermometer, graph paper

*For Activity 3*
magnifying glasses, sheets of paper

*For Expansion Activity*
6 tea bags, large jar

**Safety Precautions:** Before starting the activities, go over the following safety rules:

+ The students should call the teacher if the thermometer is dropped and broken and avoid touching broken glass or the liquid inside the thermometer.
+ Activity 3 should be done only by a teacher or other adult.
+ Avoid playing with the magnifying glass or placing a hand between the paper and magnifying glass.
+ Do not let children stare at or touch the point of light during Activity 3.

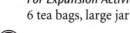

## Exploration  *Which process skills will be used?*

Predicting, observing, hypothesizing, measuring, recording and analyzing data, graphing

### What will the students do?

*Activity 1.* Ask the children to fill the pie pans with sand. Put 1 pan of sand, 1 coin, and 1 garbage bag in direct sunlight. Put the other pan, coin, and bag in shade. Predict what the differences will be between the objects in the sun and those in the shade. After a while have the children feel and compare the objects. How did the objects that were in the sun feel? What about the ones that were in the shade? Why do the things that were in the sun feel warm? Why do they feel cool if they were in the shade?

• *Temperature and Colored Surfaces*

*Activity 2.* On the second day, have the students fill 2 jars with water. Record their starting temperatures. Place one of the jars in the sun and one in the shade. Predict how much temperature change will take place in both as time progresses. Have students

• *Temperature: Sun versus Shade*

record the temperatures of the two jars every half hour for a total of 3 hours. Take a final temperature reading. Graph the results with a bar graph using different colors for the sunny and shady sites.

• *Magnifiers: Capture the Sun*

*Activity 3.* (Do this on day 2 while waiting for the results of Activity 2). On a sunny day, hold the magnifying glass over a piece of paper until the light comes to a point. Hold it there for a few seconds. What happens to the paper? What made the hole in the paper? What does this tell you about what the sun does for us? What can the sun do to your skin and eyes?

## Explanation/Concept Invention  *What is the main idea? How will the main idea be constructed?*

*Concept:* The sun produces energy in the form of heat, referred to as *radiant energy.*

What does your graph tell you about a sunny environment versus a shady one? Why do you think there were such temperature differences at the two sites? What does the sun do for the Earth? The sun provides us with *radiant energy.* Would the strength of radiant energy change if the Earth were closer to the sun? What if Earth were farther from the sun? What would life be like in either case?

## Expansion of the Idea  *Which process skills will be used?*

Predicting, observing, inferring, hypothesizing

### How will the idea be expanded?

• *Sun Tea*

Fill a large jar with water and 6 tea bags. Record its temperature. Predict what will happen to the water after a few hours. (Suggest to the students that they might want to think about more than just a temperature change.) Decide where you would place the jar if you wanted to make tea. Place the jar in that spot. Throughout the day check the jar and record the changes. Ask: "What do you think is happening inside the jar? How did the water change into tea? What part did the sun play in this process? What other ways can the sun's heat be harnessed to help things work?"

### Science in Personal and Social Perspectives

✦ Why is the sun important to us?
✦ What are some of the things we need to be aware of when we are in the sun?

### Science and Technology

✦ What are some ways in which people use solar energy? (Solar batteries, skylights, heating water to warm rooms, and so on.)
✦ Are these beneficial? In what ways?
✦ Why might we need to explore ways to use solar energy in the future?

◆ Why do clothing manufacturers create lighter-colored clothing for the summer months? Would a manufacturer make more money selling black or white T-shirts in the summer?

### Science as Inquiry

◆ Why are people more careful about being exposed to the sun during the summer than during the winter?
◆ New concepts to be identified for invention in new lessons: global warming, the ozone layer, the greenhouse effect.

### History and Nature of Science

◆ What are some careers in which people can work with solar energy?
◆ Why would it be important for a botanist, a florist, or a gardener to understand how the sun heats the Earth?

## *E*valuation  *How will the students show what they have learned?*

Upon completing the activities, the students will be able to:

◆ while blindfolded, tell which objects were in the sun and which were in shade, and give reasons for the answers;
◆ create a collage showing the many uses of solar energy;
◆ draw pictures showing ways they can protect themselves from the damaging effects of the sun.

---

## Water Cycle

GRADE LEVEL: 5–8
DISCIPLINE: Earth/Space Science and Physical Science

**Inquiry Question:** Living things need and use a lot of water, so why isn't the Earth's water supply used up?

**Concept to Be Invented:** The *water cycle* is a system in which the Earth's fixed amount of water is collected, purified, and distributed from the environment to living things and back to the environment.

**National Science Education Standards:** 5–8 Physical Science—Transformations of Energy and 5–8 Earth and Space Science—Structure of the Earth's System.

---

**Science Attitudes to Nurture:** Cooperating with others, obtaining reliable sources of information, avoiding broad generalizations

**Materials Needed:** See Project Learning Tree (PLT) lesson, "Water Wonders" in Instructor's Manual and on the companion website for this textbook: www.ablongman.com/martin4e.

**Safety Precautions:** None for Part A. For Part B, wear goggles if making the watering can. Enforce the no eating rule.

## Exploration  *Which process skills will be used?*

Communicating, predicting, identifying variables, inferring

Modify the PLT lesson into a learning cycle to help students in grades 4–8 experience the fundamentals of a learning cycle. Pose the word "cycle" to the class and ask them to help construct a list of all words they can think of containing the word "cycle." Without drawing special attention to the words Water Cycle, develop a general description of what the word "cycle" means. Use guided imagery and ask the students to imagine they have a glass of water and divide it into its smallest part: a water molecule. Prepare students to take a pretend journey as a water molecule following the instructions and using the water stations' materials as provided in the Project Learning Tree lesson, "Water Wonders." See this information on the companion website (www.ablongman.com/martin4e) or in the Instructor's Manual.

## Explanation/Concept Invention  *What is the main idea? How will the main idea be constructed?*

Using the chalkboard with the 7 water stations listed in a circular shape, ask the students to describe where they were prior to cloud; where they went after cloud. Do this for all stations and web the chalkboard diagram. Discuss the meaning of the diagram and what it represents: Water Cycle. Ask the children to describe what they think a water cycle is, what it does, and how it functions. Consult the water cycle figure in the PLT lesson. Develop the concept that a water cycle is a system in which the Earth's fixed amount of water is collected, purified, and distributed from the environment to living things and back to the environment.

## Expansion  *Which process skills will be used?*

Defining operationally, interpreting, modeling

Use Part B of the PLT lesson and the enrichment activity to expand the children's conception of water cycle. Supplement with the discussion questions provided in order to address many of the National Science Education Standards' new dimensions. The expansion can also be supplemented with a video, such as "The Wonders of Weather," commonly shown on PBS or the Discovery or Learning Channel. Also, available from

Project Learning Tree is the "Energy and Me" CD or video by Billy B, which demonstrates the water cycle among other energy transfer systems.

## Evaluation  *How will the students show what they have learned?*

Use the PLT assessment opportunity to have the children revise their definitions of the water cycle or to construct a concept map of the water cycle. Students are also challenged to write a scenario about water movement within a water cycle.

---

# Weather Forecasting

GRADE LEVEL: 5–8

DISCIPLINE: Earth and Space Science

**Inquiry Question:** How do symbols help us collect and report the weather?

**Concept to Be Invented:** Main idea—Weather data can be collected and reported.

**Concepts Important to Expansion:** Controlling variables, use of symbols, cloud types

### Materials Needed

*For Exploration*

| | | |
|---|---|---|
| barometer | wind vane | anemometer |
| thermometer | rain gauge | clinometer |
| sling psychrometer | cloud charts | nephoscope |

The students should have had prior experience with this equipment as they were learning about individual weather phenomena, such as air pressure, humidity, temperature, air masses, fronts.

*For Expansion and Evaluation*

weather instruments listed above; collection of weather maps from newspapers

**Safety Precautions:** Remind students to use care with weather instruments when collecting data; when outdoors, obey school rules, and avoid talking to strangers, and exercise caution if inclement weather prohibits data collection.

## Exploration  *Which process skills will be used?*

Brainstorming, observing, formulating models, predicting, measuring, questioning

*Teacher introduction:* How many of you have nicknames? When you write letters or your name in school, do you write your full name or your nickname? Which is easier for you to write?

Try to picture in your mind a McDonald's or a Kentucky Fried Chicken restaurant. Imagine you are in the parking lot, or you are riding down the road and you spot one of these places. What image comes to mind first? How many of you remembered a shape or a symbol for the restaurant first?

Can you think of any other things in your life, like toys, games, or bicycles, where you might remember the symbol for the manufacturer rather than the actual name of the company?

For which stores, restaurants, toys, or games do you find the symbol easiest to remember? How often do you use the item or frequent the store? Do you find that the more you use the item or frequent the store, the easier it is to remember the symbol?

Now imagine you're a meteorologist and you collect weather data every day for years. Just like you and your nickname or McDonald's and their golden arches, would it help the meteorologist to have symbols to record data with instead of words? Why or why not?

### *What will the students do?*

• *Weather Log Creation*

Challenge the students to prepare a weather log or a data chart that they will use to collect weather information. Encourage them to keep in mind the previous discussion. Allow the students to break into their own groups. This will help when the students eventually collect weather information on weekends.

Try to give as little input as possible. Give the students time to brainstorm all the factors that may be important to forecast weather. Have the instruments available for them to look over as they try to think of what they need to create a good weather forecast.

Encourage the students to use their designed chart for 1 week. At the start of the next week, ask the student groups to share the information they obtained. As a class, determine the group that was the most accurate in predicting daily weather.

## Explanation/Concept Invention *What is the main idea? How will the main idea be constructed?*

*Concept:* Weather data can be collected and reported.

Controlling variables is important in making reliable weather observations. Each separate weather measurement is a variable that cannot be controlled. Ask the students the following questions to help them invent the concept:

+ Did the weather factors you chose to observe give you enough information to forecast the weather?
+ Could you have been more accurate had you collected other types of data?
+ Which factors could increase error in your data?
+ Did you try to control any human factors that might have made your readings faulty?
+ Can you simplify the way in which you recorded your data?

## Expansion of the Idea *Which process skills will be used?*

Observing, interpreting data, inferring, creating models, making conclusions

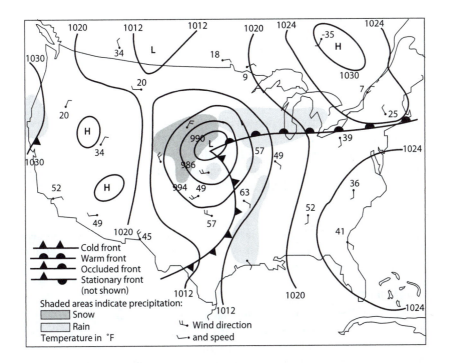

### How will the idea be expanded?

Symbols can be used to designate some weather observations. Collect a supply of weather maps from as many different newspapers as possible. Once you have a number of maps that vary in sophistication, distribute them to your students and ask if they can interpret them. Create a list on the board of all of the different symbols they observe on the maps. Encourage the students to speculate about what each symbol represents. After exploring the various symbols found on the map, break the class up into six groups. Assign each group one of the following tasks:

- Weather Map Symbols

1. Draw a station model diagram that shows wind direction and speed, type of high cloud, type of middle cloud, sea-level pressure, pressure change, type of low cloud, dew point, sky cover, present state of weather, air temperature.
2. Create a chart that shows the weather map symbols for highs, lows, fronts, isobars, and air masses.
3. Create a chart titled "Present State of the Weather" that shows and briefly describes the symbols for precipitation.
4. Create a chart titled "Sky Cover" that shows the symbols for the different fractions of cloud coverage.
5. Create a chart titled "Major Cloud Types" that shows the symbols for and names of the major cloud types.
6. Create a chart titled "Wind Scale" that lists the speed and shows the symbols for the wind.

As the student groups report on the symbols they discovered to represent the various weather phenomena, ask them to decide how they could use some of this information to make recording weather information easier. How can you use this information to predict weather?

### Science in Personal and Social Perspectives

• *Weather Data Collection*

✦ What changes have you experienced in the amount of attention you pay to weather forecasts now that you have had a chance to collect weather information yourself?

✦ Do you think you can create a family weather station at your house without spending a large amount of money on expensive weather equipment? What types of weather instruments could you create?

### Science and Technology

✦ In the summer of 1990 a sudden flood wiped out the town of Shadyside, Ohio. Could an improved weather radar system have helped to save lives? Could it have prevented the sudden flood?

### Science as Inquiry

✦ Create graphs for each of the weather factors collected over the one-week time period. Study your graphs. Do you see any great fluctuations in any of the readings over time? If so, with which weather factor?

✦ Was there ever a dramatic rise or decrease in the barometric pressure?

✦ Did you examine your graphs to see if any other factor changed dramatically when the barometer did? If you did find some changes, with what other factors?

✦ What kind of pressure system was over the area when the barometer changed dramatically?

✦ What conclusions can you draw about the relationships among different weather factors?

### History and Nature of Science

✦ Survey local radio and television stations. Where do they get their weather forecast information from? Is there a resident meteorologist who prepares the forecast? If so, see if you can interview that person. Prepare some key questions you would like to have answered in the light of the experiences you have just had collecting your own weather data.

## *E*valuation  *How will the students show what they have learned?*

Upon completing these activities, the students will be able to demonstrate the use of symbols for collecting and reporting weather data by completing the following tasks:

✦ Ask the students to look at the data they collected from the exploration phase of this lesson and consider the following questions: Is there a weather factor you did not consider collecting that you would add now? Would it be important to be consistent in your data collection? In other words, did you consider things like making sure you collect your information at the same time every day, or that at least two people in the group are responsible for reading the instruments to check for accuracy?

+ Revise your weather log to include all the factors necessary to make a sound weather forecast. You may ask the teacher for sample weather logs or suggestions on what data to collect. Be sure the variables that can be controlled are controlled!

+ Once you have revised your log, show it to the teacher. If it is judged complete, then collect weather data for a month.

Some teachers may have their students so proficient on the various weather instruments that it becomes second nature to them. Collect weather data every day for the entire school year. Your class may want to give a daily weather report to the school on the intercom each day.

# Air Mass Movement

GRADE LEVEL: 5–8

DISCIPLINE: Earth and Space Science

**Inquiry Question:** How do air masses affect our weather?

**Concept to Be Invented:** Main idea—When moving air masses of different temperature and different moisture content come in contact, it results in precipitation and other identifiable weather phenomena.

**Concepts Important to Expansion:** Fronts, cold and warm

## Materials Needed

*For Exploration*

globe of the Earth            paper                    thermometer
medicine dropper            marking pen             hammer
colored water                dry ice                  matches
flat-sided top                container of water      string

*For Expansion*

clear bottle with screw cap (small juice       cold water
  bottles work well)                             red and blue food coloring
cooking oil

**Safety Precautions:** Use extreme caution when handling the dry ice. If the students are immature, the teacher or another adult may need to handle the dry ice for that part of the experiment. Heavy-duty safety gloves should be made available for anyone handling the dry ice. Goggles should be worn. Care should be taken when handling any of the instruments. Exercise care with glass containers.

## **E**xploration  *Which process skills will be used?*

Observing, measuring, recording data, formulating models

### *What will the students do?*

- *Coriolis Effect: Globe*

*Station A.* Spin the globe quickly so that it moves in a west-to-east direction. Pretending that you are on the globe at the North Pole, use the medicine dropper to start some colored water rolling in a stream south toward the equator. Carefully record your observations, being sure to include the movement of the water both north and south of the equator.

- *Coriolis Effect: Top*

*Station B.* Obtain a small flat-sided top. On a piece of paper draw a circle the size of the top. Push this down over the handle of the top and center it on the top. As you spin the top in a counterclockwise direction (from west to east) with one hand, hold a marker in your other hand and try to draw a straight line on the paper attached to the top. Record what happens when you do this.

- *Air Movement: Dry Ice*

*Station C.* Break a piece of dry ice with a hammer and place a few small pieces into a container of water. Be sure to use caution when working with the dry ice (gloves and goggles). Observe the air around the container over a period of time. Measure the temperature of the air mass (1) just above the container, (2) about 1 meter above the container, and (3) near the base of the container. Record these readings.

Light one end of a piece of string and then blow out the flame. The end should begin to smoke. Give the smoking string to the students and have them wave it around the container. Ask them to record their observations of the movement of the smoke.

## **E**xplanation/Concept Invention  *What is the main idea? How will the main idea be constructed?*

*Concept at Stations A and B:* Air masses, low-pressure areas, and fronts move generally from west to east.

◆ At Station A, in what direction did the stream turn in the Northern Hemisphere? In the Southern Hemisphere?

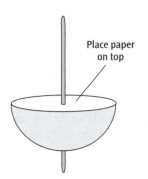

Place paper on top

◆ What effect do you think the land masses with their mountain ranges will have on the moving air?
◆ At Station B, what happened when you tried to draw a straight line on the paper from the center to the edge of the top?
◆ Because of the Earth's rotation, the motion of a body as seen from Earth appears to deflect to the right in the Northern Hemisphere. This fictitious deflecting force is also called the *Coriolis effect.* How do you think the Coriolis effect can help explain the results you obtained when trying to draw a straight line on the paper on the spinning top?

*Concept at Station C:* When moving air masses of different temperature and different moisture content come in contact, it results in precipitation and other identifiable weather phenomena.

- ◆ Where was the air mass the highest?
- ◆ What happened to the air as it cooled?
- ◆ What were your temperature readings around the container? If there were differences, why do you think they occurred?
- ◆ What happened when you waved some smoking string in the air around the container? In what direction did the air flow around the container?
- ◆ What kind of precipitation do you think could occur if warm air were blown over the cold air flowing from the container?
- ◆ From what you've discovered through your explorations at Stations A, B and C, how do you think air masses affect our weather?

## Expansion of the Idea  *Which process skills will be used?*

Manipulating materials, formulating models, hypothesizing, inferring

### How will the idea be expanded?

Fill a bottle halfway with cooking oil. Add some red food coloring, cap the bottle, and shake well. This will represent a warm air mass. In a separate container, add blue food coloring to cold water. What do you think will happen as you pour the cold water into the bottle of oil? Slowly pour the water into the bottle.

• *Oil and Water Fronts*

The following concepts can be demonstrated with this arrangement of materials:

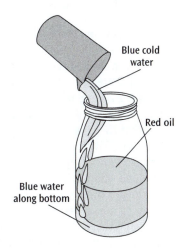

Blue cold water

Red oil

Blue water along bottom

- ◆ Lines of temperature differences between two air masses are called *fronts*.
- ◆ A *warm front* is caused by a relatively warm mass of air advancing over a mass of relatively cold air.
- ◆ A *cold front* is caused by a mass of relatively cold air displacing relatively warm air.
- ◆ Advancing cold fronts lift warm air. Advancing warm fronts result in the warm air being lifted.
- ◆ Fronts do not all move at the same speed or in the same direction.
- ◆ The amount of moisture in the air controls the kind of weather along the front.

### What questions can help students invent expansion concepts?

- ◆ What happened when you poured the cold water into the oil? Did it behave as you predicted? Which liquid is denser? How do you know?
- ◆ Place the screw cap on the bottle. Slowly turn the bottle on its side. How does the heavier liquid move, and what is its final position?

✦ If a cold air mass moves toward a warm air mass, would the leading edge of the cold air mass be at the ground level or above the ground? Why? (Remember that the blue water represents the cold air mass, and the red oil is the warm air mass.)

✦ If a warm air mass moves toward a cold air mass, would the leading edge of the warm air mass be at the ground or above the ground? Why?

✦ How would you describe a stationary front? What factors affect its formation?

### Science in Personal and Social Perspectives

✦ If you were planning a picnic for Saturday and you heard on a Thursday weather forecast that a warm front would be moving into the region on Friday evening, would you switch the day of your picnic to Sunday? Why or why not?

### Science and Technology

✦ What effect do extremes in precipitation have upon area populations (not just human)?

✦ How do you think knowledge of such weather phenomena as air masses, fronts, and precipitation have assisted in the invention of the material Gore-tex, which is now used in running clothes, tents, tarpaulins, and so on? How has this invention allowed us to enjoy our environment more, no matter what the weather conditions?

### Science as Inquiry

✦ What kind of pressure system do you think would bring your area a large amount of precipitation? A small amount? Create your own rain gauge to measure precipitation by following the steps below.

• *Create a Rain Gauge*

Use the following materials to create your own rain gauge: large straight-sided jar, long narrow jar or large test tube, meter stick, metric ruler, and masking tape. Place a ruler vertically in the large jar and pour in water until it reaches the 10 mm mark on the ruler. Pour this water into the narrow jar, to which you have attached a strip of masking tape. Place the masking tape at the exact level of the water. This represents 10 mm in the jar. Repeat this procedure for levels of 20 mm, 30 mm, and so on.

Place the large jar outside, away from any obstruction, to collect rain. Why is that important? The top of the jar should be about 30.5 cm above the ground. To read the amount of rain, empty it into the measuring jar at the same time each day. Keep a daily record in a chart form.

Do you think you can determine how much snow you would have had if you had 50 mm of rain collected in your gauge? What if you have 50 mm of snow? How much rain would that be? The student can do two things here: (1) Obtain a tall, straight-sided container, such as an empty juice can. Carefully fill it with loose snow, but do not pack the snow in the can. Heat the snow until it is completely melted. Use the rain gauge to measure the amount of water. If you know the length of the can, you can compare the amount of snow to rain. (2) The student could guesstimate the amount of rain the snow is equal to by knowing that the ratio of snow to rain is usually 10 to 1. A wet, heavy snow may have a ratio as low as 6 to 1, while in dry, fluffy, new-fallen snow, the ratio may be as high as 30 to 1.

- ✦ How is it possible for airplanes to fly in the eye of the storm during a hurricane? What kind of information do pilots need to understand about air masses in order to do this?
- ✦ Create a list of all of the types of jobs that can be affected when air masses of different temperatures and moisture contents come in contact. Are any of those jobs in areas in which you would like to work?

## Evaluation   How will the students show what they have learned?

The following parachute activity, as well as the questions covering personal development, science, technology, society, academic growth, and career awareness could be used to assess the students' knowledge of the relationships among air masses, fronts, and precipitation.

• *Air Masses and Parachutes*

### Parachute Materials

12-inch square sheet of tissue paper
8 glue-backed hole reinforcers
4 strings, 10 inches in length each

washer for weight
paper person (for decorative purposes only)

Punch a hole in each corner of the tissue with a pencil point. Place a hole reinforcer on each side of the hole. Tie the 4 strings to each hole. Tie the loose ends of the strings together around the washer. Be sure the strings end up being of equal length. Decorate with a paper person attached to the washer. You may find that a small hole in the very center of the tissue will help the parachute open more quickly.

Fold up your chute and throw it into the air. Have a partner time from the moment you release it until the moment it begins to descend. Time its descent.

- ✦ How does the parachute depend on air pressure?
- ✦ What if your parachute came from several hundred meters above the Earth's surface? Would it fall any differently?
- ✦ Would the parachute fall differently if a cold front were in the area? What about a warm front?
- ✦ What if a warm front were just moving into the area, replacing a cold front. Would it be safe to parachute during that time? Why or why not?

## Air Pressure

GRADE LEVEL:  5–8
DISCIPLINE:  Earth and Space Science

**Inquiry Question:**  What factors influence air pressure?

**Concept to Be Invented:**  Main idea—Air has weight.

**Concepts Important to Expansion:**  Air can exert pressure. Temperature and air movement are factors that influence air pressure.

**Earth Science**

## Materials Needed

### For Each Student Group

| | | |
|---|---|---|
| modeling clay | 3 balloons | straw |
| pencil | 2 books | 1 index card |
| yardstick | 1 piece of 8½-inch by | 1 glass of water |
| string | 11-inch paper | 1 sandwich bag |

### For Teacher Demonstration
1 beach ball

### For Science as Inquiry and Evaluation

2 paper lunch bags
2 balloons and string for each
    student group

1 lamp or candle
1 straw and 1 Ping-Pong ball
    per student

**Safety Precautions:** The students should take care that when blowing during the activities they don't hyperventilate and get dizzy. Have a paper bag available for any hyperventilating student to breathe into slowly. This will balance the oxygen—carbon dioxide ratio and return the student to normal.

## Exploration   Which process skills will be used?

Observing, predicting, comparing, questioning, describing, manipulating materials, recording data

### What will the students do?

• *Balloon Balance*

Provide the students with modeling clay, pencil, yard stick, 3 balloons, and a string. Ask them to manipulate these materials so that they can create a balance such as in the diagram.

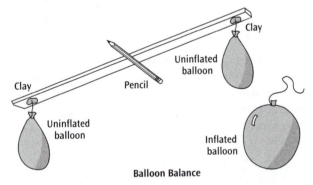

**Balloon Balance**

Suspend and balance two uninflated balloons. Ask the students to record their observations. Then ask them to predict what would happen to this balanced system if they were to replace one of the uninflated balloons with an inflated balloon. Record their predictions. Now replace one of the uninflated balloons with an inflated balloon. Record students' observations. Do they match their predictions?

## Explanation/Concept Invention   What is the main idea? How will the main idea be constructed?

*Concept:* Air has weight.

What kind of data did you collect? Did you obtain results as you predicted? Hold up an uninflated beach ball. Ask the students to help you weigh it. Now ask one of the students to blow it up. Ask for their predictions as to whether it now weighs the same. How is this demonstration similar to the balance you just created? What happened with your balance when you replaced the uninflated balloon with an inflated balloon? Weigh it. Does it weigh the same? Why? (Air has weight.)

## Expansion of the Idea  *Which process skills will be used?*

Observing, predicting, comparing, manipulating materials, recording data, hypothesizing

### How will the idea be expanded?

Ask the students to place two books (at least a quarter- to a half-inch thick) 3 inches apart on a desktop. Place a sheet of 8½-inch by 11-inch paper across the book lengthwise. Have the students predict if they can blow the paper off the books by blowing into the space between the books. Record your predictions, then try it! Repeat the experiment, this time using a straw placed just under the edge of the paper to blow between the books.

• *Paper Blowing*

What happened to the paper when you blew without the straw? With the straw? Were you able to blow the paper off the books either time? Did the paper move at all? If so, how? This activity demonstrates that air has pressure. Air moving fast, such as the air you blew out between the books and underneath the paper, creates a lower pressure than the pressure above the books. Thus you see a slight dip in the paper. When you use a straw to blow through, the straw creates a narrow high-speed path of low pressure between the books. Now the pressure underneath the paper bridge is much lower than the pressure

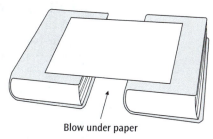

Blow under paper

above the paper; thus you observe a big dip in the paper bridge. This dip is caused by the higher air pressure on top of the paper. Thus, air exerts pressure, and the speed of the moving air will effect the air pressure.

A good teacher demonstration is to take a yardstick or some other relatively long, thin piece of wood and place it on a table top. Smooth out a large piece of newspaper over the wood. Leave about 6 to 8 inches of wood sticking out one side. Make sure there are no air spaces between the newspaper and the table top. Ask the students if they think you can hit this stick and make the paper go flying. Once you take several predictions, hit the stick. What happened? The stick broke and the paper remained on the table top. Why? Because on every square inch of that paper, air is exerting a pressure of 14.7 pounds per square inch. A full sheet of newspaper is typically 27 inches by 23 inches, or 621 square inches. If there are 14.7 pounds of pressure exerted on every square inch of the newspaper, that means that there is 621 square inches times 14.7 pounds per

• *Newspaper Strength*

square inch, or 9,128.7 pounds of pressure being exerted by the air on that paper. You would have to hit the stick with a force equal to that amount to get the paper to move!

### Science in Personal and Social Perspectives

+ What does air pressure have to do with a smooth ride on your bike or in a car?
+ What happens when your bike gets a flat tire? What does this do to the air pressure in the tire?

### Science and Technology

+ In the second activity you found that faster-moving air causes lower air pressure. How do you think this fact has influenced the design of airplanes?
+ Ask a student to demonstrate lift by taping a narrow strip of paper to a pencil. Hold the pencil by your mouth and blow over the strip of paper. What happens to it? How do you think this movement is similar to air blowing over the wing of an airplane?

### Science as Inquiry

+ Does all air have the same weight? Ask the students to replace their uninflated balloons in the balanced system with two paper lunch bags. Get the system to balance. Now place a lit lamp or candle several inches below one of the bags. What happened to that balanced system? Which weighs more: cold or hot air?

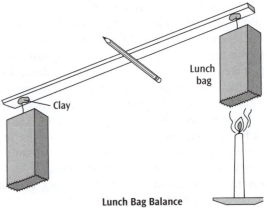

Lunch Bag Balance

+ What kind of air pressure do you think would be associated with a cold front? A warm front?

### History and Nature of Science

+ Ask the students to share information with one another on Daniel Bernoulli (1700–1782). He was a Swiss doctor, mathematician, biologist, physiologist, physicist, astronomer, and oceanographer. Can you think of any people today who are as well versed in as many areas as Daniel Bernoulli was? Do you think it is more difficult to be an expert in all of these areas today? Why?
+ Invite a pilot to speak to your class. Ask him or her to explain how knowledge of air pressure helps him or her to control an airplane.

## Evaluation *How will the students show what they have learned?*

Upon completing these activities, the students will be able to:

- predict and then explain why two balloons suspended on equal-length strings about 3 inches apart come closer together when the students blow between them; they will be able to demonstrate this phenomenon.
- look at a picture of an unbalanced system, in which one balloon is inflated and the other is uninflated, and explain why this system is unbalanced.
- demonstrate that a Ping-Pong ball can hover over the end of a drinking straw; they will also be able to explain why this happens and be able to share and explain this phenomenon to children in a primary grade.

# Solar Heating

GRADE LEVEL: **5–8**

DISCIPLINE: **Earth and Space Science**

**Inquiry Question:** Are all surfaces of the Earth equally heated?

**Concept to Be Invented:** Main idea—The Earth's surfaces are heated unevenly.

**Concepts Important to Expansion:** Uneven heating creates wind and makes the water cycle occur. The sun is the source of energy that determines the weather on Earth.

### Materials Needed

*For Exploration (Per Student Group)*

| | |
|---|---|
| 3 paper cups | 3 thermometers |
| dark soil | 1 lamp |
| light sand | satellite photographs |
| water | of the Earth's surface |

*For Evaluation*

| | |
|---|---|
| 3 metal cans | matte black paint |
| white enamel paint | Styrofoam cups |

*For Expansion (Per Student Group)*
One thermometer

**Safety Precautions:** The students should be careful when using the lamp and around electricity.

# Exploration *Which process skills will be used?*

Observing, predicting, comparing, questioning, describing, manipulating materials, recording data

### What will the students do?

Ask the students to cut the tops off the paper cups so that they are about 4 cm deep. Fill one with dark-colored soil, one with light-colored sand, and the third with water.

• *Temperature versus Surface Color*

Instruct the students to place a thermometer into each cup, covering the bulb with about 0.5 cm of soil, sand, or water. Record the temperature of each surface. Place a lit lamp so its bulb is about 15 cm from the tops of the cups. After 5 minutes, record the temperature of each cup. Identify which cup gained heat the fastest, and record this information. Remove the lamp from the cups. Predict which cup you think will lose heat the fastest. Record your prediction. Leave the cups untouched, and after 10 minutes, record the temperature of each cup. Which lost heat the fastest? Record these data. Did you predict correctly?

## Explanation/Concept Invention   *What is the main idea? How will the main idea be constructed?*

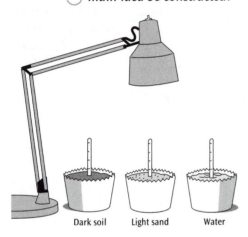

Dark soil   Light sand   Water

*Concept:* The Earth's surfaces are heated unevenly.

What kinds of data did you collect? Did you obtain results as you predicted? How do you think this activity helps explain the uneven heating of the Earth's surfaces?

Look at satellite pictures of the Earth. Describe the different surfaces. Why do dark-colored surfaces absorb more heat energy from the sun? What do lighter-colored surfaces do that would prevent as much absorption of the sun's energy as dark surfaces? (The lighter surfaces reflect more of the sun's energy, whereas dark land absorbs it. Also, dark land loses its heat faster than water.)

## Expansion of the Idea   *Which process skills will be used?*

Observing, predicting, comparing, manipulating materials, recording data, hypothesizing

### How will the idea be expanded?

• Optimum Thermometer Placement

Ask the students where they think they should place a thermometer to measure the air temperature every day. Ask the students to predict and then record air temperature taken on blacktop, grass, in the shade of a tree, a sandy area, and a gravel area. Take these readings at ground level and at 1 meter from the ground. Does this make a difference? Will the time of day make a difference? Have the students record the temperature at these various sites during different times of the school day. Which site and time gives the most accurate reading for actual air temperature? Once the class decides this, then at that site and time, daily temperature readings can be taken for a weather log for the class. The students can also practice taking temperature readings in degrees Celsius and Fahrenheit. How do these findings reinforce your answer to the inquiry question: Are all surfaces of the Earth equally heated?

### Science in Personal and Social Perspectives

✦ What are ways of staying cool on a hot day or warm on a cold day?

✦ Why are swimming pools, ponds, lakes, or oceans good places to cool off?

✦ What kinds of clothes will help keep you cool in summer? What kinds will keep you warm in winter? How and why?

### Science and Technology

✦ How do we attempt to control the temperature in our homes? What kinds of heating and cooling systems do we utilize?

✦ What alternative sources of energy, aside from fossil fuels, should we continue to develop? How efficient do you think these are or will be?

### Science as Inquiry

✦ Aside from unequal heating of the different-colored surfaces of the Earth, temperature is also determined by many other factors. Discuss how the following could affect air temperature: cloud cover, time of day, time of year, wind, latitude, altitude, and oceans or other large bodies of water.

✦ At what temperature in degrees Celsius does water freeze? Boil? At what temperature in degrees Fahrenheit does water freeze? Boil?

### History and Nature of Science

✦ Who helps supply energy to keep our homes cool in summer and warm in winter? (Coal miner, lumberjack, oil-field worker, power plant operator, heating—ventilation—air conditioning personnel, and so on.) Choose one of these jobs and identify how the workers supply energy. What raw material do they make use of?

## *Evaluation*  *How will the students show what they have learned?*

Upon completing these activities, the students will be able to:

✦ fill three identical-sized cans with tap water. Insert a thermometer through a cover made out of the bottom of a Styrofoam cup. One can should be painted dull black, one left shiny metal, and the last painted shiny white. Ask the students to predict what will happen to the temperature of the water when the cans are placed in direct sunlight or equally distanced from a 150- to 300-watt lightbulb. The students should be able to record the temperature of the water in the cans at 1-minute intervals. They should be able to write a short report of their observations.

✦ record the temperature of the cans in Celsius and Fahrenheit.

✦ choose an optimal location outdoors to record daily temperature observations.

# Air Movement and Surface Temperature

**Inquiry Question:** Does the temperature at the Earth's surface affect the movement of air masses?

**Concept to Be Invented:** Main idea—Air moves downward over cold surfaces and upward over warm surfaces.

**Concepts Important to Expansion:** A volume of warm air has less mass than an equal volume of cool air; particles of warm air are farther apart than particles of cool air. Cold air, being heavier than warm air, sinks, pushing warm air upward.

## Materials Needed

*For Exploration to Make an Observation Box*

1 cardboard box (about 30 cm × 30 cm × 50 cm)  
clear plastic food wrap

plastic tape  
1 plastic straw

Remove the top of the box. Leave a 3-cm edge for strength. Turn the box over. Cut a window in the new top, leaving half of the top intact. Cut out one side, again leaving a 3-cm edge for strength. Tape clear plastic food wrap to the side and the half window on top. In one end of the box, cut a small hole just large enough to insert a plastic straw. See figure for assistance in construction.

*Additional Materials for Exploration*

1 35-ml syringe  
1 plastic straw (cut into three even pieces)  
heavy cotton string (three 4-cm pieces)  
scissors  
matches

ice water  
hot water  
aluminum pan  
metric ruler

*For Expansion*

1 dowel rod (3 feet long × ¾-inch wide) with hole drilled exactly in center  
1 dowel rod (1 foot long × ¼-inch wide) to be placed through hole in larger rod  
1 paper clip used as a sliding clip to balance the rod  
2 small paper bags of equal size  
2 thumbtacks of equal size and weight  
1 150-watt bulb and socket  
extension cord if necessary

 **Safety Precautions:** Use caution around open flame.

## Exploration  *Which process skills will be used?*

Observing, experimenting, formulating models, questioning, communicating, inferring

### What will the students do?

Take a piece of string and fold it in half. Place the folded end into one of the pieces of straw, allowing about 0.5 cm to hang out the end. Be sure it fits snugly in the end. Do this for each piece of straw.

*• Convection Current and Surface Temperature in an Observation Box*

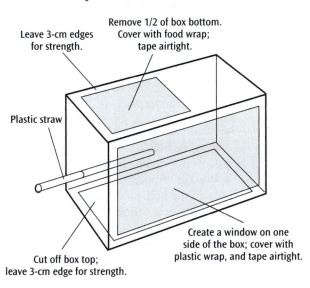

Remove 1/2 of box bottom. Cover with food wrap; tape airtight.

Leave 3-cm edges for strength.

Plastic straw

Cut off box top; leave 3-cm edge for strength.

Create a window on one side of the box; cover with plastic wrap, and tape airtight.

Slip the open end of the prepared straw onto the syringe. Light the string. Collect smoke in the cylinder by slowly pulling out the plunger. Remove the straw and lay it aside where it won't burn anything. You may need more smoke later.

Place a pan of ice water inside the observation box. Be sure the straw is in place through the end of the box, but not hanging over the pan. Let the pan sit for 3 or 4 minutes. After the wait, insert the smoke-filled syringe into the straw of the observation box. Gently force the smoke through the straw into the box. Carefully observe what happens to the smoke as it moves over the pan of ice water.

Complete the procedure using a pan of hot water instead. Once again, make careful observations of the smoke as it moves over the hot water.

## Explanation/Concept Invention  *What is the main idea? How will the main idea be constructed?*

*Concept:* Air moves downward over colder surfaces and upward over warm surfaces.

+ What path did the smoke take as it moved over the cold surface? (It spread out slowly over the pan, staying close to the pan's surface.)
+ What path did the smoke take as it moved over the hot surface? (It slowly spread out and upward.)
+ Do you think a force is acting on the smoke as it moves above the warm or cold surfaces? (A force is something that causes a change in shape or a change in motion of a body. It is easy to see the change in shape; this also shows the change in motion.)

## Expansion of the Idea  *Which process skills will be used?*

Experimenting, making conclusions, evaluating, generalizing

### How will the idea be expanded?

• *Paper Bag Balance*

Set up the dowel rod balance as in the figure. Fasten the 2 paper bags to the balance rod using the thumbtacks. Balance the rod using the sliding paper clip. Hold the rod stationary. Put the lighted bulb just below the open end of the bag on one side. Keep the bulb under the bag for 30 seconds. Then gently let go of the bar. Observe the bag for several minutes.

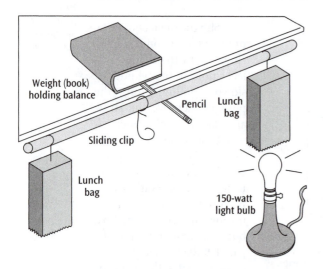

Weight (book) holding balance

Pencil

Lunch bag

Sliding clip

Lunch bag

150-watt light bulb

### What questions can help invent additional concepts?

◆ What happened to the bag on the side near the bulb?
◆ How do you know this?
◆ Was the temperature of the bag away from the bulb colder or warmer than the bag near the bulb?
◆ What happened when you gently released the balance?

◆ From your observations, which has the greater mass? Is it the bag of warm air or the bag of cool air?
◆ The bags in this activity have the same volume. Which do you think has more gas particles? Why?
◆ What do you think this activity demonstrates about what happens to a substance when heated?

Warm air has less mass than an equal amount of cool air: particles of warm air are farther apart than particles of cool air. Cold air, being heavier than warm air, sinks, pushing warm air upward.

### Science in Personal and Social Perspectives

◆ How would the absence of wind affect your life? Do you think life would be changed in any way if there never was a wind?
◆ How does the presence of wind affect you personally? How do you think strong winds would affect you if you lived in a coastal city?

### Science and Technology

◆ How has wind power become a source of energy in some regions of the world? How has this harnessing of the wind changed the lives of people living there?
◆ How has knowledge of air mass saved lives? In what circumstances?

### Science as Inquiry

✦ The students will develop process skills needed to identify moving air as wind and to determine that air has mass.

✦ The students will be able to explain the movement of air over surfaces of varying temperatures and apply this knowledge to explain why wind occurs.

### History and Nature of Science

✦ How will knowledge of wind behavior assist a pilot in flight? What kind of training must a pilot undergo in order to understand how wind behaves? Can just anyone become a pilot? What skills do you think are necessary to become a successful pilot?

✦ Read a book on Amelia Earhart. What do you think happened to her when she vanished in her plane over the Pacific Ocean?

✦ Can you list any other occupations in which knowledge of wind and its behavior is necessary?

## *E*valuation  *How will the students show what they have learned?*

Upon completing the activities, the students will be able to:

✦ answer all of the questions included in this lesson;

✦ demonstrate the movement of smoke over cold air and warm air to a group of younger students or parents and be able to explain the concept behind the movement;

✦ demonstrate that cold air sinks and warm air rises when given a thermometer, a pan of ice water, and a fan.

---

# Uneven Heating of the Earth

GRADE LEVEL: **5–8**

DISCIPLINE: **Earth and Space Science**

**Inquiry Question:** Is there a relationship between how the different Earth surfaces are heated and air pressure?

**Concept to Be Invented:** Main idea—Uneven heating of the Earth affects air pressure.

**Concepts Important to Expansion:** Uneven heating of the Earth gives rise to wind patterns that move locally and around the globe.

### Materials Needed

*For Exploration*

| | |
|---|---|
| long clear tube | clear tape |
| 2 rubber stoppers to fit tube (clear caps) | 1 tongue depressor |
| tub of water | 1 straw |
| 2 baby food jars (1 larger than the other) | scissors or knife |
| balloon | marking pen |
| 6 rubber bands | |

*For Expansion*

| | |
|---|---|
| 2 clear-glass drinking cups of the same size | 2 large can lids |
| water | clay |
| food coloring | 2 tacks |
| index card | small lamp with removable shade |
| wire | oven mitt |
| candle | glass beaker |

**Safety Precautions:** The students should take care when using any glass containers. To avoid burns, exercise extreme caution when using the hot water. Also, when using the lamp, remember that the bulb can get hot. When using the candle, be watchful of the open flame. Be sure all sleeves are rolled up, all hair is pulled back, and no shirts are dangling into the flame.

# Exploration   *Which process skills will be used?*

Observing, measuring, questioning, recording data, predicting, formulating models

### What will the students do?

The following two activities could be done ahead of time to introduce the concept of air pressure. Once the students understand this concept, then the third activity can be performed to teach the concept at hand.

* *Tower of Water*

Close one end of a long, clear tube with a stopper or cap. Stand this in a tub of water. Fill the tube with water. Seal the top end of the tube with the stopper or cap. Remove the seal at the bottom, keeping the opening of the tube under water. What happens to the water in the tube? Why? What do you think will happen if you remove the stopper from the top of the tube? Try it! Was your prediction correct? Why does all of this happen?

* *Aneroid Barometer*

Cut the open end off a balloon. Obtain a large-size baby food jar and extend the balloon over the mouth of the jar. Make sure the balloon is stretched taut. While you hold it, have your partner fasten it in place with a rubber band. Be sure to make a tight seal. Use the second rubber band to make sure the seal is tight. Why do you think a tight seal is important? Draw a sketch of your jar. Show what the balloon seal would look like if the pressure inside the jar were greater than the pressure outside of the jar. Cut one end of the straw at an angle to make it pointed. Gently place a 3-cm strip of tape on the uncut end. Place this on the center of the balloon-covered jar. Be sure it sits securely in the center. Attach a tongue depressor to the smaller jar at the top and the bottom of the jar, using two rubber bands at each location (a total of four). Place the two jars side by side on a level support so that the pointed straw is in front of the tongue depressor. Label the point where it hits 0 to show the starting position.

### What questions can be used for student activities?

✦ What do you think will happen to the pointer as the air pressure outside the jar increases?

✦ What will happen when the air pressure outside decreases?

- ✦ Try increasing the air pressure within the jar by placing your hands over the balloon jar for about 10 minutes. What happens to the pointer?
- ✦ Try decreasing the air pressure within the jar by placing the balloon jar in a pan of ice water. What happens to the pointer?

Make use of the barometers created in the second activity or provide the students with commercially made aneroid barometers. After the students have had a chance to observe how their barometers work, divide the class into three groups. In the very beginning of the school day, instruct one-third of the students to place their barometer in the same safe place in the playground in the sun on the blacktop or gravel; one-third in the same safe place in the playground in the shade on the grass near a tree; one-third in the same area of the classroom. Instruct each group to place a thermometer in their area also. Ask the students to take readings from their barometers and thermometers throughout the course of the school day. Instruct the students to note any changes that occur in the area where they placed the barometer, such as the amount of sunlight, changing shade conditions, or wind picking up or dying down. Remind them about the importance of keeping a careful record of their observations.

• *Uneven Heating and Air Pressure*

## Explanation/Concept Invention *What is the main idea? How will the main idea be constructed?*

*Concept:* Uneven heating of the Earth affects air pressure.

If the students have made careful observations and recorded their data accurately, you should be able to create a class chart of data collected at the three sites. Ask the students from each of the groups to examine their data as a group first. If their data for the different time readings are not all the same, ask them to average the readings for that time period. These averages could be placed on the chart.

Through careful questioning and calling attention to the group data, the children may find that the barometric readings as well as thermometer readings were different at each of the sites. Ask them if they see some sort of relationship between the temperature at the site and what was happening with the barometer. What happened to the barometric reading as your temperature increased? As it decreased? Were the barometer readings any different in the shade than in the sun or the classroom? Why or why not?

The Earth is heated unevenly due to varying types and colors of surfaces found on the Earth. What was the color of the site where you placed your barometer and thermometer? Which color site had the warmest temperatures? The coolest? Were the barometer readings different for these sites? What conclusions can you draw about uneven heating of the Earth and air pressure?

## Expansion of the Idea *Which process skills will be used?*

Observing, hypothesizing, predicting, communicating

*How will the idea be expanded?*

*Concept:* Uneven heating of the Earth gives rise to wind patterns that move locally and around the globe.

Set up stations around the classroom so that the children can practice the following:

- *Air Pressure versus Water Temperature*

Fill 2 clear glasses with water. Place an index card on the top of one. Holding the card in place, invert the cup and place it on top of the other cup. Remove the card. Obtain some very hot water. Put food coloring in it. Use this water to fill one of the clear glasses from your practice session above. Do the same with cold water and a different color of food coloring. Place a card over one glass. Be sure to wear an oven mitt to hold the hot glass. Try inverting the cold over hot and hot over cold. What happens in each set of cups? Why?

- *Air Temperature versus Movement of Air*

Draw a spiraling line on an index card. Cut out this snake and tape a thread to the center of it. Blow on the snake from the bottom. What happens to the snake? What do you think will happen if you suspend it above a burning candle? Try it! Why is this snake moving?

- *Heat Transfer on a Wire*

Light a candle and allow the melting wax to harden at different spots on a wire. Hold one end of the wire in a candle flame. What do you think will happen to the wax drops on the wire? Does something happen to all of the drops at the same time? How is heat transferred from one end of the wire to the next?

- *Heat Movement Through Air*

Remove the shade from a lamp and plug it in. Place your hand carefully near the side of the bulb, keeping the light off. Turn on the lamp. Did you notice a change in the temperature of your hand? Place a cool beaker around the lit bulb. Can you feel the heat from the bulb?

- *Heat Transfer Through Metal*

Cover one side of a large tin can lid with candle soot. Fix a tack to the opposite side with candle wax. Fix a tack to the side of a clean tin can lid. Support each lid in a clay mound so the tacks are directly opposite the candle flame, a small but equal distance away. Which tack do you think will fall first and why? Did it occur as you predicted?

As the students rotate through the five stations, set up a sixth demonstration area so that the small groups can observe the teacher perform the following activity.

Make an observation box before beginning the demonstration. The following materials will be needed: one cardboard box (about 30 cm × 30 cm × 50 cm), clear plastic food wrap, plastic tape, one plastic straw.

Remove the top of the box. Leave a 3-cm edge for strength. Turn the box over. Cut a window in the new top, leaving half of the top intact. Cut out one side, again leaving a 3-cm edge for strength. Tape clear plastic food wrap to the side and the half window on top. In one end of the box, cut a small hole just large enough to insert a plastic straw. See figure for assistance in construction.

## Additional Materials

| | |
|---|---|
| 1 35-ml syringe | matches |
| 1 plastic straw (cut into 3 even pieces) | ice water |
| heavy cotton string (three 4-cm pieces) | aluminum pan |
| scissors | metric ruler |

## Teacher Demonstration

1. Take a piece of string and fold it in half. Place the folded end into one of the pieces of straw, allowing about 0.5 cm to hang out the end. Be sure it fits snugly in the end. Do this for each piece of straw.

2. Slip the open end of the prepared straw onto the syringe. Light the string. Collect smoke in the cylinder by slowly drawing out the plunger. Remove the straw and lay it aside where it won't burn anything. You may need more smoke later.

3. Place a pan of ice water inside the observation box. Be sure the straw is in place through the end of the box but not hanging over the pan. Let the pan sit for 3 or 4 minutes. After the wait, insert the smoke-filled syringe into the straw of the observation box. Gently force the smoke through the straw into the box. Carefully observe what happens to the smoke as it moves over the pan of ice water.

4. Complete the procedure using a pan of hot water instead. Once again ask the students to make careful observations of the smoke as it moves over the hot water.

*• Movement of Smoke over Hot and Cold Surfaces: Clouds*

Remove 1/2 of box bottom. Cover with food wrap; tape airtight.

Leave 3-cm edges for strength.

Plastic straw

Create a window on one side of the box; cover with plastic wrap, and tape airtight.

Cut off box top; leave 3-cm edge for strength.

## Additional Activity/Demonstration Materials Needed

| | | |
|---|---|---|
| observation/convection box | tape | scissors |
| drinking straws | index cards | empty soda bottle |
| straight pins | clay | small fan |
| paper clips | | |

Remove the pan of water used in the activity above and replace it with a candle. Cut a 10-cm hole in the observation box in the lid directly above the candle so that the observation box now looks like the figure below. Light the candle and place it inside the box directly under the hole. Once again, inject air through the straw to keep the wick smoking. Observe the behavior of the smoke in the box. Which direction is the smoke in the straw coming from: horizontal or vertical? Place a pan of ice cubes directly below the smoking wick and leave the burning candle in place. What happens to the smoke as it moves over the pan and on toward the candle?

*• Movement of Smoke over Hot and Cold Surfaces: Wind Patterns*

*Concept:* Uneven heating of the Earth gives rise to wind patterns that move locally and around the globe. *Convection* is hot air rising above cold. *Conduction* is heat transferred through surface of objects. *Radiation* is heat energy that travels in waves.

### What questions can be used for student activities?

- ◆ What three types of heating did you experience in the above activities?
- ◆ When warm air rises over cold air, what type of current does this represent?
- ◆ If you had a choice of the type of heating for your home, would you choose one that made use of conduction, convection currents, or radiation? Which do you think is the most efficient? The least efficient?
- ◆ How can a toaster be used to demonstrate the three different types of heating?

### What questions can the teacher use for the demonstration?

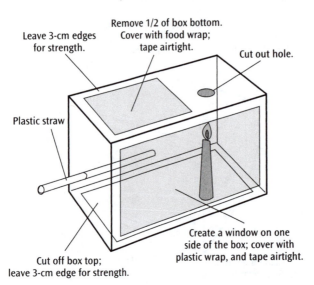

Leave 3-cm edges for strength.

Remove 1/2 of box bottom. Cover with food wrap; tape airtight.

Cut out hole.

Plastic straw

Create a window on one side of the box; cover with plastic wrap, and tape airtight.

Cut off box top; leave 3-cm edge for strength.

- ◆ What path did the smoke take as it moved over the cold surface? (It spreads out slowly over the pan, staying close to the pan's surface.)
- ◆ What path did the smoke take as it moved over the hot surface? (It slowly spread out and upward.)
- ◆ What path did the smoke take as it moved over the ice and on toward the candle? (It stayed close to the pan's surface and then rose up over the candle.)
- ◆ Do you think a force is acting on the smoke as it moves above the warm or cold surfaces? (A force is something that causes a change in shape or a change in motion of a body. It is easy to see the change in shape; this also shows the change in motion.)
- ◆ What name could you give this change of motion? Why do you think it occurs? (Wind is caused by the uneven heating within the observation box. The teacher should elaborate on this concept of local and global winds.)

### Science in Personal and Social Perspectives

- ◆ Do you think you could run a mile in Denver, Colorado, as easily as you could in Chicago, Illinois? Why or why not?
- ◆ On a hot summer day, can you feel a difference in your comfort level when you are wearing a dark-colored shirt compared to a light-colored shirt? Why?
- ◆ Why do you think you have to bake a boxed cake mix at a different temperature when you are in a place at a high altitude compared to a place closer to sea level?

### Science and Technology

+ What causes winds?
+ Why is a desert climate different from a forest climate?

### History and Nature of Science

+ Who was Bernoulli and how did his work explain the concept of air pressure?

## Evaluation  *How will the students show what they have learned?*

Upon completing these activities, the students will be able to:

+ compare cloud patterns of different areas when given satellite photographs;
+ look at an aerial map of a coastal state and be able to predict where most of the clouds will form;
+ demonstrate the ability to read a barometer;
+ explain the difference in barometric readings over land and sea;
+ explain why you would expect the air to be warmer in the daytime over land than sea;
+ engage in a reflective discussion on the cause of wind and its importance.

# National Science Education Standards: Content Standards for K–4 and 5–8

## K–4 Physical Science Standards

**Content Standard B—K–4:**

All students should develop an understanding of:

✦ Properties of objects and materials
✦ Position and motion of objects
✦ Light, heat, electricity, and magnetism

### Properties of Objects and Materials Concepts

✦ Objects have many observable properties, including size, weight, shape, color, temperature, and the ability to react with other substances. These properties can be measured using tools such as rulers, balances, and thermometers.
✦ Objects are made of one or more materials, such as paper, wood, and metal. Objects can be described by the properties of the materials from which they are made, and these properties can be used to separate or sort a group of objects or materials.
✦ Materials have different states—solid, liquid, and gas. Some common materials such as water can be changed from one state to another by heating or cooling.

### Position and Motion of Objects Concepts

✦ The position of an object can be described by locating it relative to another object or the background.
✦ An object's motion can be described by indicating the change in its position over time.
✦ The position and motion of objects can be changed by pushing or pulling and the size of the change is related to the strength of the push or pull.

✦ Vibrating objects produce sound. The pitch of the sound can be varied by changing the rate of vibration.

### Light, Heat, Electricity, and Magnetism Concepts

✦ Light travels in a straight line unless it strikes an object. Light can be reflected by a mirror, refracted by a lens, or absorbed by the object.
✦ Heat can be produced in many ways, such as burning, rubbing, and mixing chemicals. The heat can move from one object to another by conduction.
✦ Electricity in circuits can produce light, heat, sound, and magnetic effects. Electrical circuits require a complete loop through which the electrical current can pass.
✦ Magnets attract and repel each other and certain kinds of metals.

## K–4 Life Science Standards

**Content Standard C—K–4:**

All students should develop an understanding of:

✦ The characteristics of organisms
✦ Life cycles of organisms
✦ Organisms and environments

### Characteristics of Organisms Concepts

✦ Organisms have basic needs, which for animals are air, water, and food. Plants require air, water, and light. Organisms can only survive in environments in which they can meet their needs. The world has many different environments, and

National Resource Council. (1996). Science content standards, *National Science Education Standards.* Washington, D.C.: National Academy of Sciences, pp. 123–160.

distinct environments support the life of different types of organisms.

◆ Each plant or animal has different structures which serve different functions in growth, survival, and reproduction. For example, humans have distinct structures of the body for walking, holding, seeing, and talking.

◆ The behavior of individual organisms is influenced by internal cues such as hunger and by external cues such as an environmental change. Humans and other organisms have senses that help them detect internal and external cues.

### Life Cycles of Organisms Concepts

◆ Plants and animals have life cycles that include being born, developing into adults, reproducing, and eventually dying. The details of this life cycle are different for different organisms.

◆ Plants and animals closely resemble their parents.

◆ Many characteristics of an organism are inherited from the parents of the organism, but other characteristics result from an individual's interactions with the environment. Inherited characteristics include the color of flowers and the number of limbs of an animal. Other features, such as the ability to play a musical instrument, are learned through interactions with the environment.

### Organisms and Their Environments Concepts

◆ All animals depend on plants. Some animals eat plants for food. Other animals eat animals that eat the plants.

◆ An organism's patterns of behavior are related to the nature of that organism's environment, including the kinds and numbers of other organisms present, the availability of food and resources, and the physical characteristics of the environment. When the environment changes, some plants and animals survive and reproduce, and others die or move to new locations.

◆ All organisms cause changes in the environment where they live. Some of these changes are detrimental to themselves or other organisms, whereas others are beneficial.

◆ Humans depend on both their natural and their constructed environment. Humans change environments in ways that can either be beneficial or detrimental for other organisms, including the humans themselves.

## K–4 Earth and Space Science Standards

### Content Standard D—K–4:

All students should develop an understanding of:

◆ Properties of Earth materials
◆ Objects in the sky

### Properties of Earth Materials Concepts

◆ Earth materials are solid rocks and soils, liquid water, and the gases of the atmosphere. These varied materials have different physical and chemical properties. These properties make them useful, for example, as building materials, as sources of fuel, or for growing the plants we use as food. Earth materials provide many of the resources humans use.

◆ Soils have properties of color and texture, capacity to retain water, and ability to support the growth of many kinds of plants, including those in our food supply. Other Earth materials are used to construct buildings, make plastics, and provide fuel for generating electricity, and operating cars and trucks.

◆ The surface of the Earth changes. Some changes are due to slow processes, such as erosion and weathering and some changes are due to rapid processes such as landslides, volcanoes, and earthquakes.

◆ Fossils provide evidence about the plants and animals that lived long ago and nature of the environment at that time.

### Objects in the Sky Concepts

◆ The sun, moon, stars, clouds, birds, and airplanes all have properties, locations, and movements that can be described and that may change.

◆ Objects in the sky have patterns of movement. The sun, for example, appears to move across the sky in the same way every day, but its path changes slowly over the seasons. The moon moves across the sky on a daily basis much like the sun. The shape of the moon seems to change from day to day in a cycle that lasts about a month.

◆ The sun provides the light and heat necessary to maintain the temperature of the Earth.

◆ Weather can change from day to day and over the season. Weather can be described by measurable quantities, such as temperature, wind direction and speed, precipitation, and humidity.

## 5–8 Physical Science Standards

**Content Standard B—5–8:**

All students should develop an understanding of:

+ Properties and changes of properties in matter
+ Motions and forces
+ Transformations of energy

### Properties and Changes of Properties in Matter Concepts

+ Substances have characteristic properties such as density, boiling point, and solubility, which are independent of the amount of the sample. A mixture of substances can often be separated into the original substances by using one or more of these characteristic properties.
+ Substances react chemically in characteristic ways with other substances to form new substances (compounds) with different characteristic properties. In chemical reactions the total mass is conserved. Substances are often placed in categories or groups if they react in similar ways, for example, metals.
+ Chemical elements do not break down by normal laboratory reactions such as heating, electric current, or reaction with acids. There are more than 100 known elements which combine in a multitude of ways to produce compounds, which account for the living and nonliving substances that we encounter.

### Motions and Forces Concepts

+ The motion of an object can be described by its position, direction of motion, and speed.
+ An object that is not being subjected to a force will continue to move at a constant speed and in a straight line.
+ If more than one force acts on an object, then the forces can reinforce or cancel one another, depending on their direction and magnitude. Unbalanced forces will cause changes in the speed and/or direction of an object's motion.

### Transformations of Energy Concepts

+ Energy exists in many forms, including heat, light, chemical, nuclear, mechanical, and electrical. Energy can be transformed from one form to another.
+ Heat energy moves in predictable ways, flowing from warmer objects to cooler ones until both objects are at the same temperature.
+ Light interacts with matter by transmission (including refraction), absorption, or scattering (including reflection).
+ In most chemical reactions, energy is released or added to the system in the form of heat, light, electrical, or mechanical energy.
+ Electrical circuits provide a means of converting electrical energy into heat, light, sound, chemical, or other forms of energy.
+ The sun is a major source of energy for changes on the Earth's surface.

## 5–8 Life Science Standards

**Content Standard C—5–8:**

All students should develop an understanding of:

+ Structure and function in living organisms
+ Reproduction and heredity
+ Regulation and behavior
+ Populations and ecosystems
+ Diversity and adaptions of organisms

### Structure and Function in Living Systems Concepts

+ Living systems at all levels of organization demonstrate complementary structure and function. Important levels of organization for structure and function include cells, organs, organ systems, whole organisms, and ecosystems.
+ All organisms are composed of cells—the fundamental unit of life. Most organisms are single cells; other organisms, including humans, are multicellular.
+ Cells carry on the many functions needed to sustain life. They grow and divide, producing more cells.
+ Specialized cells perform specialized functions in multicellular organisms. Groups of specialized cells cooperate to form a tissue, such as a muscle. Different tissues are in turn grouped together to form larger functional units, called organs. Each type of cell, tissue, and organ has a distinct structure and set of functions that serve the organism as a whole. The human organism has systems for digestion, respiration, reproduction, circulation, excretion, movement, control and coordination, and for protection from disease.
+ Disease represents a breakdown in structures or functions of an organism. Some diseases are the

result of intrinsic failures of the system. Others are the result of infection by other organisms.

### Reproduction and Heredity Concepts

+ Reproduction is a characteristic of all living systems; since no individual organism lives forever, it is essential to the continuation of species. Some organisms reproduce asexually. Other organisms reproduce sexually.

+ In many species, including humans, females produce eggs and males produce sperm. An egg and sperm unite to begin the development of a new individual. This new individual has an equal contribution of information from its mother (via the egg) and its father (via the sperm). Sexually produced offspring are never identical to either of their parents.

+ Each organism requires a set of instructions for specifying its traits. Heredity is the passage of these instructions from one generation to another.

+ Hereditary information is contained in genes, located in the chromosomes of each cell. Each gene carries a single unit of information, and an inherited trait of an individual can be determined by either one or many genes. A human cell contains many thousands of different genes.

+ The characteristics of an organism can be described in terms of a combination of traits. Some traits are inherited and others result from interactions with the environment.

### Regulation and Behavior Concepts

+ All organisms must be able to obtain and use resources, grow, reproduce, and maintain a relatively stable internal environment while living in a constantly changing external environment.

+ Regulation of an organism's internal environment involves sensing external changes in the environment and changing physiological activities to keep within the range required to survive.

+ Behavior is one kind of response an organism may make to an internal or environmental stimulus. A behavioral response requires coordination and communication at many levels, including cells, organ systems, and whole organisms. Behavioral response is a set of actions determined in part by heredity and in part from past experience.

+ An organism's behavior has evolved through adaptation to its environment. How organisms move, obtain food, reproduce, and respond to danger, all are based on the organism's evolutionary history.

### Populations and Ecosystems Concepts

+ Populations consist of all individuals of a species that occur together at a given place. All of the populations living together and the physical factors with which they interact compose an ecosystem.

+ Populations of organisms can be categorized by the function they serve in an ecosystem. Plants and some micro-organisms are producers—they make their own food. All animals, including humans, are consumers, which obtain food by eating other organisms. Decomposers, primarily bacteria and fungi, are consumers that use waste materials and dead organisms for food. Food webs identify the relationships among producers, consumers, and decomposers in an ecosystem.

+ For ecosystems, the major source of energy is sunlight. Energy entering ecosystems as sunlight is converted by producers into stored chemical energy through photosynthesis. It then passes from organism to organism in food webs.

+ The number of organisms an ecosystem can support depends on the resources available and abiotic factors such as quantity of light and water, range of temperatures, and the soil composition. Given adequate biotic and abiotic resources and no disease or predators, populations, including humans, increase at very rapid (exponential) rates. Limitations of resources and other factors such as predation and climate limit the growth of population in specific niches in the ecosystem.

### Diversity and Adaptations of Organisms Concepts

+ There are millions of species of animals, plants, and microorganisms living today that differ from those that lived in the remote past. Each species lives in a specific and fairly uniform environment.

+ Although different species look very different, the unity among organisms becomes apparent from an analysis of internal structures, the similarity of their chemical processes, and the evidence of common ancestry.

+ Biological evolution accounts for a diversity of species developed through gradual processes over many generations. Species acquire many of their unique characteristics through biological adaptation, which involves the selection of naturally occurring variations in populations. Biological adaptations include changes in structures, behaviors, or physiology that enhance reproductive success in a particular environment.

◆ Extinction of a species occurs when the environment changes and the adaptive characteristics of a species do not enable it to survive in competition with its neighbors. Fossils indicate that many organisms that lived long ago are now extinct. Extinction of species is common. Most of the species that have lived on the Earth no longer exist.

## 5–8 Earth and Space Science Standards

### Content Standard D—5–8:

All students should develop an understanding of:

◆ Structure of the Earth's system
◆ Earth's history
◆ Earth in the solar system

### Structure of the Earth's System Concepts

◆ The solid Earth is layered with a thin brittle crust, hot convecting mantle, and dense metallic core.

◆ Crustal plates on the scale of continents and oceans constantly move at rates of centimeters per year in response to movements in the mantle. Major geological events, such as earthquakes, volcanoes, and mountain building, result from these plate motions.

◆ Land forms are the result of a combination of constructive and destructive forces. Constructive forces include crustal deformation, volcanoes, and deposition of sediment, while destructive forces include weathering and erosion.

◆ Changes in the solid Earth can be described as the rock cycle. Old rocks weather at the Earth's surface, forming sediments that are buried, then compacted, heated, and often recrystallized into new rock. Eventually, these new rocks may be brought to the surface by the forces that drive plate motions, and the rock cycle continues.

◆ Soil consists of weathered rocks, decomposed organic material from dead plants, animals, and bacteria. Soils are often found in layers, with each having a different chemical composition and texture.

◆ Water, which covers the majority of the Earth's surface, circulates through the crust, oceans, and atmosphere in what is known as the water cycle. Water evaporates from the Earth's surface, rises and cools as it moves to higher elevations, condenses as rain or snow, and falls to the surface where it collects in lakes, oceans, soil, and in rocks underground.

◆ Water is a solvent. As it passes through the water cycle it dissolves minerals and gases and carries them to the oceans.

◆ The atmosphere is a mixture of oxygen, nitrogen, and trace gases that include water vapor. The atmosphere has different properties at different elevations.

◆ Clouds, formed by the condensation of water vapor, affect weather and climate. Some do so by reflecting much of the sunlight that reaches Earth from the sun, while others hold heat energy emitted from the Earth's surface.

◆ Global patterns of atmospheric movement influence local weather. Oceans have a major effect on climate, because water in the oceans holds a large amount of heat.

◆ Living organisms have played many roles in the Earth system, including affecting the composition of the atmosphere and contributing to the weathering of rocks.

### Earth's History Concepts

◆ The Earth's processes we see today, including erosion, movement of crustal plates, and changes in atmospheric composition, are similar to those that occurred in the past. Earth's history is also influenced by occasional catastrophes, such as the impact of an asteroid or comet.

◆ Fossils provide important evidence of how life and environmental conditions have changed.

### Earth in the Solar System Concepts

◆ The Earth is the third planet from the sun in a system that includes the moon, the sun, eight other planets and their moons, and smaller objects such as asteroids and comets. The sun, an average star, is the central and largest body in the solar system.

- Most objects in the solar system are in regular and predictable motion. These motions explain such phenomena as the day, the year, phase of the moon, and eclipses.
- Gravity is the force that keeps planets in orbit around the sun and governs the rest of the motion in the solar system. Gravity alone holds us to the Earth's surface and explains the phenomena of the tides.
- The sun is the major source of energy for phenomena on the Earth's surface, such as growth of plants, winds, ocean currents, and the water cycle. Seasons result from variations in the amount of the sun's energy hitting the surface, due to the tilt of the Earth's rotation axis.

# NSTA Position Statement: Guidelines for Responsible Use of Animals in the Classroom*

These guidelines are recommended by the National Science Teachers Association for use by science educators and students. They apply, in particular, to the use of nonhuman animals in instructional activities planned and/or supervised by teachers who teach science at the precollege level.

Observation and experimentation with living organisms give students unique perspectives of life processes that are not provided by other modes of instruction. Studying animals in the classroom enables students to develop skills of observation and comparison, a sense of stewardship, and an appreciation for the unity, interrelationships, and complexity of life. This study, however, requires appropriate, humane care of the organism. Teachers are expected to be knowledgeable about the proper care of organisms under study and the safety of their students. These are the guidelines recommended by NSTA concerning the responsible use of animals in a school classroom laboratory:

✦ Acquisition and care of animals must be appropriate to the species.
✦ Student classwork and science projects involving animals must be under the supervision of a science teacher or other trained professional.
✦ Teachers sponsoring or supervising the use of animals in instructional activities—including acquisition, care, and disposition—will adhere to local, state, and national laws, policies, and regulations regarding the organisms.
✦ Teachers must instruct students on safety precautions for handling live animals or animal specimens.
✦ Plans for the future care or disposition of animals at the conclusion of the study must be developed and implemented.
✦ Laboratory and dissection activities must be conducted with consideration and appreciation for the organism.
✦ Laboratory and dissection activities must be conducted in a clean and organized work space with care and laboratory precision.
✦ Laboratory and dissection activities must be based on carefully planned objectives.
✦ Laboratory and dissection objectives must be appropriate to the maturity level of the student.
✦ Student views or beliefs sensitive to dissection must be considered; the teacher will respond appropriately.

For additional information concerning the responsible use of animals in the classroom, check the following Web sites:

http://www.nsta.org/handbook/animals.html
http://www.etsu_tn.edu/ospa/exosubf.html

*Adopted by the NSTA Board of Directors in July, 1991.

# NSTA Position Statement: Liability of Teachers for Laboratory Safety and Field Trips*

The National Science Teachers Association (NSTA) issued the following position statement regarding liability and emphasizing the importance of safety in 1985:

> Laboratory investigations and field trips are essential to effective science instruction. Teachers should be encouraged to use these instructional techniques, as physical on-site activity is important to the development of knowledge, concepts, processes, skills, and scientific attitudes. Inherent in such physical activities is the potential for injury and possible resulting litigation. As such, liability must be shared by both school districts and teachers, utilizing clearly defined safety procedures and a prudent insurance plan. The NSTA recommends that school district and teachers adhere to the following guidelines:

> I. School districts should develop and implement safety procedures for laboratory investigations and field trips.
> II. School districts should be responsible for the actions of their teachers and be supportive of the use of laboratory activities and field trips as teaching techniques.
> III. School districts should look to NSTA for help in informing teachers about safety procedures and encouraging them to act responsibly in matters of safety and related liability.
> IV. School districts should provide liability and tort insurance for their teachers.
> V. Teachers, acting as agents of the school districts, should utilize laboratory investigations and field trips as instructional techniques.
> VI. Teachers should learn safe procedures for laboratory activities and field trips and follow them as a matter of policy.
> VII. Teachers should exercise reasonable judgment and supervision during laboratory investigations and field trips.
> VIII. Teachers should expect to be held liable if they fail to follow district policy and litigation ensues.
> IX. School districts and teachers should share the responsibilities of establishing standards and seeing that they are adhered to.

*Adopted by the NSTA Board of Directors in July, 1985.

# NSTA Position Statement: Laboratory Science*

The National Science Teachers Association (NSTA) issued the following position statement regarding the importance of laboratory science for all grade levels (K–16). Their position on Laboratory Science for grades Pre-K–8 states:

> The inquisitive spirit of science is assimilated by students who participate in meaningful laboratory activities. The laboratory is a vital environment in which science is experienced. It may be a specially equipped room, a self-contained classroom, a field site, or a larger place, such as the community in which science experiments are conducted. Laboratory experience is so integral to the nature of science that it must be included in every science program for every student. Hands-on science activities can include individual, small, and large group experiences.

Problem-solving abilities are refined in the context of laboratory inquiry. Laboratory activities develop a wide variety of investigative, organizational, creative, and communicative skills. The laboratory provides an optimal setting for motivating students while they experience what science is.

Laboratory activities enhance student performance in the following domains:

+ process skills: observing, measuring, manipulating physical objects
+ analytical skills: reasoning, deduction, critical thinking
+ communication skills: organizing information, writing
+ conceptualization of scientific phenomena.

Since the laboratory experience is of critical importance in the process of enhancing students' cognitive and affective understanding of science, the National Science Teachers Association makes the following recommendations.

## Preschool/Elementary Level

+ Preschool/elementary science classes must include activity-based, hands-on experiences for all children. Activities should be selected that allow students to discover and construct science concepts; and, after the concept is labeled and developed, activities should allow for application of the concept to the real lives of students. Provisions also need to be included for inquiry activities in which students manipulate one variable while holding others constant and establish experimental and control groups.
+ Children at all developmental levels benefit from science experiences. Appropriate hands-on experiences must be provided for children with special needs who are unable to participate in classroom activities.
+ A minimum of 60 percent of the science instruction time should be devoted to hands-on activities, the type of activities where children are manipulating, observing, exploring, and thinking about science using concrete materials. Reading about science, computer programs, and teacher demonstrations are valuable, but should not be substituted for hands-on experiences.
+ Evaluation and assessment of student performance must reflect hands-on experience. The full range of student experience in science should be measured by the testing program.
+ Hands-on activities should be revised and adapted to meet student needs and to enhance curricular goals and objectives. There should be ongoing dissemination of elementary science education

*Adopted by the Board of Directors, January 1990, found at http://www.nsta.org

research results and information about supplementary science curricula.

+ Hands-on activities must be supported with a yearly building science budget, including a petty cash fund for immediate materials purchase. Enough supplies, for example, magnets, cells, hand lenses, etc., should be purchased, permitting each child to have hands-on experiences. Many science activities can also be taught using easily accessible, free and inexpensive materials.
+ Reasonable and prudent safety precautions should always be taken when teachers and students are interacting with manipulative materials. (See NSTA publication: *Safety in the Elementary Science Classroom*)
+ Preschool/elementary science should be taught in a classroom with sufficient work space to include flat moveable desks or tables/chairs, equipment, and hands-on materials. Consideration should be made for purchase and storage of materials with convenient accessibility to water and electricity. Computers, software, and other electronic tools should be available for children's use as an integral part of science activities.
+ Parents, community resource people, and members of the parent/teacher organizations should be enlisted to assist preschool/elementary teachers with science activities and experiences. For example, these individuals could act in the role of field trip chaperones, science fair assistants, material collectors, or science classroom aides.
+ The number of children assigned to each class should not exceed 24. Teachers and children must have immediate access to each other in order to provide a safe and effective learning environment.

## Middle Level

+ All middle-level science courses must offer laboratory experiences for all students. Students at all developmental levels benefit from the laboratory experience.
+ A minimum of 80 percent of the science instruction time should be spent on laboratory-related experience. This time includes pre-lab instruction in concepts relevant to the laboratory, hands-on activities by the students, and a post-lab period involving communication and analysis.

Computer simulations and teacher demonstrations are valuable but should not be substitutions for laboratory activities.

Investigations should be relevant to contemporary social issues in science and technology. (Note the *NSTA Position Paper on Science-Technology-Society*.) In those schools where team teaching is practiced, science topics should be integrated with the other academic areas.

+ Evaluation and assessment of student achievement in science should reflect the full range of student experiences, especially laboratory activities.
+ Laboratory activities in science need to be subjected to continual professional review. A need exists for ongoing research to evaluate the merit of certain laboratory activities, especially some traditional verification labs. Laboratory activities should be screened for safety and new activities need to be developed. An emphasis must be placed on disseminating new information to teachers.
+ An adequate budget for facilities, equipment, and supplies must be provided to support the laboratory activities. The budget needs to provide funds for the purchase of locally available materials, as needed, during the course of the school year.

Training in laboratory safety must be provided to the teacher. Necessary safety equipment, such as safety goggles, fire extinguishers, and eye washes, must be provided and maintained.

+ Due to the nature of middle-level science activities, teachers should not have to share a laboratory with other teachers. A combination science-laboratory room should be used by only one teacher. This room should have at least one resident computer.

In schools where students are grouped together in interdisciplinary teams, it is more important for science to be taught in a well-equipped science laboratory than to have all students in a team in close proximity to one another learning science in a regular classroom.

+ A competent student laboratory assistant should be provided to assist with laboratory preparation. It is a valuable experience for the student and helps alleviate some of the teacher's time spent setting up and cleaning up activities.

The number of students assigned to each class should not exceed 24. The students and teacher must have immediate access to each other for there to be a safe and effective learning environment.

Arbor Scientific Company (ASC). (1996). *Arbor Scientific—innovation in science education.* Ann Arbor, MI: Arbor Scientific.

Bank Street College of Education. (1995). *The voyages of Mimi I and II.* Pleasantville, NY: Sunburst Communications.

Berger, C. F., Lu, C. R., Belzer, S. J., and Voss, B. E. (1994). Research on the uses of technology in science education. In D. L. Gabel (Ed.), *Handbook of research on science teaching and learning* (pp. 466–490). New York: Macmillan.

Corporation for Public Broadcasting. (1995). *The Annenberg/CPB math and science project—the guide to math and science reform; EE toolbox, interdisciplinary education access (IDEA), parks as classrooms* (Computer disc). Available through the Corporation for Public Broadcasting.

Ediger, M. (1994). *Technology in the elementary curriculum.* U.S. Department of Education (ERIC Reproduction Document No. ED 401882).

Edmark. (2001). *Thinking Science Software.*

Gerlovich, J. & Hartman, K. (1990). *Science safety: A diskette for elementary educators.* Waukee, IA: JaKel.

———. (1998). *The total science safety system: Elementary, 4th edition* [computer software]. Waukee, IA: JaKel, Inc.

Gerlovich, J., Hartman, K., & Gerard, T. (1992). *The total science safety system for grades 7–14* [computer software]. Waukee, IA: JaKel, Inc.

International Society of Technology Education. (1994). *National Education Technology Standards for Students.* http://www.cnets.ISTE.org

MECC. (2001). *Amazon Trail Software—Bring the Rainforest to Life. 3rd ed.*

Mullis, I. V. S., Martin, M. O., Beaton, A. E., Gonzalez, E. J., Kelly, D. L., & Smith, T. A. (1997). *Mathematics achievement in the primary school years: IEA's third international mathematics and science study (TIMSS).* Chestnut Hill, MA: Center for the Study of Testing, Evaluation, and Educational Policy, Boston College.

National Association of Biology Teachers. (1990). *NABT guidelines for the use of live animals.* Position Statement of NABT, January 1990.

National Geographic Society. (2003). *National Geographic Explorer.* Washington, DC: Author.

National Research Council. (1996). *National Science Education Standards.* Washington, DC: National Academy Press.

National Science Teachers Association. (1990). *Postion Statement on Lab Safety.* Washington, D.C. http://www.nsta.org

Nickerson, R. S. (1995). Can technology help teach for understanding? In D. N. Perkins, J. L. Schwartz, M. M. West, & M. S. Wiske (Eds.), *Software goes to school—teaching for understanding new technologies.* New York: Oxford University Press.

O'Sullivan, C. Y., Reese, C. M., & Mazzeo, J. (1997). *NAEP 1996 science report card for the nation and the states.* Washington, DC: National Center for Educational Statistics.

Snir, J., Smith, C., & Grosslight, L. (1995). Conceptually enhanced simulations: A computer tool for science teaching. In D. N. Perkins, J. L. Schwartz, M. M. West, & M. S. Wiske (Eds.), *Software goes to school—teaching for understanding new technologies* (pp. 106–129). New York: Oxford University Press.

U.S. Department of Labor, Occupational Safety and Health Administration. (1990). 29 CFR Part 1910, Occupational Exposures to Hazardous Chemicals in Laboratories. *Federal Register.* Washington, DC: U.S. Government Printing Office.

———. (1991). 29 CFR Part 1910.1030, Occupational Exposure to Blood borne Pathogens: Standard Summary Applicable to Schools. *Federal Register.* Washington, DC: U.S. Government Printing Office.

Western Regional Environmental Education Council. (1992). *Project WILD and Aquatic Project WILD.* Golden, CO: Author.

———. (1994). *Project Learning Tree.* Golden, CO: Author.

———. (1995). *Project WET.* Golden, CO: Author.

**index**